Lost Wings of WW I: Downed Airmen on the Western Front 1914-1918

Because these wings are no longer wings to fly
But merely vans to beat the air
The air which is now thoroughly small and dry
Smaller and dryer than the will
Teach us to care and not to care
Teach us to sit still

Ash Wednesday, T. S. Eliott

Lost Wings of WW I: Downed Airmen on the Western Front 1914-1918

Martin W. Bowman

Pen & Sword
AVIATION

First Published in Great Britain in 2014 by
Pen & Sword Aviation
an imprint of
Pen & Sword Books Ltd
47 Church Street, Barnsley, South Yorkshire S70 2AS

ISBN 9781783831951

A CIP catalogue record for this book is
available from the British Library.

Typeset in 10/12pt Palatino
by GMS Enterprises

Printed and bound in England by
CPI Group (UK) Ltd, Croydon, CR0 4YY

Pen & Sword Books Ltd incorporates the Imprints of Pen & Sword
Aviation, Pen & Sword Family History, Pen & Sword Maritime, Pen & Sword
Military, Pen & Sword Discovery, Wharncliffe Local History, Wharncliffe
True Crime, Wharncliffe Transport, Pen & Sword Select, Pen & Sword
Military Classics, Leo Cooper, The Praetorian Press, Remember When,
Seaforth Publishing and Frontline Publishing.

For a complete list of Pen & Sword titles please contact
PEN & SWORD BOOKS LIMITED

47 Church Street, Barnsley, South Yorkshire, S70 2AS, England
E-mail: enquiries@pen-and-sword.co.uk
Website: www.pen-and-sword.co.uk

Contents

Acknowledgements

I am indebted to all the contributors for their words and photographs. Thanks also go to my fellow author, friend and colleague, Graham Simons, for getting the book to press ready standard and for his detailed work on the photographs; to Pen & Sword and in particular, Laura Hirst; and Jon Wilkinson, for his unique jacket design once again. Equally, I am most grateful to Anna Malinovska & Mauriel Joslyn for their kind permission in allowing me to quote from their book *Voices In Flight: Conversations with Air Veterans of the Great War* (Pen & Sword Aviation 2006) and to Terry Treadwell for his permission to quote his research into the USAS airmen. Also, to *RAF Flying Review*, Nigel McTeer; The Norfolk & Suffolk Aviation Museum, the Shuttleworth Trust; and the Second Air Division Memorial Library, Norwich.

On 1 June Lieutenant Wheatley and Carter of 'B' Flight were killed about 6 am. Due to engine failure, their machines side-slipped into the ground. About this time the Squadron evenings were considerably enlivened by the Jazz Band which Captain Burney, the Flight Commander of 'B' Flight, got together and conducted in the mess of an evening. On 15 June the Squadron left Le Hameau about dawn and travelled to its new aerodrome at Longavesnes on the Somme. I remember feeling how disappointed I was at learning that the observers had to travel by road, whilst the pilots flew the machines. The policy was a short-sighted one, because one or two pilots lost their way and were involved in crashes which would have 54 been avoided, in all probability, had they had observers aboard.

On 13 July HM The King visited Peronne and I flew with Lieutenant Oliver over the town and took a few photographs at 12,000 feet. He and I had previously been photographing the German front line on that day. On 15 July the Squadron left Longavesnes for Mons-en-Chausee. We were now serving with the Third Corps of the Army, Lieutenant General Sir William Pulteney in command. Periodically about this time, we used to play football matches under both codes, even in the height of summer - cricket was out of the question because we had no ground fit to play on. Deck tennis was also another game which was well supported and keenly contested.

59 Squadron at this time was serving on the extreme right of the British position in France, the French joining us somewhere in the region west of and opposite St Quentin. No.3 Squadron in the meantime had taken our old aerodrome at Longavesnes and were flying Morane-Parsols there. It was just about that time that we observers were detailed to fly regularly with particular pilots and I flew with Lieutenant J.A. Craig. We did not get on very well at first, I recollect and he took an opportunity of reporting me to Captain Roberts for failing to open fire on a German plane at the time he felt I should have done. At the subsequent interview with Captain Roberts I explained to him that I was following the instructions which I had learned whilst training at Brooklands. How different the theory at home was, in comparison with that adapted in practice, I was to find out as I gathered experience with the Squadron.

After this little contretemps, Craig and I settled down together very well indeed and we worked most harmoniously with, I think, some measure of success. Anyway, I have since heard that Craig was recommended (though without avail) to receive the Military Cross on two or three occasions, whilst he was serving with 59 Squadron. Eventually he was awarded, in 1918, the Distinguished Flying Cross and was one of the first to be granted that decoration.

About 7 o'clock on the evening of Saturday, 18 August word came through that the wire in front of Gillemont Farm was insufficiently cut and Craig and I were ordered to go up and register No. 40 Siege Battery to deal with the situation, before the attack early next morning. As we taxied across the aerodrome the pin on the left wheel sheared through and the wheel came off just as we were leaving the ground. I happened to be facing the tail-plane, noticed this and advised Craig, with whom I was flying as usual.

It was vitally important that the shoot should be proceeded with, since dusk was approaching and there would be no further opportunity left. The Squadron was concerned as to our well-being and went to endless trouble to advise us of our predicament. Major Egerton, the CO, informed the Central Wireless Station to get into touch with us and even went to the trouble of placing on the aerodrome large white strips formed to shape the letters 'A5 WHEEL OFF'. It was about 8 o' and darkening when we reached the aerodrome and as I had no message b board, I fired Very lights to those on the ground as a signal that we had seen their message Craig circled the aerodrome once or twice and then gave me the signal that he was about to go down and land, advising me to hold on as tightly as I could. The whole of the personnel of the Squadron appeared to be on the aerodrome to see what happened, since the R.E.8 was notoriously nose-heavy and prone to catching fire. Craig had a very difficult task, since darkness was approaching, making the landing more hazardous. I felt our sole remaining wheel touch 'terra firma' and everything went quite smoothly until the axle dropped and cut into the soil. Immediately this happened, the whole world appeared to turn upside-down and the plane went over onto its back. As a matter of fact, both Craig and I were unhurt and we scrambled out to be welcomed with the congratulations of the other fellows in the Squadron, led by the ambulance.

In the early morning of Sunday, 19 August our infantry attacked the German lines at The Knoll and Gillemont Farm (near Hargicourt) and for a number of days previously the Squadron was much engaged in registering the guns on the German batteries. Our artillery fire at that time was excellent. Many guns were ranged by the Squadron during that period and it was quite the usual thing to be in the air for two sessions of 3-4 hours each. The Knoll and Gillemont Farm were captured by the British Forces, but the Huns counter-attacked in the evening. We lost two of our fellows that day, one of our R.E.8s being brought down by anti-aircraft fire, piloted by Lieutenant Tipping with his observer, Lieutenant Gordon. This was a grievous loss to the Squadron. Also, Tipping was our violinist and used to perform remarkably well.

On 21 August the Squadron suffered a further misfortune. Captain Pemberton, OC 'C' Flight and his observer, Lieutenant Manners-Smith, being shot down by a German plane whilst taking photographs in the morning, north of Vendhuille. I heard subsequently (although I was never able to verify it) that Pemberton was killed and that Manners-Smith, although wounded, brought down the plane safely. On 24 August the Squadron received a letter of thanks from the Army Corps, thanking the Squadron for its valuable help in recent operations. On 25 August the Huns retook Gillemont Farm from us.

On 26 August Craig and I, having received instructions the night previously, took off at 5.15 am and were engaged on contact patrol (with, I believe, the 34th Division), attacking Cologne Farm, again near Hargicourt. When we arrived over the line we were flying through our own artillery barrage, which was the thickest I had ever seen. The Huns were firing machine guns at us from the flanks, I recollect, as we went down calling 'A.A.' continuously on the klaxon. I was able to mark the positions of the advanced infantry units, who had marked them by lighting red flares, just as the day was dawning. These positions were entered on maps in triplicate and copies were dropped by me at the Headquarters of the 34th Division and of the 3rd Corps. Our fellows captured Cologne Farm all right. The 35th Division, however, on the left of the attacking front advised us that they believed the Germans were massing for a counter attack. We went over but could see nothing and I dropped a message to that effect at the Headquarters of the Division.

On 27 August, Craig and I again took off at 5.30 am and went on contact patrol with the 34th Division, as yesterday. We flew very low over the trenches at a few hundred feet only and were pleased to note that our men had kept their gains. Maps pointing out the position were dropped by us at the Headquarters of the Division, Corps and at 59 Squadron. On 31 August, the Germans were reported as having retaken part of The Knoll.

At the beginning of September our pilots were engaged on night flying, bombing Cambrai and other places and although I was warned for this, the instructions were subsequently cancelled, no observers being allowed on this work.

On 15 September I went home on leave and when I returned on 1 October I found that Captain Roberts had returned home. Also, that during my absence one of our pilots, Lieutenant Baker, in taking off, had taxied into a plough at the edge of the aerodrome, the plane catching fire. He was rescued by a French ploughman and suffering from burns he was sent to hospital. Our new Flight Commander arrived to take charge of my Flight (A). On 11 October, Craig and I fell foul of the CO for flying in bad weather and sending a message, not in code, to the effect that conditions were good for all classes of the Squadron's work. A severe 'ticking off by the CO resulted. On the afternoon of 17 October, Captain Fales (A Flight Commander) and I went over the lines and took oblique photographs. These were some of the first oblique photographs taken on the Western Front, so I heard. We flew down the line towards St Quentin at just under 1,000 feet and returned home at about 200 feet. The light was bad and we were constantly machine-gunned whilst the photographs were being taken.

On 19 October, Craig and I went on Army patrol at 6 am with two other machines, to Gavrelle (north of Arras) and we dropped bombs on Cherisy. At this time the Squadron was engaged on Army work. On 21 October, the first United States troops arrived and some of them visited our aerodrome in the afternoon. That day I received my orders to return to England and there was a farewell dinner in the evening. On 22 October, I left the Squadron. (Later, Craig wrote and told me that the machine in which we had done so much flying together, was taken up by a new pilot who crashed, killing himself and writing off the machine completely).'

Corporal Ralph Wilson, of Ramnoth Road, Walsoken, served in the Royal Fusiliers. He was captured during the German advance in spring 1918 and spent eight months as a prisoner of war. As a former reporter he was able to pen a vivid account of his life as a prisoner, which appeared in his local paper. He wrote:

'The small party that I was captured with was marched, after a night's sleep in the line that the Germans had advanced from, to a prisoners' cage at Esnes, a small French town, where the women secretly and gladly gave us a share of their small food supplies to supplement our first experience of semi-starvation rations, which have been typical all along of what the Germans have regarded as sufficient for human beings - other than themselves. Our next march was to Caudry, where we spent three days in a rather comfortable factory and when we walked from there to a prisoners' cage at Le Quesnoy, the mounted escort relieved the monotony of the journey by chasing women and children who were trying to give us pieces of bread and biscuits. And in that occupation they were ably assisted by the lances they carried. Our numbers had by this time been considerably augmented.

'At Le Quesnoy we were left in open cages for two days and nights and before we entrained from there we had become saturated with rain. It was a frightfully uncomfortable journey in locked-up cattle trucks, with exceedingly limited food supplies, to Munster, in Westphalia, where is a very large camp. For about eighteen days we lingered there, on rations that were very scanty in quantity and very unsatisfying in quality. In addition, we suffered severely through loss of sleep, for a bath and the fumigation of our clothing were of course non-effectual against the hordes of fleas that infested the wood-shaving mattresses and blankets that constituted our bed. Before we left this camp we were scarcely able to walk and when we departed to another place we merely tottered to the station as a result of our weakness. We were removed to Limburg (on the river Lahn), a promising looking camp which fed us better as regards quantity, though the food itself was extremely poor. Again we were troubled with fleas in the dirty barracks that we were unable to clean because the means were not provided to sweep them out.

'By this time we had been informed of something that we had no knowledge of while we were at the Front: that our public and other authorities at home, through the Red Cross Society, kept us supplied with rations weekly from England and we began to look for them. Already we had had two small issues of what were known as 'emergency rations' - food from England sent in bulk but we knew that our own people were doing their very best to fortify us against the inadequate feeding of our enemies. So we had to await as patiently as possible for our own parcels of food to arrive. At Limburg, all information concerning us was again taken, as a form of registration and once more when we arrived at Parehim, on May 3rd, after over two days railway journey. In Springhirsch lager we seemed to be miles from anywhere. The surrounding country is only partially developed agricultural land, very marshy and at one time covered by pine forests, thousands of acres of which still remain. The camp stands on the side of the very picturesque and very straight main road running from Hamburg to Neumunster. It consists of two compounds, with the German sentries' quarters (numbering about 160) outside the barbed wire at one end.

'Gradually the original number of prisoners (about 300) was increased to just under 1,500 and some idea of the state of over crowdedness there may be imagined when I mention that our space for exercise was three square yards per man. But our chief objection was not so much to outside overcrowding, as the fearful lack of space inside the barracks. The beds there, in the middle of the room, were constructed after the fashion of ships' bunks, one above the other; three feet high and there were other bed spaces along the floor on each side. There were insufficient tables, inadequate heating and lighting apparatus and most of us had to have our meals upon our bunks. All we had to sweep out with were bunches of heather gathered a few times a week from a neighbouring wood. We were free from vermin when we arrived there, but before long we were considerably troubled with lice. On two occasions only did we have our clothing and blankets fumigated and the fumigation apparatus was only a partial success. It was useless too, for every nook and cranny seemed to contain the irritating parasites, so we could never be free from the filthy vermin. Two hours daily we had compulsory exercise. That, I think now, was for our benefit, though in those days, when we were very hungry, we had scarcely strength to walk around the compound for the period laid down.

'This compulsory exercise resulted in many fellows having troubles piled on to them in the way of close confinement. In many instances, being too weary to walk about - more vigorous exercise was demanded of us until the Germans found it useless to urge us - men rested or hid themselves and being caught, were put in cells on reduced rations for periods varying from seven to twenty one days. The German camp comedian was an aggravating toadying interpreter, whose chief occupation seemed to be seeking out exercise-defaulters, threatening them with 'Eine und zwanzig tagen' and then taking their names. Sentence followed without us having any chance whatsoever of defending ourselves or presenting an excuse; and there was no appeal. When I speak of ill-treatment I do not mean actual physical violence, for there was very little of that. I can remember only a few cases where Germans assaulted any of our men and then not of a serious nature. But ill-treatment was meted out in a rather more subtle fashion - by the issuing of extremely unjust orders, which could not often for human reasons be complied with.

'During the very hot weather, the suffocating atmosphere of the huts was intolerable. We could not sleep or rest: yet if we went outside to get fresh air after a certain hour at night, we rendered ourselves liable to imprisonment for being out of barracks after what was, ironically enough, termed 'Lights Out', though in those days we never had lights, for German time was so far advanced that for a long time it was daylight until after ten o'clock at night. Other discomforts were seriously deficient sanitary arrangements and parades that were totally unnecessary and were held at inconvenient hours. It is impossible to go into much detail, for detail would fill volumes. But of all the suffering that we had, that of hunger was the worst. Until August and September, the majority' of us were dependent on German rations and here I think you will be particularly interested. I still cannot understand how the country can have held out so long during the war on such rations. Not only was the quantity small, but the quality was extremely low. 'Substitute' was a word stamped across every article of diet. The feeding of prisoners could not have been a very difficult problem. I cannot accuse them of doing their best to keep us alive, but I charge them with doing their very worst to prevent us from starving. I further declare in all seriousness that were it not for the sending of food from our own country, we should gradually have died and I cannot imagine a more agonising death than that of slow starvation. As it was, some few, to our own knowledge, died through want of nourishment. We should have shared the fate of the unfortunate Russian and Italian prisoners (who, we were told by some Germans, had, through want of food developed consumption and other diseases and gradually expired to the number of thousands), were it not for the hopes we placed in our sympathetic people back home.

'The best food we had would not compare favourably to the worst in England. Under the category of the best come the bread, oats, potatoes, beans and horse meat, all of which were issued in very sparing quantities. The worst, of which we naturally had most, though often not enough, in spite of the fact that it was practically uneatable, were sauerkraut and pickled mangolds and swedes. There were other 'foods', the names for which I know not, because they were a mysterious substitute. The bread, which averaged 250 grammes a day, was a black, heavy, solid, sour substance, but there were times when we regarded it as cake, for often it was all we had for the whole day, the other food being uneatable, hungry as we were. We generally had that for breakfast, with nothing to put on it, unless we were lucky enough to have a little salt. To drink with it, we usually had a hot fluid, which we dignified by the name of coffee, but was nothing of the sort. It was, we believed, a drink made from burnt ground acorns. There was no taste to it, but we drank it because the water supply in the camp was polluted: though often we went days together without taking anything to drink at all. Occasionally we had a distasteful herb tea, sweetened with a little saccharine.

'The horse-flesh was rare, but valued because it was meat. Sometimes it was served up like sausages, boiled in with potatoes or oats or sauerkraut. More often than not it was strongly tainted, visibly green, before it was cooked. It had a disagreeable flavour, but we had to eat it or nothing at all. Most of the food was served up as a sort of soup, served up in huge coppers. A mixture of beans, potatoes, meal and meat was accepted as a great luxury and it was possible for a couple of litres of that to satisfy us for half-an-hour almost. There were occasional small issues of something resembling butter and jam, but as there was never enough to go round, they were used for flavouring the 'soups'. The filthiest of all foods was sliced mangolds, preserved in some kind of acid and boiled up as it was, or with a little meal, it was disgusting to smell and extremely difficult to swallow. It was that we existed on mainly and for one period of a month we had it for dinner and tea. Ultimately our stomachs revolted against it, so that we had nothing the whole day long save that 250 grammes of bread.' [1]

Footnotes Prologue

1   Quoted in *Norfolk in the First World War* Frank Meeres (Phillimore & Co Ltd 2004).

Chapter 1

'Not So Quiet On The Western Front'

Dead horses and shapeless bundles of clothes lay scattered in the mud. Streams of scarlet tracer-bullets leaped endlessly upwards. The air was heavy and agitated by shells whose wakes hurled the aircraft about in their passage. Ever and again some machine, cut short in its flight, crashed into the ground and flared with a sudden blaze. Many more, like blackened skeletons, burnt fitfully or lay on their backs with buckled wings. Despite the cold, the pilots sweated with the exertion of weaving stick and rudder-bar. Those who survived returned to their aerodromes time after time for more ammunition and fuel; then back to the lines and the beehives of smoke mixed with flying lumps of flesh...
Too Busy Fighting John Gurdon DFC

The Royal Flying Corps was constituted by royal warrant In April 1912. It consisted of a naval wing and a military wing. (In time the naval wing was re-named the Royal Naval Air Service). An experimental branch of the Royal Flying Corps was formed in March 1913 and in the spring of 1914 a headquarters flight was placed at its disposal. When the War came the Royal Flying Corps took the field with the British Expeditionary Force in August 1914 under Sir David Henderson. The original force consisted of 105 officers and 755 other ranks, with 63 aeroplanes. Of these 36 were flown over the Channel with singularly few mishaps. After a brief period at Amiens, the majority of the corps moved to Maubeuge and began to carry out reconnaissances over Belgium. The early reports of the observers gave valuable information as to the movements of the German troops. During the retreat from Mons the headquarters was moved from Maubeuge to Le Cateau and afterwards to various other places. Besides following the movement of the German advance, pilots were also able to watch the positions of the British in retreat and inform the corps commanders of the state of their rearguards. Later valuable work was done in the photographing of enemy positions and the early photography of the Royal Flying Corps was the forerunner of that immense photographic map of the Western Front in thousands of sections, constantly renewed, which played a great part in the later stages of the War.

With the improvement both in material and organization and the increase of artillery power, the airmen of the Allies were able to show to better advantage. The work of the aerial scouts went on incessantly. They preceded both armies in the long race to the sea which began west of the Aisne in the third week in September and ended on the Yser in the second week in October, strategical reconnaissance being by far the most important part of their work, while tactical observation and photography also occupied them continually. There was also the unceasing work of directing the fire of the artillery. Now and then, when occasion offered, the airmen came out in large machines, carrying a store of bombs, with which they tried to disrupt enemy railway communications.

About the middle of October 1914 there was a series of German aeroplane raids on St. Omer, Dunkirk, Calais and Boulogne. During this early period of the War a German cavalry division was defeated by a few airmen. The large force of horsemen were pursued and harassed from the sky during the whole of 15 October and as evening drew on a well-aimed bomb attack completed their discomfiture.

The superiority in the air won by the Allies at the beginning of the War was partly due to the fact that their opponents were at first using old machines which they had kept at their frontier stations. They had mainly old-type Taube monoplanes, Aviatrik biplanes and early-type Albatros and L.V.G. biplanes. These were heavy and slow and many of them had only four-cylinder engines of 70hp. In the middle of October a large supply of superior machines arrived in the German lines. Some of them had been built before the War; others had been completed after it had started. Progress in construction, however, had continued in England. British airmen had the Sopwith Scout, the Bristol Scout, the remarkable Avros, so light and yet so strong and the new Martinsyde Scout. Later the Royal Aircraft Factory developed a small machine with the then enormous speed of well over 100 mph. In November 1914 a combined squadron of British and French airmen made an attack upon the forts of Lille. On 4 November they blew up Fort Englos. The next day they destroyed Fort Carnot. The forts were being used as magazines by the Germans and were important as points of support in the enemy's line of entrenchments. Their sudden destruction by aerial bombardment was an affair of some significance. The Germans got new machines about the middle of October 1914 and In the middle of November especially they devoted much attention to the British Army Service Corps, killing men and transport horses. It seemed as though the British had then lost for a while the supremacy of the air through not having enough fast and powerful aeroplanes to attack all the German pilots who approached their lines.

The first Zeppelin raid on England took place on 19 January 1915 when the Norfolk coast was bombarded. On 14 April a more serious attack was made in Northumberland, the airship proceeding over Blyth, Wallsend and South Shields and dropping several bombs without, however, doing much damage. The following night a Zeppelin visited Essex and Suffolk and dropped bombs on Maldon and Lowestoft. On 16 April a biplane dropped bombs at Faversham and Sittingbourne in Kent. Later in the month a Zeppelin attempted to visit Northumberland again but failed and early on 30 April another airship dropped bombs at Ipswich and Bury St. Edmunds. On 10 May the Zeppelins began a new serious succession of raids. On 31 May the Zeppelin raiders approached their principal goal, the outlying district on one side of London and bombs were dropped at places in Essex and Kent. On the night of 6/7 June 1915 Zeppelin LZ37 became the first airship to be shot down. In company with LZ38 and LZ39, the airship set out from Bruges to bomb London but adverse weather later forced them to alter course for their secondary targets - railways in the Calais area. LZ37 was located and attacked by Flight Sub-Lieutenant Reginald Alexander John

Warneford of 1 Squadron RNAS flying a Morane-Saulnier Parasol from Dunkirk. Warneford's only means of attack were six 20lb bombs; he followed the airship from Ostend to Ghent, being forced to keep his distance by fire from the airship's gunners. He made a single pass over the airship as it began to descend to its base at Gontrode, dropping all six bombs from about 150 feet above it. The sixth exploded and the airship fell in flames on a suburb of Ghent killing four people on the ground. Only one member of Oberleutnant Otto van de Haegen's crew survived. Warneford returned safely to base after making a forced landing to repair a broken fuel line. He was informed the following evening that he had been awarded the Victoria Cross; he died twelve days later when the tail of a Henry Farman pusher biplane collapsed in mid-air.

The last Zeppelin raid of the year took place on 15 October when Zeppelins again visited the London area and the eastern counties. Joachim Breithaupt, commander of Zeppelin L-15 tells of the fate which befell him and his crew.

'Clear for action!'

The speaking tubes carry my urgent command to all parts of the great airship. We are over the outskirts of London - the city we have come to bomb on this night in March 1916. The fierce searchlight beams flash past the gondola and guns are firing at us from all directions. Shrapnel shells burst to both sides and below us, passing under the ship in elegant, parabolic curves. The officer of the watch lies on his stomach, observing the ground through his pendulum telescope; the sentries on the platform eagerly scan the skies for hostile aircraft and pass their observations through the speaking tube to the pilot in the gondola.

Closer and closer come the shell-bursts. Then we are hit. Several shells crash through the middle part of the ship over our heads. By some miracle my Zeppelin, L-15, does not catch fire. But the steering gear is put out of action and four of the gas bags are emptied. The carrying capacity of our ship is greatly reduced and our time in the air is limited. Our machine guns fire sharply at a British aircraft which is shadowing us and trying to reach our height, but soon our guns and every other jettisonable metal part, have to be thrown overboard to make the ship lighter.

We are now over Ipswich and the antiaircraft guns open fire again, but this time without success. Still L-15 is sinking rapidly. We have lost 10,000 feet already and are now wallowing along only 2,000 feet above the ground. All hope of reaching the Continent safely has to be abandoned. But we must do our utmost not to crash where the English can salvage valuable parts of the airship and gain knowledge of its construction. Can we reach the open sea...?

This was my third raid over England, my second on London. My first London raid had been a great success from our point of view. With other Zeppelins we arrived over the city on the night of 15 October 1915. At first London lay dark beneath us, but we could make out several landmarks like Regent's Park and the Serpentine. Shells were thrown up at us continually and the fire increased as we flew over Tottenham, so we decided to attempt the attack from another side. A sea of houses was now clearly visible below us, for the searchlights had been turned on. We stood out to the west and steered over the suburbs in the direction of the city. On either side other Zeppelins stood out brilliantly against the night sky, lighted up like ours by the searchlights. My height when passing Waterloo

Bridge was 11,000 feet. I should have liked to have flown higher, but the air temperature was greater than we had expected and our carrying capacity was not so good.

That night I dropped a stick of bombs which caused damage in a long line stretching from Hyde Park down to Lime-house in the docks area. A long strip of fire below us showed clearly the effect of our work. We suffered no damage on that trip, but a thick fog covered Germany on our return to base and this almost caused our downfall. We began to run short of fuel as we neared Terschelling and two of our motors were working irregularly. It was essential that we found the landing ground as soon as possible. It was five hours after this before we saw the captive balloon which marked the landing ground, soaring above the thick clouds of fog. By then, only one of our four motors was working. I forced my way down through the fog and at that last moment the remaining engine failed. The ship lost driving power and rose again to 1,500 feet. The southerly wind drove it like a drifting balloon over the impenetrable clouds towards the sea. The only chance left was for me to make an immediate blind landing and hope that there was no town below. I opened the gas-valves and the ship fell, slowly at first and then faster. The altimeter indicated a descent of twenty feet per second - over 13 mph. There was no ballast left to check our fall. Down we went. At one hundred feet we saw the ground and immediately struck it hard. The framework was forced down over the gondola, but we all escaped with slight wounds. Luck was with us, for there were no houses or trees in the area and the ship was dragging slowly over a far-stretching heath. I sent some crew members overboard to anchor the ship, which was eventually towed back to base over three miles away.

My second attack on England was in January 1916 and was directed against the western industrial districts. Bad visibility and a faulty compass prevented us from reaching our target - Liverpool - and my bombs fell on Burton-on-Trent. The orders for my third and what was to prove my last raid on London came on the evening of 30 March 1916. Senior Captain of Airships, Captain Matthy, received a message from Commander Strasser, Chief of Naval Airships: 'In the event of constant weather, all available airships will rise tomorrow to attack central and southern England. Chief objectives are London and the districts of Lincoln, Nottingham and Derby.'

Dawn the next day and the landing place suddenly springs to life. Shed doors are thrown open and motors start with a growl for a few seconds' trial run. Benzine, gas and water ballast are piped in; fire and high-explosive bombs trundled to the ships on heavy barrows. At 11am we discuss the weather and it is decided that the raid is on. Whistles and horns sound the 'Stand-to' for the five hundred men of the aerodrome staff and ship's crews make their way on board. As I climb into the gondola the officer of the watch greets me with the report, 'Ready to start, sir.' There is one last-minute wait while the air conditions in the higher regions are tested by pilot balloons. 'Airship march!' The order is given and one ship after the other is pulled with ropes out of the shed. The slightest touch of the framework against the shed could mean disaster and the greatest care must be taken. By repeated weighing off - that is, by letting out some of the water ballast - our ship is made lighter than air. The side motors growl as they are started and then L-15 rises majestically by the prow up into the air. Over the Frisian Isles we steer, keeping low. Even at 200 feet the ground is hidden by a thick fog. But this is good, because we avoid inquisitive eyes. At 2,000 feet the weather clears and we cruise sedately along among the mountains and valleys formed by the clouds. We see another airship bound on the same errand as ours and wave greetings and 'good luck' messages to each other. Towards 6pm the clouds clear a little and we are nearing the English coast. We drop ballast and increase height slowly to 5,000 feet. The bombs are prepared for their drop. Our orders are not to cross the coast until after dark. As the last rays of the sun disappear over the horizon we drop our remaining ballast. The instruments show that we have reached 9,000 feet and we can feel the extra height by the increase in cold. As we cross the coast the English batteries fire at us, but there are no bursts near enough to worry us. From time to time a searchlight flashes past the gondola, but, once inland, there is darkness and silence.

'Occasionally we are forced to drop a light bomb to fix our position and its split-stars illuminate the country below dazzlingly for one minute. But we do not like doing this because it shows our position to the enemy as well as to ourselves. We steer towards the Thames and then turn westwards - towards London and the intense barrage which we know awaits us... Then the first well-aimed broadsides of shells had crippled our ship I suppose that each member of the crew had a momentary feeling of danger. But as Captain I was far too busy to feel frightened although I could already foresee the dire consequences of our damage. In no time it seemed as if the nose of our ship was dipping through twenty degrees. The steering gear was quite useless. Although there was now no hope of reaching the Continent, I had to do all in my power to prevent the L-15 falling on land when the inevitable crash came, to prevent valuable parts reaching British Intelligence. The rate of descent was not, at that moment, alarming, but we were losing gas all the time. Every removable object had been thrown overboard and all secret maps and papers destroyed.

'After what seemed a lifetime of aimless drifting we found ourselves once more over the Thames and there seemed a chance that I could pull off a 'soft' landing, save the crew and then sink the ship. All the men who could be spared were ordered up into the ship, which would float when we hit the water. Only myself and two helmsmen remained in the gondola. At midnight our height was only 1,000 feet and all we could do was to wait for the end. Suddenly it happened. L-15 had lost so much gas that, without warning, the framework doubled in two and we began a vertical plunge towards the cold waters of the Thames. There was no sound except the roar of the wind as the airship fell out of the sky. Without warning, I was thrown violently on to the floor of the gondola. We had hit the water. The gondola was completely submerged and I could feel my body being tossed around like a cork by the masses of water which roared in. Somehow I found myself on the surface and my crew hauled me up into the ship. One of the two helmsmen also reached the surface, but he had lost all his teeth in the struggle. The other helmsman we never saw again. L-15 was sinking slowly all the time while we huddled together on the top of the ship. The centre section was completely covered by the water. For hours we waited for ships to come and rescue us, but not until dawn was breaking did we see four trawlers approaching. As we waited for them to draw near we cut the gas bags. The airship sank a few minutes after we had been taken off. Zeppelin L-15 had made her last bombing raid on England and for us, her crew the war had come to a premature end'. [2]

In France meanwhile, the first British bombing raid in direct tactical support of a ground operation occurred on 10 March 1915, comprising attacks on railways bringing up German reinforcements in the Menin and Courtrai areas during the Neuve Chapelle offensive. Improved Aviatiks and twin-engined battle-planes carrying guns suddenly appeared towards the end of April 1915 but the German staff thinned its western lines of fast, scouting aeroplanes in order to exercise an overwhelming superiority in the war against the Russians. A more defensive attitude was maintained against British and French airmen and German battle-planes were less frequently seen over the British trenches. The first air Victoria Cross was awarded posthumously to 2nd Lieutenant William Bernard Rhodes-Moorhouse, pilot of a B.E.2 of 2 Squadron RFC for gallantry in a low-level bombing attack on Courtrai railway station on 26 April 1915.

By the end of the battle of Loos in October 1915 a marked improvement in the performance of German aeroplanes began to make itself felt British and French pilots found that their machines were no match for the new, swift aeroplanes with which the German pilots were being supplied and consequently the successes obtained by the enemy constituted a grave menace. The main reason for the German ascendancy was the improved Fokker E.III 'Eindecker', or monoplane. A remarkably fast machine, it was able to attain great heights and make long vertical dives. Moreover, most of these machines were fitted with interrupter gear, by which the firing of the machine gun was synchronized with the engine, thus allowing the pilot to fire through the blades of the propeller. This innovation gave the Fokker a marked fighting superiority.

Three men of the Fokker aircraft company manufactured a mechanical interrupter gear which relied on the propeller itself to operate a machine-gun's firing mechanism, thus preventing the gun from firing when a blade aligned with the gun barrel. The gear was fitted to a Fokker M.5K monoplane scout and on 1 July 1915 Leutnant Kurt Wintgens used the new gun gear to destroy a French Morane. His victory was soon repeated by other Fokker pilots, including Oswald Boelcke, the first true fighter leader of the First World War; Max Immelmann or 'The Eagle of Lille' as he was known, Germany's first great fighter ace; and Max Mülzer. [3] It was the start of what came to be called the 'Fokker Scourge', when the British and French flying services suffered rapidly increasing losses to the agile Eindeckers.

When the Fokker crisis arose in the autumn of 1915 the British pilots often operated scarcely higher than 8,000 feet. In their new Fokkers, with engines of 200hp, Immelmann, Boelcke, Wintgen and other German pilots used to hover over their own lines at an altitude of 12,000 feet and dive down on the B.E. machines like hawks and approach their enemy from an unguarded angle, usually from the direction of the sun, whence they were invisible and poured a hail of lead into him before he was even aware of the danger. The manoeuvre, known as the 'Immelmann turn', named after Leutnant Max Immelmann, was perfected by the German pilots. [4] At first most confusing to the British and French airmen, this skilful manoeuvre caused the loss of many machines. But the real danger of the Fokker lay, not so much in its fighting ability as in the moral effect it exercised over its rivals. In 1916 only a comparative handful of German pilots were operating the Fokker scouts; yet so great was the superiority of the agile single-seater, with its synchronised forward-firing machine gun, that the 'Fokker Scourge' became a major disaster for the Allies.

In Great Britain the best available material from private and foreign sources was ordered in considerable quantities and the personnel of the RFC was quickly expanded. A private British machine, the de Havilland, began to be used on active service in large numbers before the improved official F.E. machine arrived. The new Martinsyde, the fighting Maurice and the new Sopwith were placed at the service of the pilots of the RFC. Meanwhile, the Rolls-Royce Company had produced a 250 hp aero-engine of an original kind. It was fitted into a government machine and in May 1915 was entrusted to a pilot who had never flown to France. Being ordered to fly to the front, he lost his way, strayed over Lille, was attacked by German guns and coming down, presented the enemy with a valuable sample of the new aero-engine on which Great Britain was largely relying to regain her dominion of the air.

By this time the B.E.2C machine, a product of the Royal Aircraft Factory, had become antiquated owing to the progress made by German, British and French manufacturers, as were the hundreds of British machines manufactured to the order of the government by firms new to the art of aeroplane construction. Some of these firms had been delayed in production by late alterations and even by downright errors in the drawings supplied to them by the Royal Aircraft Factory. Sir Hugh Trenchard, however, the chief of the RFC, devised a method of operation as soon as he obtained from private British firms a few battle-planes capable of assisting the Bristol Bullet pilots and Vickers gun-bus pilots and manoeuvring against the new Fokker. The old, slow machines were sent out in flocks of from six to 12. High above the weak flock of workers circled two or three of the battle-planes, ready to engage any Fokker that swooped into the field. By the first week in May 1916 duels in the air began to grow infrequent; instead, combats took place between squadrons of fast fighting machines at high altitudes, while far below them there was often a flight of almost defenceless working planes waiting the issue of the battle.

Gradually the number of British fighting planes increased; the perils of the British scouts, spotters and bombers were diminished and for a time Great Britain and France held a practical dominion of the heavens. Meanwhile some remarkable battle practice went on behind the British front in the late spring and early summer of 1916. From aerial photographs a good reproduction of the German system of fortifications was constructed on the practice field and over the lacework of trenches the British infantry manoeuvred in attack, in conjunction with low-flying, directing airmen known as contact patrols. As a result of organization in the field the RFC was thoroughly rearranged. Six distinct orders of machines were developed. Fighting planes were divided into two classes, one of which operated over the British lines in a defensive manner, while the other swept out over the German lines to attack Fokker pilots and at the same time protect British working machines. The working machines were, as a general rule, arranged in scouting groups, artillery observation groups, aerial photography groups, bombing raid groups and infantry contact groups.

By the nature of things the fighting pilots came most brightly into the limelight of fame. The tale of their exploits is a long record of singular daring, of daily hazard cheerfully faced and conquered. Chief among them was Captain Albert Ball, who ranked in the summer of 1916 above all French and German fighting pilots in regard to his record of victories. Only 19 years of age, he had taken part in 100 air combats and had brought down 30 enemy aeroplanes.

Albert Ball VC DSO** MC was the first high-scoring fighter pilot whose exploits became widely known on the home front. His fighting philosophy usually involved an unhesitating charge straight at the enemy, whether equally matched or outnumbered six or seven to one. Born in Nottingham in 1896 and a good shot while still a boy, Ball joined the Sherwood Foresters on the outbreak of war. During a visit to Hendon he became fired with enthusiasm for flying and secured a transfer to the RFC. He joined 13 Squadron in France on 15 February 1916 and flew B.E.2Cs on artillery-spotting flights. In May he was posted to 11 Squadron, which had on charge a Nieuport scout and this little machine became his preferred mount throughout his career. His first two successes came on 22 May; he shot down (but could not get confirmed) an Albatros DI and forced a two-seater to land. On 1 June he flew over the German airfield at Douai; a Fokker and an Albatros rose to challenge him. Though he did not destroy them he completely out-flew them and returned safely. On 25 June he shot down a balloon and his MC was gazetted two days later. He shot down a Roland CII on 2 July. While on a brief 'rest' on 8 Squadron he forced an enemy balloon observer to take to his parachute while on an artillery-spotting flight. Given a new Nieuport on his return to 11 Squadron on 10 August, Ball resumed his private war against the Rolands. He then took his Nieuport to 60 Squadron and was given a roving commission. Uncaring of odds, he would charge at enemy formations and deliver a devastating fire at close range, generally from a position immediately below the belly of the enemy machine, with his wing-mounted Lewis gun pulled down and back to fire almost vertically upwards.

His DSO and Bar were gazetted simultaneously on 26 September and a second Bar on 25 November. (During 15-28 September he shot down four Rolands and forced a third to land and he destroyed two Albatros and forced down three more). By the time he left France on 4 October Ball was credited with the destruction of ten enemy aircraft and with forcing down 20 more. On 7 April 1917, after a period spent instructing pupil pilots in England, he returned to the front as a Flight Commander on 56 Squadron. This unit had flown out to France at the beginning of April 1917 and first flew the new S.E.5 scout at Vert Galand. Ball did not at first view the change of equipment with enthusiasm. He acquired a Nieuport for his personal use, but as he continued to increase his score while using both types of aircraft he became reconciled to the S.E.5. His 44th and last victory on 6 May 1917 was nevertheless gained in his beloved Nieuport. He flew close beneath an Albatros scout of Jasta 20, hauled the gun back and shot it out of the sky near Sancourt.

Late the following evening three flights consisting of eleven S.E.5As were drawn up to patrol offensively east of Lens. 'B' flight comprised Arthur Percival Foley Rhys Davids, born on 26 September 1897, at Honour Oak Park in South London, who was flying his first combat patrol and three other pilots, led by

Captain Crowe. One of these, Lieutenant Musters disappeared early on. Rhys Davids saw him dive, apparently in pursuit of another aeroplane and he was never heard from again. As combat ensued Rhys Davids was preparing to dive on an Albatros with Captain Crowe and Lieutenant Leach when the experienced German appeared. Rhys Davids found his plane full of bullets, his engine in bad shape and the rest of the aircraft badly damaged. Both of his guns had jammed and had his opponent not abruptly left he may have found his combat career at an end before it had even started. His engine stopped completely and he managed to glide into a field. Rhys Davids, who had reported for duty as a 2nd Lieutenant, RFC Special Reserve on 28 August 1916 in Oxford, had been delighted at the prospect of joining Major Richard Blomfield, CO of 56 Squadron at London Colney, which he dramatically referred to as 'The Land of The Gods.' In particular Rhys Davids was ecstatic to find himself serving with Captain Albert Ball.

The 7th September was a sad day for 56 Squadron. Only five aircraft returned to Vert Galand. News came in that both Rhys Davids[5] and Captain Crowe were down safe on the British side of the lines, but another pilot, Leach, was in a critical condition in hospital. They did not yet know that Musters was not to return and Albert Ball was already dead. Captain Ball, flying his S.E.5, had dived into dense cloud while chasing a German single-seater near Lens. He emerged upside down from low lying cloud and crashed apparently without prior injury in the air. His back was broken, his chest crushed and he suffered numerous broken bones on impact. He died shortly afterwards at the scene. The enemy later discovered his wrecked aircraft and his body. His death remains a mystery. Lothar Freiherr von Richthofen was officially credited with the victory, but he denied it, maintaining that the aircraft he shot down was a triplane; an opinion confirmed by other witnesses. Ball's body bore no wound and what caused his aircraft to crash has never been established. He was 20 years and 9 months old when he died; his Victoria Cross was gazetted on 3 June 1917.

Rittmeister (Cavalry Captain) Manfred, Freiherr von Richthofen - the so-called 'Red Baron' was the greatest ace of the First World War. The eldest son of an aristocratic Silesian family, he was born on 2 May 1882. Early in the War Richthofen served on the Eastern Front as an officer in a Uhlan Regiment before transferring to the Air Service in May 1915. His first operational posting was to Feldfliegerabteilung Nr. 6g; with this unit he flew two-seater reconnaissance machines in the East and he continued to serve in general purpose units until September 1916 when he was selected for Jagdstaffel 2, the single-seater scout squadron trained and led by the brilliant Oswald Boelcke. By this time it was probable that Richthofen had already gained two victories, a Maurice Farman S.11 over Champagne in September 1915 and a Nieuport 11 near Douaumont on 25 April 1916 - but for lack of ground confirmation these were not included in his official list of victories. His first officially recognised victory was over an F.E.2b of 11 Squadron RFC; Richthofen, flying an Albatros D II scout, shot this aircraft down on 17 September 1916 and the crew, 2nd Lieutenant L. B. F. Morris and Lieutenant T. Rees, were killed. Richthofen's score continued increasing and in January 1917 he was awarded the coveted 'Blue Max', the Ordre pour le Mérite and given command of Jagdstaffel 11. His considerable fame spread; a cold and calculating fighter, he brought to air combat the attitudes of the aristocratic huntsman; he maintained a collection of silver cups, each engraved with the particulars of a victim. During 'Bloody April' in 1917 he shot down 21 aircraft. The most famous pilot to fall victim was Major Lanoe G. Hawker VC DSO commanding officer of 24 Squadron RFC, who has been called 'the English Boelcke' for his skill, vision and organising ability. Hawker, flying a D.H.2, had scored nine victories when he was shot down after a prolonged and unequal dogfight with Richthofen on 23 November 1916 to become the 'Red Baron's' eleventh victim. Late in June 1917 Richthofen was given command of a new formation, Jagdgeschwader Nr. 1, comprising Jastas 4, 6, 10 and 11 which became known to the Allies as 'Richthofen's Flying Circus', partly on account of the bright colours used by various pilots to decorate and identify their aircraft. Contrary to popular legend Richthofen did not invariably fly a personal aircraft painted blood red overall; he flew several aircraft, Albatros D IIIs and Fokker Dr Is and one of each type is thought to have been painted red overall; but he also used several which were only partially finished in red. [6]

Other great British fighters included Captain R. N. Adams, who attacked six enemy machines over the enemy's lines, set one on fire and drove off the others. While still a learner he went out with Lieutenant Savage and saw his comrade brought down by the ace of the Fokker fighters, Leutnant Immelmann. Lieutenant Dirk Cloete first acted as observer to Adams and later, promoted pilot, saw his former chief engaged with six enemy machines. Diving into the affray, he sent one enemy crashing to earth and helped to fight away the other five, another of which Adams himself brought down. In fights against odds Captain W. A. Summers as pilot and Lieutenant W. O. T. Tudor-Hart as observer, appear almost to have topped the list. Quite unsupported, they attacked over the German lines, a formation of ten enemy aeroplanes. Under constant fire from as many as four hostile machines at one time, they broke up the formation and though their own machine was badly damaged, they continued their extraordinary struggle until all their ammunition was expended.

The first Albatros scouts reached the front in September 1916, superseding the Fokkers and Halberstadts and one of the first units to be re-equipped was Jasta 2 led by Kapitän Oswald Boelcke who led the first 'circus' across the Allied lines on 17 September 1916. The de Havilland D.H.2 pusher scouts were helpless against the new fighter and Boelcke rapidly took heavy toll of his opponents. The D.H.2 was a primitive machine with no windscreen, no brakes and no throttle. It climbed as high as 14,000 feet, went at 90 mph, fought vicious battles and survived the most violent manoeuvres without breaking. The pilots had to be optimists, however, for the planes were made of wood, the fuel tank was unshielded, incendiary bullets were in use and there were no parachutes. Nevertheless, air power became a reality.

Geoffrey de Havilland reached manhood in an age of change, when the first motor-buses were beginning to jerk noisily pas horse-drawn trams. He went to an engineering school at Crystal Palace and the first result was a hand-made motor bike, on which he roared off every week-end to his home in Hampshire. He took a job designing buses and got married. The pattern of his life looked unremarkable. Then the young motor-engineer became a man possessed. He was able to persuade his grandfather to advance him £1,000 so that he could leave his job and design an aero engine. Then, together with a friend, Frank Hearle, who remained his partner for 50 years, he built an aeroplane out of wire, wood and linen. Young Mrs. de Havilland stitched the fabric for the wings, conscious that her husband's life might depend on every seam. When the plane was finished in the year 1909, de Havilland took it off, flew 40 yards - and crashed. Undaunted, he built another and he and that plane learned to fly together. Sitting unprotected on the wing, cap jammed backwards on his head; his sharp face seeming to cut into the wind, the tyro pilot knew his first sweet victory over his lifelong friend and enemy, the air. It coincided with the birth of his first son, Geoffrey, destined to become the most famous test-pilot in Britain. The heady excitement continued until the £1,000 ran out; but the success of his first aircraft had landed him a job at the Royal Balloon Factory (later the Royal Aircraft Factory) and he and Hearle set to work to produce Britain's first military planes. De Havilland's later models, the D.H.4 and the D.H.9, were the workhorses of the war and many hundreds of de Havilland machines saw service over France. [7]

The new Albatros D.III arrived on the Western Front early in 1917 and the opinion of many was that 'it is easy to fly and superior to all enemy aircraft at the front.' But aerial superiority was not to remain permanently with the German air service for, in the early spring of 1917 the Albatros scouts were no longer superior to their opponents; the Allies had introduced the SPAD S.VII, Sopwith's Camel and Triplane and the S.E.5. 8 Louis Bechereau designed the SPAD in 1916 around the new 150 hp Hispano-Suiza 8Ac 8-cylinder water-cooled engine. The SPAD VII flew for the first time in May that year and became one of the most famous French fighters used by the escadrilles de chasse (fighter squadrons) in the First World War. Large numbers also saw action with the RFC, US Army Air Service and Belgian and Italian air arms. The most famous unit to use the SPAD was the elite Group de Combat No 12, which was known generically as 'Les Cicognes' (The Storks'). Among its ranks was Capitaine Georges Guynemer, of SPA3 and the second top French ace with 54 confirmed kills, who flew the Spad VII in early 1917. In the late summer of 1917 the SPAD XIII made its appearance on the Western Front. Its high-aspect-ratio wing permitted a favourable rate of climb but the thin aerofoil and wing arrangement produced such bad gliding characteristics that pilots had to land the SPAD with engine on. Fortunately its robust construction enabled aviators to dive their machines with little worry of structural failure. RFC units equipped with the SPAD VII did not re-equip on the new type. No 23 Squadron was the only British squadron wholly equipped with the SPAD. It was plagued by the unreliability of its Hispano-Suiza engine and after an undistinguished career 23 Squadron replaced the SXIII in May 1918 with the Sopwith Dolphin. The SVII outlived the Spad XIII in the RAF, continuing in post-war service with 72 Squadron in Palestine and Nos. 30 and 63 Squadrons in Mesopotamia.

The loss of Spad XIII orders for the RFC was more than made up for by the introduction of the type into service with eleven squadriglie of the Italian 'Aeronautica del Regio Esercito', one Belgian squadron and sixteen squadrons of the American Army Air Service after the US entered the war in April 1917. Capitaine René Fonck, of Escadrille SPA103 of Groupe de Combat No 12 and the leading French ace with 75 confirmed kills, used the Spad SXIII to shoot down six aircraft each on two days in September 1918. Other SPAD aces included Major Maggiore Baracca, CO of the 91 a Squadriglia during the winter of 1917-18. His Spad XIII carried his famous prancing horse insignia in which his score rose to 34 confirmed victories. He was killed in June 1918 and was Italy's leading ace of the First World War.

The SPAD XIII was a favourite mount of the American contingent on the Western Front. Second Lieutenant Frank Luke Jr, of the 27th Aero Squadron, flew Spad XIII fighters to score 21 aerial victories in just seventeen days. He finished as the second top American ace to Captain 'Eddie' Rickenbacker, last CO of 94th Aero Squadron who achieved most of his record 26 confirmed kills in a SPAD SXIII.[9] Third highest American scorer with seventeen confirmed kills was Major Gervais Raoul Lufbery who was killed on 19 May 1918. Born of French parents, Lufbery served with the SPA12 'Escadrille Lafayette' until America's entry into the war and he subsequently became CO of the 94th Aero Squadron where he flew a SPAD XIII painted with a Sioux Indian head and swastikas as his personal good luck symbol. Although 8,472 SVIIs and SXIIIs were built, only 1,141 of these were produced by SPAD.

The Camel was a classic dog-fighting aircraft, developed as a successor to the Pup. It got its name from the 'hump' over the gun breeches of the two fixed, synchronized Vickers machine-guns. The nickname 'Camel' was later officially adopted by the Royal Flying Corps. From the outset excellent manoeuvrability was all important so most of the Camel's weight (engine, fuel tanks, machine-guns, ammunition and pilot) was concentrated well forward near the centre of gravity. Its short fuselage and the high torque of the large rotary engine could easily trap the unwary pilot but in the hands of an experienced aviator it was a close rival to the Fokker DRVII, which is generally regarded as the finest fighter of the First World War but the Camel was the most successful, destroying a record total of 2,800 enemy aircraft on the Western Front alone. The Camel first went into action with the Royal Flying Corps in July 1917 with 70 Squadron. By October 1918 the RAF had more than 2,600 Camels on charge, equipping 32 squadrons. The type also served on the Western Front with the 'Aviation Militaire Belge' and the US Air Service. Camels also equipped ten Royal Naval Air Service squadrons which subsequently became RAF squadrons in April 1918. The RNAS Camel first saw action on 4 June 1917 during a single combat by Flight Commander A. M. Shook. On 4 July that year five F1 Camels from the RNAS station at Dunkirk attacked a formation of Gothas returning from a raid over England. The F1 Camel served with both the RFC and the RNAS but the 2F1 was designed especially for operation as a shipboard fighter. It differed from the previous model in having tubular centre-section struts instead of wooden struts and the fuselage was constructed in two halves, the rear half being detachable to conserve space aboard ship.

Since 1914 the air defence of Great Britain was entrusted to the RNAS, until the RFC took over the responsibility again and the main operational function of the 2F1 Camels was to intercept Zeppelins over the North Sea. As a result many Camels were carried aboard warships and flown from platforms mounted above gun turrets. The last Zeppelin to be destroyed in air combat was shot down on 10 August 1918 by Lieutenant S. D. Culley flying a 2F1 Camel from a lighter towed out to sea by a destroyer of the Harwich Force. By the end of the war these comparatively 'hot' aircraft were able to operate safely from the first conventional carriers of the Royal Navy. On 17 July 1918 seven 2F1's, each carrying two 50lb bombs, flew off from the deck of HMS *Furious* and six successfully destroyed two Zeppelins during a bombing raid on the airship sheds at Tondern. By October 1918, 129 2F1 Camels were serving in the RNAS and 112 were carried aboard Royal Navy ships. Most Naval Camel squadrons were disbanded in 1919. A total of 5,490 Camels was built.

The SE5a, developed from the SE (Scout Experimental) 5, was one of the finest single-seat fighters of the First World War and the favourite mount of many British aces. One exception was Captain Albert Ball who flew the prototype SE5 in November 1916. He claimed the large celluloid windscreen impaired vision and he later had his own SE5 modified. Ironically, Ball was killed in an SE5 on 7 May 1917. His Squadron, No 56, was the first to receive the SE5, at London Colney, Hertfordshire on 13 March 1917. Next month 56 Squadron was posted to France and became the first of fourteen squadrons to use the type on the Western Front. Deliveries of the SE5a began in June 1917 and eventually the type equipped 24 squadrons of the RFC and RAF in France, Palestine, Macedonia, Mesopotamia and the United Kingdom. It also equipped one squadron of the Australian Flying Corps and two squadrons of the US Air Service. The SE5a was a very powerful and robust fighter which owed its combat success to a combination of speed and its stability as a gun platform. A total of 5,205 machines (SE5/SE5a) were built. Plans for a further 1,000 SE5a aircraft to be built by the Curtiss Company in America were cancelled after the cessation of hostilities.

From the end of March to the middle of October 1916 the new British machines enabled the officers of the RFC to recover their former superiority. On some sectors the range of enemy vision extended only a few hundred yards beyond their fire-trenches, while the aerial eyes of the British and French armies ranged over hundreds of miles of German activities. The Krupp works at Essen were bombarded by two French airmen on 22 September 1916; and on 17 November, Captain de Beauchamp, in his Sopwith biplane, carried out a raid on Munich.

It was now the turn of the Germans to take steps to recover their lost supremacy. Late in 1916 new fighting machines began to appear in German Jagdstaffeln (literally, Hunting Squadrons) the streamlined Albatros D.I and D.II scouts with plywood-skinned fuselage and twin synchronised machine-guns firing through the propeller arc and the Halberstadt D. Series with a 240hp engine. In the first week of October 1916 the new aircraft soared above the British fighting planes. Possessing terrific speed and extraordinary power of climb, they enabled the German pilots to operate at the amazing working height of 17,000 to 20,000 feet and to swoop upon all British battle-planes that could not cruise at more than 12,000 or 15,000 feet. Casualty lists began to show that the RFC was again losing heavily and Haig, in his communiqués, admitted day after day serious losses in machines. In a dispatch written in the last week of December 1916 the British commander-in-chief significantly remarked: 'I desire to point out that the maintenance of the mastery of the air, which is essential, entails a constant and most liberal supply of the most up-to-date machines, without which the most skilful pilots cannot succeed'.

The loss of the mastery of the air for six months from October 1915 to March 1916 was due to the fact that the old Royal Aircraft product B.E.2c was not so fast or so handy as the Fokker. There were some machines at the front capable of dealing with the Fokker on equal terms, but they were not available in sufficient numbers. The first de Havilland fighter, answering the Fokker, was shot down by the enemy in the spring of 1916, the day after it arrived at the front. On 3 January 1917 the first British machine of superior power to the Spad and Halberstadt was given to the Germans. It was a Handley-Page super-aeroplane, with two Rolls-Royce engines, giving together 500 hp and its RNAS pilot lost his way in the mist and landed within the enemy's lines.

The year 1916 culminated in the Battle of the Somme, when the British troops went 'over the top' in their thousands to take the German front-line trenches, which they were assured would have been obliterated by artillery bombardment. Unfortunately they had not been obliterated: the Germans rushed from dug-outs to their trenches and mowed down the advancing British forces. Almost 20,000 of them were killed.

The struggle for supremacy in the air which had been raging so fiercely during 1916 continued unabated into the next year.

In the early days of 1917 it became known that the Germans intended, by the spring of 1918, to maintain a total of 3,500 machines at their front. This would have required a steady output of 1,350 machines a month. In the first six months of 1917 the Allies on the Western front claimed to have brought down 1,401 German machines and 52 kite balloons, while the Germans claimed to have destroyed 955 machines and 45 kite balloons. During the early months of 1917, Britain carried the air war into German territory; but despite the skill and courage of the British aces the experiment was a costly one. From 56 in January, British casualties among airmen rose to 119 in February and to 152 in March, while on one single day in April 117 casualties were reported. April was a very black period for the RFC and the situation became extremely grave. The German scout pilots were aggressive and seldom hesitated to attack the British machines even when outnumbered. The fact that they were equipped with very fine aeroplanes, the Albatros D III single-seater and the Halberstadt, gave them confidence and the frequent successes which came to them in combats encouraged them to further efforts. In a similar way the scout machines of the British squadrons were at that time definitely outclassed. The little DH 2, which had done so well, was now obsolete; it was too slow and its armament of a single Lewis gun was inferior to the twin synchronized machine - guns of the German scouts.

The German Air Force began to lose the ascendancy that it had held over the Western Front in the early summer of 1917. The Allies had introduced the Spad S-7 and the S.E.5 and the situation was considered by the German High Command to be so serious that new fighter equipment had to be found with the least possible delay. German aircraft manufacturers were ordered to develop a new fighter with all haste. From the late summer the Fokker Dr.I triplane had been adopted by Jasta 1 led by Manfred von Richthofen. Richthofen himself had selected the Dr.I, despite his aversion for rotary engines. But this hope faded after Gontermann and Pastor lost their lives when their Fokker triplanes disintegrated in the air and when suspicion arose that certain losses in air combat may have been due to similar structural failures, the Fokker Werke was accused of criminal negligence. The promising Dr.I, which was perfectly sound structurally, was thus banned until November-December, 1917, when improved wings had been supplied.

The new Albatros scouts meanwhile, offered little improvement in performance and precious time had been lost in providing better fighters for use on the Western Front which was now a source of bitter complaints. In consequence, even as late as May 1918 newly established Jagdstaffeln had to be equipped with the hopelessly obsolete Albatros D.Va. Vizefeldwebel Jentsch, one of Jasta 61's pilots, wrote of this period: 'The SPADs usually fly and manoeuvre at about 20,000 feet. With our Albatros we can only just reach 16,500 feet!' Leutnant Osterkamp, a most successful pilot of the Naval Fighter Wing, had already reported in 1917 that 'The Albatros D.III is no longer sufficient. The Camel and the SPAD are its superiors and the new de Havillands are so fast that they run away from us. The newer Albatros D.V. is better, more elegant but weakly constructed and several structural failures have occurred in the air.'

The Albatros D-VI was almost a duplicate of the earlier D-V and no improvement. The Pfalz was obviously too weak for combat flying, while the L.F.G. had no visibility and the A.E.G. was an out-and-out flop. Anthony Fokker (a Dutchman) and Reinhold Platz's VII design, based on the tri-decker Dr I, won the single-seat fighter competition in January 1918. Extremely manoeuvrable at high altitudes, complete flying control could be maintained at low flying speeds. Its 'N'-shaped interplane struts eliminated drag-producing rigging wires in the wings. The first D.VIIs began to reach the Western Front in May during Germany's abortive spring offensive, at a time when the morale of Germany's fighter pilots had reached its lowest ebb. Allied squadrons proved superior but throughout the summer and autumn the D-VII replaced inferior fighting scouts in the majority of Germany's Jagdstaffeln. Germany's fighter pilots soon took advantage of the D-VII's fast turn and other flying characteristics. A favourite form of attack was to hang the aircraft on its propeller below an Allied aircraft while firing the two synchronized Spandaus. By July swarms of D.VIIs were preying on Allied aircraft and soon, almost every Jagdstaffel serving on the Western Front had been re-equipped with the formidable new weapon. The D.VII's ability to retain sensitive control at low flying speeds (it could virtually 'hang on its prop' and pump bullets into its enemy whilst so doing) and extreme altitudes; its rapid climb and remarkable dive recovery, its nicety of control; all contributed to the ascendancy which it immediately gained over all Allied fighters.

Rittmeister Manfred Freiherr von Richthofen's famous 'Flying Circus' flew the Fokker D-VII in the Second Battle of Aisne in mid-1918. The D-VII was also the favourite mount of other German aces such as Leutnant Carl Degelow, CO of Jagdstaffel 40 who scored over twenty of his thirty confirmed victories flying a D-VII over a five-month period. Another was Hauptmann Rudolf Berthold, CO of Jagdgeschwader Nr 2, who finished the war with 44 confirmed victories.

By November 1918 almost 800 D-VIIs were in service with the German Army Air service but the type had arrived too late to influence the outcome of the air battle on the Western Front. It had proved such an outstanding adversary that the D-VII was specially referred to under the reparation clauses at the Treaty of Versailles. However, some examples managed to reach Holland where Fokker continued producing this outstanding fighter in limited numbers. The Fokker D-VII is generally regarded as the finest fighter of the First World War.

On 27 March 1918 King George V sent a telegram to Sir Douglas Haig, commander of British Forces in France which said: 'I wish to express to General Salmond and all ranks of the Air Services of the British Empire in France today my gratification at their splendid achievements in this great battle. I am proud to be their Colonel-in-Chief.' Five days later, on 1 April, the Royal Air Force officially came into being as a separate service. To the flying men themselves, however, the actual birthday was March 26, the day of the 'great battle' to which King George V referred. It is interesting to note that General Eric von Ludendorff, in his War Memoirs, also refers to this same offensive as the 'great battle.'

Those who did the flying in this battle, the men of the RFC and the Royal Naval Air Service, entered the lists as rivals. But so intense was the heat of the battle that all pettiness was burnt away and the erstwhile rivals had already become one in spirit before, on 1 April, they became one in name.

To appreciate the violence and vital significance of that battle it is only necessary to record two plain facts: one is that never before or since has Britain been so close to final and overwhelming disaster; the other is that the battle would quite certainly have been lost but for the active participation of aircraft and 'active participation' means getting down to the job of actually fighting the enemy - not just helping the ground forces by reconnaissance, artillery observation and bombing behind the lines.

Why, though, was the situation so desperate? It must be remembered that an all-out German offensive on the Somme had been expected since the first fortnight in February and that by 20 March every man in the Fifth British Army, commanded by General Sir Hubert Gough, was perfectly sure that the blow would be struck on that front. The Staff, in fact, knew for certain that the 21st was to be the fateful day.

Thick fog shrouded the lines at 4 am when the battle suddenly broke with a shuddering crash on a front of about 44 miles between Croiselles and La Fere. By Sunday, the 24th, the situation at the junction between the left flank of the Fifth Army and the right flank of the Third had become extremely critical, for a gap nearly three miles wide had opened and the enemy were driving a wedge between the two armies.

The night of 25/26 March was wild with hail and snow, yet the RFC received the following order: 'A concentration of enemy troops has been located just west of Bapaume. Every available machine will leave the ground so as to attack this concentration at dawn with bombs and small-arm ammunition and break it up before any attack develops.' Nor was that all. Between the 25th and 27th nine new divisions reinforced the German Second Army on the Cambrai Front, while further south a massive attack developed on the Fifth Army's right flank and another wedge was thrust between themselves and the French at Roye - a wedge aimed at capturing Montdidier and so cutting the lateral railway which served the whole front. Had those two wedges not been stopped, the Allied line would have been broken into two halves by the extinction of the entire Fifth Army. Each half would have been outflanked, with the result that the French would have been rolled back southwards towards Paris while the Commonwealth Forces were pressed northwards towards the Channel ports. The war would have been lost with the loss of the ports.

That, then, was the situation on the 26th when the RFC and the RNAS were assigned the task of helping to hold the line and when Major General Salmond sent this order to his squadrons: Bomb and shoot up everything you can see... Very low flying essential. All risks to be taken. Urgent.

To this the squadrons responded by swarming into the gaps in such numbers that collisions were a constant hazard and flying was so low that some of the enemy were knocked out by undercarriage wheels. A case of this was recorded by a bugler of the 8th German Grenadier Regiment, who wrote: 'Several Tommies flew so low that the wheels of their aeroplanes touched the ground. My company commander, Lieutenant Nedee, had to fling himself 'flat on the ground, but for all that he was struck on the back by the wheels of one machine, thus being literally run over.'

And what was it like from the point of view of the men who did the flying? Messes were full with groups who talked excitedly and discussed the war news. Now it was that the Germans had advanced ten miles and that every man, gun and beast was being hurried up to stop them; now that they were being decoyed by a skilful retreat into a trap that was to end the war.

Every day, from March 21, recorded more cases of aerodromes shelled and captured; of kit - and even personnel that had to be abandoned; of confusion and lack of communications; heroic counter-attacks that failed to stem the advance; loss of men, guns spiked and left for the enemy; machines burnt. Then came the 26th, when the squadrons took-off at dawn and flew east at a height of five hundred feet. They passed over little villages whose cottages showed furtively between the wintry skeletons of trees. Along every road wound an interminable string of lorries, past which there occasionally flashed some furiously-riding motor-cyclist. Like graves on the bleak countryside were freshly - dug trenches. All was clammy, sodden, grey and yellow.

When the aircraft reached the battleground, little puffs of smoke thickly dotted the mud, suddenly appearing and slowly melting away. Occasionally some explosion, mightier than the others, would throw up red tongues of flame that changed to sullen black smoke. No definite trenches could be seen - only scratches in the earth connecting shell-holes. Dull green water filled their hollows and round their muddy circumferences lay dark specks, some of which moved and some lay still... Roads did not exist in this wilderness. They entered from the west, but grew fainter and fainter in outline as they were battered into the surrounding swamps until they vanished completely. Over all the chaos the mist drove slowly.

Dead horses and shapeless bundles of clothes lay scattered in the mud. Streams of scarlet tracer-bullets leaped endlessly upwards. The air was heavy and agitated by shells whose wakes hurled the aircraft about in their passage. Ever and again some machine, cut short in its flight, crashed into the ground and flared with a sudden blaze. Many more, like blackened skeletons, burnt fitfully or lay on their backs with buckled wings. Despite the cold, the pilots sweated with the exertion of weaving stick and rudder-bar. Those who survived returned to their aerodromes time after time for more ammunition and fuel; then back to the lines and the beehives of smoke mixed with flying lumps of flesh...

On the evening of Tuesday the 26th General Gough spoke on the telephone to the Chief of the General Staff and told him that the energy of the attacks was weakening and that the Germans were nearing exhaustion. And it was in the last throes of the battle that a new service was born - or, to be more accurate, its birth was officially registered. What did they think about this change, the men of the RFC and RNAS? The answer is quite simple and perhaps a little unexpected. They were much too busy fighting to think about it at all!

Monday, 1 April 1918 dawned a fair enough day on the Western Front and visibility was good. The new service had been in operation since the first minute of its registration with bombing attacks made during the night by the 3rd, 5th, 7th and 9th Brigades on Douai railway station and the German barracks there. Then, after sun-up came reports of enemy air activity south of the Somme. The aircraft were mainly two-seaters, which were flying low, firing at British troops. But there was a promise of some good air-to-air combats, with the further report of enemy scouts flying high. The British pilots were not disappointed. Captain G. E. H. McElroy of 24 Squadron spotted three enemy scouts while on patrol in his S.E.5. McElroy, who was to notch up an unofficial score of 52 enemy aircraft before being killed at the end of July, held the advantage of height. Swiftly he dived. McElroy picked one aircraft and was able to get within one hundred yards without being spotted. He took aim carefully and then poured 100 rounds into the German. It was with great satisfaction that McElroy watched his prey fall gracefully off on to one wing and crash in a field just north of Ignaucourt. Nearby, at Beaucourt, Lieutenant Viscount Glentworth found himself involved in a hair-raising ground-level chase with a German scout. He had discovered four Germans attacking two SE5s and had chosen one of the enemy as his victim. Glentworth dived, but the German saw him coming and swooped to within fifty feet of the ground. The British pilot stuck to his tail, oblivious of the trees and shrubs flashing past perilously close. At last Glentworth had the enemy in his sights and let off fifty rounds. The German flew straight into a group of trees, where his aircraft disintegrated. A ground chase with different results was the lot of Lieutenant W. J. A. Duncan. He had dived on to an enemy aircraft which was firing at British troops. A low-level chase ensued, lead-behind the British lines and unexpectedly, the German landed in an open field. Not to be baulked, Duncan came down, too and ran up to the German, brandishing his revolver. But the German pilot had been wounded and was in no mood for resistance.

By sunset on 1 April the RAF had shot down seventeen enemy aircraft. By the end of the first week the total was 57 German aircraft destroyed and a further 37 driven down out of control. Against this total, the RAF had lost 47 aeroplanes. It was during this week, on 4 April, that General Eric von Ludendorff himself admitted that Germany had lost the war.

Meanwhile, far away from the front, at the Hotel Cecil in London (disrespectfully known as 'Bolo House'), no fewer than fifteen different committees were simultaneously sitting and debating such matters as new badges of rank and a suitable colour for the new uniform. But the men who really mattered - the men who were flying the Camels, the SE5s, the Bristol Fighters, the R.E.8s, the Dolphins and the rest - just went on (flying and doing their job. There is something of a lesson to be learned from that fact and it goes right back past

1918 to 5 June 1912. On that day the Royal Flying Corps suffered the first of many thousands of casualties. Captain Eustace Loraine and his passenger, Staff Sergeant R. H. V. Wislon crashed and were killed near Stonehenge. Immediately, the order was issued that flying would go on as usual that evening.

And flying has been going on ever since. [10]

Footnotes Chapter 1

2   Adapted from *Tales of Hazard* (John Lane, Bodley Head Ltd) in *RAF Flying Review* (December 1956).

3   Boelcke was born in 1891. He gained his pilot's certificate at the Halberstadt Flying School on 15 August 1914. He was posted to La Ferte to join Feldftiegerabteilung 13 in September, and, with his brother Wilhelm as observer, soon amassed a considerable number of sorties in army co-operation Albatros B II biplanes. By early 1915 he had 42 sorties in his log-book and had been awarded the Iron Cross, 2nd Class. In April, having received the Iron Cross, 1st Class, he secured a posting to Hauptmann Kastner's Feldftiegerabteilung 62, where he flew an armed machine for the first time - an Albatros C I. He displayed great spirit and enabled his observer to shoot down a Morane by his skilful and aggressive flying. He was selected to fly early examples of Fokker's E-series armed monoplane scouts; few were available and Boelcke, Kastner and Immelmann at first took turns to fly them. Boelcke's success as a combat pilot was matched by his grasp of technical matters and his organising ability. His ideas for the use of squadrons composed entirely of fighting scouts commanded attention in high places; until mid-1916 most units operated mixed equipment, and the concept of an offensive force of single-seater scouts carrying the war directly to the enemy's air forces was entirely new. After a tour of other fronts early in 1916, Boelcke returned to the West and was given command of the new Jagdstaffel Nr. 2. He trained his pilots personally and revealed a great gift for patient and inspiring instruction, so that his hand-picked group of pilots, flying the sleek new Albatros D I and D II scouts, became the scourge of the Western Front. Many of the greatest aces of the Luftstreitkrdfte served their apprenticeship in Jasta 2 and Boelcke commanded great respect and affection among his young subordinates. He was killed on 28 October 1916 when the wing of his Albatros D.II was struck by Erwin Boehme's Albatros and the aircraft broke up before he could land. He was 25 years old and the victor of 40 aerial combats. *Air Facts and Feats: A Guinness Record of Aerospace Achievement*, compiled by Francis K. Mason and Martin C. Windrow (Guinness Superlatives Ltd 1970).

4   Immelmann was serving with Fl. Abt. 62 at Douai when the first Fokker monoplane scouts became available. On 1 August 1915 Immelmann scored his first victory while flying an E I, when his comrade was forced to drop out of the fight with a defective machine gun. Thereafter he and Hauptmann Oswald Boelcke ranged over their sector of the front, sometimes together, sometimes alone, hunting the enemy from the sky. Immelmann was idolised in Germany. He finally met his death, after shooting down 15 Allied aircraft on 18 June 1916. Flying near Lens, Immelmann attacked an F.E.2b of 25 Squadron RFC flown by 2nd Lieutenant George R. McCubbin with Corporal J. H. Waller as gunner. The Fokker made an attacking pass and then went into a dive and broke up in mid-air. Some sources claim that his death was caused by technical failure, but the RFC credited Waller with the victory. *Air Facts and Feats: A Guinness Record of Aerospace Achievement,* compiled by Francis K. Mason and Martin C. Windrow (Guinness Superlatives Ltd 1970).

5   On 5 June 1917 Arthur Rhys Davids received a telegram informing him that along with Captain Crowe and 2nd Lieutenant Hoidge, he had been awarded the Military Cross. Arthur proved modest about the whole affair. He claimed that although he was excited, he didn't consider that after a month at the front he deserved such an award when Crowe had been to France on three separate occasions.

6   *Air Facts and Feats: A Guinness Record of Aerospace Achievement*, compiled by Francis K. Mason and Martin C. Windrow (Guinness Superlatives Ltd 1970).

7   *Geoffrey de Havilland; the unconquerable pioneer of the air* by Francis Vivian Drake, writing in *RAF Flying Review* in 1959.

8   The letters SPAD indicate that the machine was built by the 'Societe Pour Aviation et ses Derives', a firm founded by M. Bleriot on the wreck of the business of M. Armand Deperdussin. Originally the firm was called the 'Socie'te Pour les Appareils Deperdussin'.

9   Edward Vernon Rickenbacker was born in 1890 in Columbus, Ohio. He made a considerable name for himself between 1910 and 1917 as one of America's leading racing motorists. In England to negotiate the establishment of a Sunbeam racing team in 1917, he became interested in flying; and when America's entry into the war sent him back to the United States, he advanced the idea of a squadron composed entirely of racing drivers. The idea did not arouse official interest, but a meeting with General Pershing in Washington led to Rickenbacker's enlistment and sent him to France as the General's chauffeur. In August 1917 he transferred to the Aviation Section, and his mechanical expertise led to a posting to the 3rd Aviation Instruction Centre at Issoudun as Chief Engineering Officer - a post he filled with great competence, but much impatience. In his own time he completed advanced flying and gunnery courses and in March 1918 he finally secured a transfer to the 94th Aero Squadron - the 'Hat-in-the-Ring' squadron commanded by Raoul Lufbery, the Escadrille Lafayette ace. With Lufbery and Douglas Campbell, Rickenbacker flew the first American patrol over enemy lines on 19th March; and on 29th April he shot down his first victim, an Albatros scout. On 30 May his fifth victory qualified him as an ace, but it was to be his last for four months. An ear infection put him in hospital and convalescence until mid-September, when he returned to the squadron as a Captain and Flight Commander. On 14 September he shot down a Fokker and by the end of the month had sent three more Fokkers, a Halberstadt and a balloon to join it. He took over command of the 94th on 25th September and continued to score heavily until the Armistice. *Air Facts and Feats: A Guinness Record of Aerospace Achievement*, compiled by Francis K. Mason and Martin C. Windrow (Guinness Superlatives Ltd 1970).

10   *We Were Too Busy Fighting* by John Gurdon DFC writing in *RAF Flying Review,* April 1918.

Chapter 2

The Grim Game of Escape

J. R. Ackerley

According to one source [11] 'more British prisoners of war (168,846 British and Commonwealth other ranks and 6,778 officers) were taken on the Western Front than in any other theatre. Many of the 1918 prisoners did not travel to Germany, but remained just behind the German lines on the Western Front, where they were forced to work. By the end of the war 319,138 Germans and 10,429 Austrians had been captured on the Western Front, while German naval prisoners numbered 6,410 and nine from Austria. By 1918 over 250,000 enemy PoWs were being held in over 500 camps in Britain... Approximately 192,000 British and Commonwealth servicemen became PoWs in World War I. Over 16,000 did not return and those that did were often reluctant to talk. A spate of books were written during and after the First World War but most of the literary output relating to the prison camp experience concentrated almost entirely on escapes and successful 'home runs'. This was evidently seen as being the area of most interest to the reading public. The relatively mundane existence of boredom, deprivation and daily struggle for survival, described by Captain J. R. Ackerley of the 8th East Surrey Regiment, as 'that gloomy general background of monotonous waiting and wasting' was clearly not regarded as a subject that would sell. Comparatively few men escaped, although many would have dreamt of doing so.'

'Although I was a prisoner of war in Germany I never attempted to escape' wrote Captain J. R. Ackerley in 1932 . [12] 'In fact, as far as I can recall those times, which now seem so remote and unreal, I never even thought of doing so. Perhaps the fact that I was taken rather late in the war, in the middle of 1917, had something to do with that, for by that time I may well have been too stunned and frightened to do anything more than 'stay put.'

Ackerley, the author of *Hindoo Holiday and The Prisoners of War*, a play,[13] had joined up in October 1914 at the age of 17. He was wounded on the Somme on 1 July 1916. Again wounded and taken prisoner in May 1917 he spent eight months in Germany, first in hospital at Hanover and then at prison-camps of Karlsruhe, Heidelberg and Augustabad. Invalided to Switzerland, he was interned for the rest of the war. 'Not only did I not try to escape myself, but I do not remember that anyone else tried to escape from any of the three camps in which I found myself. Perhaps these two facts are to some extent related, for the Germans tried to segregate the 'bad boys' (persistent escapers and such) into special camps where a stricter discipline and closer supervision were kept and where the atmosphere of unrest they generated would not affect 'good boys' like myself.

Generally speaking, there seem to have been three separate problems connected with escaping; breaking camp, reaching the frontier and crossing the frontier and the comparative difficulties attaching to these three problems varied with period, camp and country. Chance, of course, always played a pretty large part in each of them, but in the last two it sometimes took almost complete charge. To break out of most of the camps in Turkey, for example, was not the most serious problem of the three. The real questions there, in the heart of Asia, were how to cross several hundred miles of waterless desert and mountainous, robber-infested country and perhaps worse still, what on earth to do when one reached the Black Sea, or Marmora, or the Mediterranean, or whatever shore one was making for. Both these problems were very chancy indeed. One had to leave a lot - far too much - on the knees of the Gods. The difficulties and hardships were, in fact, so dark and incalculable that a number of prisoners in Turkey devised other methods of escape which involved securing the unconscious assistance of their captors themselves. That is the story of Lieutenant E. H. Jones IARO of *The Road to En-Dor* fame and he describes how he hoodwinked the Turks into setting him free. In these islands, too, there was one of those exceptional and daunting difficulties; the coast. Up to that point the escaper could foresee, calculate; the difficulties were much the same as those confronting our own men in Germany; but then, at the coast, little more than chance remained. That is why so few of the prisoners we took managed to escape completely; it was due to our 'splendid isolation,' as one of them told me.

In Germany and of course in other inland countries too, the three problems were, so to speak, more fairly set. Although there was an element of chance in all of them, in none did it play so disproportionate and discouraging a part as in Turkey and England. The actual camp-breaking was undoubtedly, I think, the main problem in Germany, though the subsequent difficulties mustn't be under-estimated. They were very ticklish indeed and required a very high degree of caution, patience and endurance; in fact, I believe that as many, if not more, attempts to escape were scotched outside the German camps as inside them. The distances to the frontiers varied, of course; but, long or short, the time the journeys took was greatly prolonged, since the escapers could only march by night and in a roundabout way across country, avoiding roads and villages. During the daytime - sixteen or seventeen hours - they had to lie up in hiding, in whatever cover came to hand before dawn broke. That may not sound much, but it was, I can well believe, the worst part of the whole journey. Try it and see how long you can stick it, lying close in one place and then imagine the effect on men who were hunted and hungry and whose nerves were already ragged with anxiety and impatience. At this rate it sometimes took them as long as three or four weeks to reach the frontier and they lived all this time on whatever condensed foods they could carry, eked out with raw vegetables from the fields.

They got lost, hungry and tired; they were exposed to all weathers and they became so dirty and unshaven that a single glimpse of them must inevitably have aroused suspicion and betrayed them. It was, in fact, a very nerve-racking journey and the frontier problem, if they got that far, was even more ticklish, for how does one find a frontier in total darkness, in the country, with a compass and small-scale map? How does one find it, that's to say, especially when one is already fagged out and impatient, without blundering into the arms of one of the numerous, invisible sentries, who may be a yard or a mile away, or without attracting their attention by some small noise; the snapping of a twig? How the devil was one to know, as one crawled along, on hands and knees, in and out of ditches, whether one had reached and crossed it or not for there was often nothing, deep in the country, to mark the boundary at all, except this close but invisible ring of sentries? Indeed, it sometimes happened that escapers did crawl across into safety without knowing it and then, owing to some twist in the line, crawled back into Germany and captivity again. So these two problems were by no means negligible; they required the greatest care and patience; but they did not require, I think, the ingenuity needed for breaking out of camp and the escapers from Germany in this volume, since they have not a great deal of space at their disposal, will concentrate mainly upon that. That was the real nut; that was where the fun came in and I think you will be amused and surprised at the skill with which they tackled it.

They burrowed under the defences of the camps like moles; they swooped over them like bats; they swam the moats in broad daylight under the noses of the sentries with their faces painted white and green to resemble water-lilies. But was there any expedient they did not think of? Any impudent trick they did not play in all the countries concerned? No Raffles or Arsene Lupin can lay claim to anything like the resource, the ingenuity, the inexhaustible invention shown by these prison-breakers in their stories. And not merely that. Consider too the patience and determination required. For these were seldom reckless acts, suddenly undertaken on the spur of the moment. They were usually most carefully planned and months and months of thought and work went to their preparation. The smallest detail of disguise or equipment was painstakingly considered; the remotest adverse contingency prepared against as far as possible. And all the time they were being watched.

Imagine yourselves in these circumstances digging a hundred foot tunnel with a table-spoon, for instance, or cutting through an iron window-bar with a saw made out of a broken razor-blade, for it must be remembered, too, that they started their careers as prison-breakers with nothing and the collecting together of tools and an escaping kit alone was a long and complicated business. Artful code messages were sent home in letters asking for such things as maps and compasses, which were smuggled back in the food parcels. Needless to say the contents of these parcels were most carefully examined before the prisoners were allowed to have them - tins of food were opened and emptied and things prodable were prodded with skewers. But much of the contraband got through to them nevertheless. What couldn't be procured in this and other ways they had to make for themselves. More than that, they had to make the very tools with which they made them. And all out of nothing; out of odds and ends. And that is what comes out most in these stories: patience and determination. For schemes which had taken months of hard work to prepare often failed at the last moment. The conspirators were suddenly ordered to another camp, or the tunnel fell in during its last few yards, or the plot was discovered, or the escapers, having achieved the first part of their plan and broken out of the camp, were retaken before they crossed the frontier. But no sooner had one of these schemes failed and the punishment for it been served, than another scheme was at once set afoot. They enjoyed it; undoubtedly they enjoyed it. It kept them going and apart from the serious object of it all, they extracted from it a great deal of fun. The game was very like one of those board games we used to play as boys; the game was tireless. The camp was the board. Picture it. It varied in detail from place to place, but the general plan was always much the same. Here is a description of one prison camp, chosen at random.

'It was bounded all round by a fence of solid boarding, about eight feet high, with six strands of overhung barbed wire on top. Outside this was a twenty-strand barbed wire fence about ten feet high; in all about thirty-one miles of wire were used for a perimeter of six hundred yards. There was one sentry or more at every angle outside and sentries inside at every point where buildings stood close to the board fence. There were big arc lights dotted about all over the inside and small electric lamps at about twenty yard intervals along the board fence...'

That is the kind of thing. Another camp might be an old fortress surrounded by a moat to add to the difficulties; but the general scheme of defence was much the same.

And inside, in blocks of buildings or huts, were the prisoners, men of all nationalities, intent on getting out. How did they do it? Sometimes, particularly in some of those special camps in which most of the persistent escapers were segregated, the problem that confronted them as they prowled round the defences simulating innocent perambulation, but in reality keenly investigating for weak spots, the problem seemed insoluble. So many various attempts had already been made, even here, that the captors seemed wise to every possible move and had taken counter precautions. Extra sentries and arc lamps had been placed; Alsatian police dogs added; surprise searches were constantly made; extra roll-calls at particularly inconvenient times instituted. The situation seemed hopeless. Was there any move left? There was. It seems there always was. How was it done? The escapers themselves will tell you.

A good many of the books which have been published in all countries about escaping, especially those published during or soon after the war, are coloured with the animosities and prejudices of that time and I believe that a number of their authors could now wish this otherwise.

Prisoners of war were treated the same in every country that took part in the war and when they received, as they occasionally did receive in all countries, real kindness and consideration, then we may be surprised and grateful that such good qualities managed to survive the poison and the pettiness of those times. That is the most that can be said. For war is not intended to bring out the best and kindest in men; the emotions it deliberately calls forth and fosters hatred, fear, greed, revenge are not pretty emotions and do not beget pretty manners. But in any case such matters are irrelevant to this book, for it was never from hardship or injustice, where they existed, that these men were escaping though such conditions may sometimes have supplied a purely artificial stimulus.

The urge to escape sprang from something much deeper than physical conditions; it sprang from a very deep human instinct indeed - the need for self-expression; and that is why these stories must appeal to all of us, for they touch a universal note which inspires our own actions, not only in war but in peace. Prisoners of war were on the shelf and they felt it all the time. They were unimportant, they were unused and especially to educated men that is a very dreadful thing indeed. It was not just being separated from countries, families, friends; it was not just being out of the war; it went deeper than that; it was a thwarting of the free and natural growth of individual life and it has permanently stunted many a once eager and ambitious spirit.

The danger was not an indefinable, ubiquitous, helpless danger such as that run, for instance, by a wiring party in No-man's land or raiders upon enemy trenches. Death would not drop from out of the skies or mine the ground under their feet. It was, comparatively speaking, locatable, accountable and therefore a danger against which they could, to some extent, pit their wits. And that is the point: the success or failure of their efforts all through did largely depend upon their own skill and abilities; they could and did use their wits; they had usually what is called a sporting chance. But modern war itself can hardly be said to be liberal with its sporting chances and the soldier in his trench or the sailor on his ship may be as clever as paint, but how far will that help him against gas and mines and long range guns?

Perhaps these adventure tales are the last war-escape stories that will ever be told, for it may not be fanciful to suppose that if ever there is another great war there will be no more prisoners, except in so far as nations can be imprisoned within the boundaries of their lands and dart about from end to end in their efforts to escape the poisons that fall from the sky.'

These words recalling the 'war to end all wars' were published in 1932. Only seven years' later history was repeated when the German Blitzkrieg unleashed World War Two and nations fought a bitter conflict which was to last for six long years. Captain J. R. Ackerley and millions like him could not possibly have imagined the horrific poisons that would fall from the sky, at Guernica in the Spanish Civil War, in Warsaw, Rotterdam. London, Coventry and Hamburg, Berlin and Dresden and finally, the atomic holocaust that ended the war in the Far East in 1945. And yes, The Grim Game of Escape, as Ackerley describes it, was manifest in all of these theatres of war; in Britain, Poland and Germany and in Singapore and in a hundred other places.

Footnotes Chapter 2

11   *Tracing Your Prisoner of War Ancestors; The First World War, A Guide for Family Historians* by Sarah Paterson (Pen & Sword 2012).

12   *Escapers All; Being the personal narratives of fifteen escapers from war-time prison camps 1914-1918* John Lane The Bodley Head Ltd 1932.

13   Both published by Chatto and Windus.

Chapter 3

Trapped In Belgium

Harry Beaumont

Harry Beaumont enlisted in the (Queens Own) Royal West Kent Regiment in February 1904 and served with the 2nd Battalion November 1904 to November 1912 in China, Singapore and India. He transferred to the Army Reserve in December 1912. Rejoining as a private on the outbreak of war in 1914, he went to France with the 1st Battalion, which was part of original British Expeditionary Force. He transferred to the RFC in 1917.

On the morning of 24th August 1914, the first day of the Retreat from Mons, I have a very hazy recollection of being put out of action by the combination of a German shell and a brick wall. I was picked up about twenty-four hours later and taken to a hospital by Belgian civilians. I was put to bed there suffering from a slight wound in the groin and concussion from which I recovered in a week. The hospital was at the pit head of a colliery in the village of Wasmes, about seven miles south west of Mons and the staff consisted of one nurse, two doctors (both very old) and a few voluntary workers of both sexes. The leader of this little band was named D'Capiaux, a young Belgian engineer who had been educated in England and spoke very good English.

There were about forty British patients, most of whom were officers and NCOs and there was also one German patient, a Prussian. Things were very disorganised just then and it was some days before the Germans noticed our hospital. They were too busy elsewhere but they soon took over control and we British automatically became 'Prisoners of War.' They made the Belgians responsible for supplying us with food and medical comforts, but there was very little of either available. Most of the patients were in a pretty bad way and six out of eight amputation cases died of tetanus. A German doctor used to come visiting and after one of these visits a few men were transferred to prison camps in Germany; but I always managed to be absent when he came round, so I stayed on. The hospital was unguarded, as every man was supposed to be incapable of escape and the responsibility for our safe custody was placed upon the Belgians. The hospital authorities gave me the job of nursing one of the British officers. He was totally paralysed and the Belgians could do very little for him. I nursed him until he died about three weeks later. Doing this kind of work made me helpful to the Belgians and they used to give me the tip whenever the German officer came visiting. He always commenced at the officers' building and by the time he arrived at our end, my bed was rolled up and stowed away in the storeroom and I was well hidden in the scrap iron yard.

I went on dodging this fellow up to about the second or third week in October; then, one day, he checked the roll and suddenly discovered there was one man in that hospital that he had never seen. He was in a terrible rage and ordered the Belgians to search the colliery and produce me. They knew, of course, where to find me and I was taken before him. He glared at me and in very good English said, 'Why have you been absent from this hospital every time I've visited it?' I made the first excuse that came into my head: 'I didn't know you were coming. I'm fond of fresh air and spend most of my time in the grounds.' He said: 'Fresh air! Fresh air! You'll get all the fresh air you want very soon! I shall send you to Stettin-on-Oder! 'I said: 'Thank you' and returned to my ward with something to think about. I made up my mind there and then that I was not going to Stettin, but I had not the slightest idea what to do about it. Next day the answer came without my seeking. Lance-Corporal Arthur Heath of my regiment, who was one of the patients, had got very friendly with a Belgian and his wife by the name of Neusy, who used to visit the hospital. Heath took me into his confidence. He told me that if he could get to the Neusy's house they were going to look after him and get him out of the country when he was well enough. He was shot through the thigh and could not walk. Someone therefore would have to carry him from the hospital to the Neusys' house and I was the man he chose to do the job. I said I would do it, but would the Neusys look after me too. Heath said he did not know, but thought it would be all right. We then started getting ready. Heath practised walking up and down the ward with a couple of sticks and I looked round for a civilian suit.

Our ward was opposite the gas retorts and the stoker used to come in about 8 o'clock every night, change into overalls and hang his suit up near the door. He worked until about 3 o'clock in the morning and would then fall asleep until it was time to go home; so that suit was mine for the taking. On 26 October we were suddenly ordered to be in readiness to proceed to Germany at 10 o'clock on the following day, so there was now no time to be lost and we fixed 4 o'clock in the morning as the time for our escape. We arranged that as I was to do all the hard work, I should go to bed and Heath would keep awake and rouse me about ten minutes to four. I have already told you that one of the patients in the hospital was a Prussian and this Prussian was in our ward. He was badly wounded and seldom went to sleep and I was very much afraid that he would see us going and give the alarm. But a funny thing happened. That night he beckoned me to his bedside to help him turn over, which I had often done before. As soon as I had made him comfortable, to my surprise he gripped me by the hand and placed his finger on his lips. This was his way of telling me that he knew what was going on and would keep silent. It was decent of him; we were just brothers in distress.

At ten minutes to four I was roused by Heath, who quietly left the ward on his crutches. I saw him clear and then went to the stokehold and bagged the stoker's suit. I emptied everything out of the pockets and tied them up in a bundle in the old chap's red handkerchief and left it on the hook beside him. I did not want to rob him of more than I could help. He was still dreaming about the end of the war, when I crept away.

I joined Heath at the gate. He had discarded his crutches for his sticks, which had been put there for him overnight. The Neusys' house was about four miles away and we had a rough sketch of the road to it on a sheet of ordinary notepaper. I carried Heath on my back; but it was no fun for him either as he was in great pain. At every turn of the road we struck a match and consulted our map. I well remember those matches; they were the old-fashioned twinklers of the 'wait a minute' kind. After two hours, we reached our destination, which was the second house with iron railings in the Rue Calvary in the village of Petite Wasmes. We hadn't been able to warn the Neusys that we were coming and we found the outer gate was locked. So I scaled the wall and threw some gravel at the bedroom window. After two or three throws Neusy put out his head and in a few moments we were inside.

Emil Neusy was a heavily built man with a fresh complexion and a jolly disposition. His wife Marie was a slim little woman with the heart of a lion. They seemed pleased to have us and soon made us comfortable but the difficulty was conversation. They knew no English and we knew no French, so we had to talk to one another with our hands, which was a very slow job. However, we were not allowed to rest for long. At about 9 o'clock a Belgian from the hospital arrived in a very excited state and the Neusys at once hid us behind some thick curtains. They then invited him into the room and after a long and apparently heated conversation, he left the house again. Neusy went out soon after and came back with a cab and took Heath away. I followed almost immediately, led by Neusy's son, a boy of thirteen, who took me to some woods and told me to stay there until he came back for me. After dark that night I was collected and taken to a cafe on the outskirts of the wood, where I found Heath, who had also spent the day in the woods.

We spent several days together in the woods returning to the raft at night for food and shelter. Heath still suffered great pain from his wound and found it very difficult to move about. By this time German patrols and the Belgian police had got tired of searching the district for us, so we moved by easy stages to the village of Paturage, where we were put up for a time by a Madame Godart, a friend of the Neusys. We returned to the Neusys' house at the end of November. By this time the food shortage was acute. Everyone was rationed, except us of course but we had many friends by now and never went short. We were already beginning to pick up a certain amount of French, which eased our position considerably and Heath had been attended by a doctor and his wound was now on the mend.

One day Neusy showed me a British rifle and several rounds of ammunition which he had souvenired from the battlefields. I did not think it was a wise souvenir and said so and advised him to get rid of it. I told him that if the house was searched it would be his death warrant and possibly that of others as well and although he would not take this seriously at first I never let the subject drop until the rifle was eventually cemented into the wall under the window-sill of the front bedroom. The room was then repapered to remove any traces of tampering with the walls.

Just before Christmas 1914 the Germans began to realise that there were a good many British soldiers being hidden by the Belgians in occupied territory, so they issued a warning through the Local Authorities that any British soldier who gave himself up before a certain date would be treated as a prisoner of war but that if he failed to surrender and was caught he would be shot as a spy whether in uniform or not. It also warned the inhabitants that the penalty for harbouring the enemy was death. I never saw this order, but it was discussed by the Neusys and they decided to take the risk. So we sat tight.

About the middle of February 1915 Marie received a visit from the mayor of the district. He said that it had come to his knowledge that two English soldiers were hiding in her house and that as he was responsible for his district being clear they must go. He said he did not care where they went so long as they left the district. The same night I left for Paturage to live with Madame Godart again. Heath preferred to stay where he was. A fortnight later a neighbour of the Neusys came round to me there and between fits of weeping told me that the Germans had taken Heath. This was very bad news and as soon as it got dark that night I moved to a place called La Bouverie, about five miles distant, to the house of Madam Godart's mother. This old lady was eighty years of age. At dawn the next morning there was a terrific banging at the front door. I naturally thought the Germans had come for me and was halfway out the window when I heard the voices of Heath and Emil Neusy.

Heath had not been caught after all and this is what had happened at the Neusys' house. At 9 o'clock the previous morning, two German detectives had entered by the back gate. They had given the correct secret signal, which was the opening of the gate three times, which automatically gave three peals on the bell in the kitchen. They had then walked straight into the house, covered Marie Neusy with an automatic and said: 'You've got English in your house.' Marie had denied this at once, although Heath was in bed in the room above. However, the detectives had wasted no time in argument; one remained with Marie and the other started searching the house. Luckily for Heath he began from the cellar. Heath had heard their conversation and knew he was in a hole. He had no time to put on his clothes, so in only his socks he climbed out of the landing window and fled on to the roof of the scullery, which jutted out from the kitchen. Unfortunately the slates of the roof gave way with a fearful crash and Heath nearly came through into the scullery. The German in the kitchen at once rushed to the backdoor. So did Marie. She got there first, turned the key in the lock and put her back to the door. There was a brief struggle and then the German pushed her aside and opened the door. Unfortunately - or fortunately - this was the moment chosen by Heath to jump off the roof. He jumped on top of the detective and they fell to the ground. Heath was up first and raced down the garden, zigzagging from side to side, his shirt flapping in the wind. The German who was still on the ground, fired four shots at him but he never got a hit. Heath jumped a low wall into the neighbour's garden, at the top of which was another wall; a high one with glass on top. He leapt at this, but missed his hold. By this time the German was after him and had reached the bottom of Neusy's garden, only a few feet away. He covered Heath with his automatic and said: 'Hands up.' Heath took no notice. He decided not to be an Englishman at any price. The German gave the order again, this time in French and up went Heath's hands.

Meanwhile the German inside the house had reached the landing window and saw what was happening outside. He at once started to shout orders to the one in the garden, who turned round to reply. This gave Heath another chance. He made one more leap at the wall, gained a hold and was over the top. The German in the garden turned round just in time to see his last leg disappearing. He had one more shot but was far too late.

Heath had then done a record sprint across a ploughed field, down a lane and through a forge, until he came to a cottage. The back door stood invitingly open, so in he went and locked the door behind him. The good lady of the house came down from upstairs and had a bit of a shock to find a stranger with no trousers on seated in her kitchen. However, he explained his position and she soon fixed him up with one of her husband's suits. Heath had left the house at dark and gone to Madame Godart's, where he found Neusy. They had remained there until next morning, when they came to me. Marie Neusy was arrested and taken to Mons, where she was committed for trial. The Germans ripped her house to pieces and took away several hundred francs. They didn't, however, find that rifle and for all I know it's there still. They left word with the maid that if Emil Neusy came to Mons for his money he could have it. He went next day and they arrested him too.

After a few days at La Bouverie, we returned to Madame Godart, where we anxiously awaited the result of the trial. Marie smuggled a letter to us from her prison, concealed in a piece of bread, in which she said we were not to worry about her, for what she had done was for her country and not for us. These were brave words from a woman who was expecting her death. But when the trial eventually came off, the first witness, who was Marie's maid, a girl of only twelve, stated with great presence of mind, that the man who had escaped was a Belgian and that he was the lover of Madame Neusy and stayed in the house when the master was away on business. As soon as Neusy heard this he jumped up in court and demanded a divorce and acted the part of the wronged husband so well that as the Germans had no evidence to the contrary they had to accept the story. Marie was sentenced to one month's imprisonment for obstructing the police and Neusy was charged the costs of the trial. A few days later we were visited by D'Capiaux, the engineer: from the hospital and I learnt what happened there when we escaped. He said the Germans were furious and fined everyone connected with the hospital and removed all the prisoners into Germany. He then told us that he had made arrangements to get us away. He took our photographs and presented us next day with a certificate of identity, which changed our nationality to Belgian. This certificate was an absolute forgery, but complete in every detail even to the police stamp. He had even gone so far as to append our signatures without ever having seen our handwriting.

In a few days a guide came for us and we left for Brussels, where we were taken to a hospital. The matron in charge of this hospital was Nurse Edith Cavell. I'm afraid I can't tell you much about Nurse Cavell. She was very busy all the time and so we didn't see very much of her, but she seemed a very homely woman with a smile and a cheery word for everyone. Brussels was teeming with Germans and here under their noses were at least a score of helpless British Tommies waiting to be smuggled across the frontier.'

'We were only in the hospital for three days and then there was a sudden alarm and we were all cleared out in two's and three's and conducted to the homes of various Belgians, who were all members of the same wonderful organisation. This organisation was linked up from Northern France, right across Belgium to the Dutch frontier and existed solely for the purpose of helping British, French and Belgians out of the country. In this sudden move I was separated from Heath and left the hospital accompanied by Michael Carey, of the Munster fusiliers. The Munsters were cut off during the Retreat from Mons and many of them had remained at large until picked up by the organisation.

A week later we left our house in the Avenue de Longchamps with a guide and made an attempt to reach the frontier. On the way we picked up four more Irishmen, which made our party seven and we soon left Brussels behind and reached the open country. The order of march was for the guide to go ahead and the remainder to follow in pairs at intervals of 200 yards. We passed through Louvain and Aerschot and in the late afternoon arrived at the Monastery of Averabode, where we received food and shelter for the night. There were over 200 monks in this monastery and only two could speak English.

The next morning our party was joined by a young Belgian who also wanted to get out of the country. We set off at daybreak, left the main road and made our way across country. Our destination was Turnout, a town near the Dutch frontier. At about mid-day we came to a railway crossing, where a sentry examined our forged identity cards. He just compared the face with the photograph and allowed us to pass.

The two Belgians, the three Irishmen and myself got through without a hitch; but one of the Irishmen of the last pair could not for the moment find his identity card and while he was fumbling in his pockets, he accidentally dropped a five-franc note. No sooner had it reached the ground than the sentry promptly put his foot on it, looked round at the guard house behind to see that no one was watching and passed the Irishman on with a movement of the hand. That was accidental bribery.

Two hours later we struck the main road again and here our guide gave instructions to the other Belgian and left us. Soon afterwards we entered

Turnout, which was packed with Germans. We at once proceeded to the address which had been given us of the man who was the next link in the chain of the organisation. But when we got there we found, to our dismay, that the house was full of German soldiers. It had been taken over as a billet. This floored us: our guide had gone and we had no other addresses so we retired to a cafe in a quiet part of the town to discuss the situation. The Belgian made enquiries as to the possibility of our crossing the frontier by ourselves, but he was told that we should have to swim a canal and pass two chains of sentries, which was considered an impossibility without an experienced guide. It was very dangerous to remain in Turnout, so the only thing to do was to return to Brussels. But we were all footsore and weary after our two days' march, so we found an old woman with a horse and cart and she agreed to take the risk and give us a lift back to the Monastery of Averabode for the sum of 12 francs 50 per head.

As soon as it was dark we set off and got along all right until we were halted by a mounted patrol at about one o'clock. I was on the front seat and the officer-in-charge of the patrol walked up to me with an electric torch and a revolver, both of which he pointed at me. He questioned me in Flemish, which I didn't understand, so I kept my mouth shut. The old woman and the Belgian butted in, with explanations and we were ordered off the cart and lined up by the roadside, where our identity cards were examined. The officer seemed satisfied with these and allowed us to pass on our way. It was a narrow shave, for there were three things we should have been caught out on. Only two of the party had spoken at all; we were on the road during prohibited hours without a special permit and we were many miles from the place of our registration.

We arrived at the convent four hours later and when we had had some food turned in for a well needed rest. That evening the Belgian left us to return to Brussels and promised to report our position to Nurse Cavell. We were well treated by the monks. We slept in the laundry at night and retired to a room at the top of the building by day, where we passed away the time by playing cards for buttons. We couldn't play for money as the cost of our journey back from Turnout had broken the lot of us. Seven days passed and no word came from Brussels, so one of the monks volunteered to go in and find out what was to be done. He returned the next day with the guide who had conducted us to Turnout.

The following day we returned to Brussels. Michael Carey and myself were taken to another house in the Rue du Brasserie. The other four Irishmen went somewhere else and I never saw them again. Our hostess was a very wealthy woman. Her house was stocked with everything of the best and for eight days we lived like lords. Then, with two Frenchmen who were already in the house when we arrived, we were picked up by the same old guide and made another attempt to reach the frontier. We passed up through Malines this time and everything went smoothly until we reached an examining post at a bridge-head over a canal, about six miles south of Antwerp. There were two sentries, one on each side of the road. The guide had already passed and the Frenchmen were following behind Carey and myself. We looked at the two sentries as we approached and weighed them up carefully. The fellow on the right looked less intelligent than the other, so we decided to give him the honour of inspecting our identity cards. He just compared the face with the photograph and allowed us to pass. A little further on, round a bend in the road, we waited for the two Frenchmen to catch up. We waited ten minutes and then our guide became alarmed and went back to see what had happened. He learnt that the two Frenchmen had been arrested by the sentry on the left. They had identity cards the same as ourselves and we never knew the reason for their arrest or their fate. It was just luck that had made us choose the sentry on the right, instead of the one on the left.

When we reached Antwerp we found our next link, which was a Red Cross building which had been used during the siege. The building was empty, however and the man-in-charge told us that it was being taken over by the Germans next day as a clearing station for the Belgian refugees who were returning from Holland. This was another disappointment. He allowed us to stay there that night and early next morning our guide took us to the Hotel d'Esperance, which soon belied its name. This was on a Saturday towards the end of April, six months after I'd escaped from the hospital at Wasmes.

After we had some lunch our guide told us to remain where we were until he returned on Monday. He said we had nothing to worry about; that everything had been arranged and there was nothing to pay. On Sunday night the proprietress presented us with the bill, which included the cost of the guide's food for the day before. As this took place in the public dining room and there were a good many Germans there, we couldn't argue the point, so we retired to our bedroom followed by the proprietress and induced her to wait for her money until our friend returned on Monday. I needn't add we never saw him again. There were further arguments with the proprietress on the Monday and Tuesday and the good lady informed us that if we didn't pay by 12 o'clock on Wednesday she'd inform the police. I'm pretty certain she'd have done this at once if she'd known who we were.

Carey and I couldn't muster five francs between us and our position was serious. On the Wednesday morning I told her I was going out to find my friend. Where I really went to was a house nearby, which was tenanted by the American Commission for the relief of the Belgians, but there were too many Germans about the building for my liking and I returned to the hotel. About 11.30 Carey decided to go round and try his luck. I told him not to return if he was unsuccessful and that I'd try and make a 'get away' on my own, but he wouldn't agree to that. He returned just before twelve with a face wreathed in smiles and I knew he'd been successful. He'd gained audience with the Commissioner, who had given him enough cash to meet our immediate expenses, which we did without delay and had promised to help us too in other ways. Half an hour later we were visited by a Belgian who owned a cafe in another part of the city. He said the Commissioner had sent him to look after us until such time that we could be passed over the frontier. The commission would allow us twenty francs a day, he said, but we were not to visit it again and any communication was to be made through him. After this, our prestige at the hotel went up by leaps and bounds; our meals were served in a private room and there was no more trouble with the proprietress.

We roamed all over Antwerp for three weeks and then on 16 May 1915 we were introduced to the guide who was to take us over the frontier. He was a small withered old man over 60 years of age and almost a dwarf. The following night we met at the cafe of our friend who had been our link with the American Commission and after cracking the best bottle of champagne in the house, Carey and I and the guide accompanied by the cafe proprietor boarded a tram for the outskirts of the city. Here our friend bid us God speed and returned to his home. It was now nine o'clock, pitch dark and raining in torrents. We left the main road and soon realised that our guide was a marvel. In spite of his age he moved quickly, in fact we had difficulty in keeping pace with him. He could see like a cat and appeared to know every inch of the country. After three hours of zigzagging down railway tracks, wading ditches and trespassing over private property, we emerged from some undergrowth by a deserted cottage and saw the frontier barrier a few feet ahead. It was still raining heavily and we were soaked to the skin. The church clocks in Holland were striking midnight and we could see the electric lights on the Dutch roads 500 yards away. Our guide motioned us to lie down and left us for about ten minutes. When he returned he took off all his clothes except his shirt, under-pants and boots and told us to do the same. This was to make it easier for us to crawl through the wire. We tied up our discarded clothes and threw them over the top of the barrier, which appeared to be fifteen to twenty feet in width. It was thickly meshed and very close to the ground. Each of us then selected a spot and commenced to crawl through. This could only be done by lying flat on the stomach, stretching the arms at full length, grasping the wire and pulling the body forward two or three inches at the time. It took us quite twenty minutes to reach the other side. My underclothes were ripped to ribbons and my body smarted from head to foot where it had been torn by the barbs. We rested a few moments, then grabbed our bundles and made a bolt towards the lights in the distance. Five hundred yards further we waded a ditch, stepped over a couple of strands of barbed wire and saw a sentry in blue uniform a few yards away. We were in Holland. The sentry came up, patted us on the back and said: Goot Engleesh. We put on our clothes and an hour later, were being cared for at a Dutch inn.

The following morning our wonderful guide, who had taken us through without having seen or heard a German sentry, handed us over to the Belgian Consul at Roosendael and bid us goodbye. These guides were paid by the organisation at the rate of three pounds a head for everyone they got safely across. The same day we were sent to Flushing and when I was signing my name in the Strand Hotel register I saw the signature of Arthur Heath, whom I'd left in Brussels. A day after I caught him up at Rotterdam and we both came home together on 21 May 1915. This was the end of my journey.

I had been told by the guide who took me from Nurse Cavell's hospital that I was known as No. 83 on her books; but out of that number I was only the thirteenth to get safely across the frontier.

D'Capiaux, who forged the identity cards, was sentenced to twenty years' imprisonment just after Nurse Cavell was shot. He was released at the Armistice. Emil and Marie Neusy left the country and came to England as refugees in August 1915. They were afterwards compensated by the British Government. Marie Neusy and Madame Godart received special medals and illuminated addresses from both the British and Belgian Governments. As for me I was officially reported by the War Office as killed in action on 24 August 1914 and when I reached England I found my wife a widow.

Chapter 4

Patriotism Is Not Enough

Edith Louisa Cavell (4 December 1865-12 October 1915) was a British nurse and patriot. Her strong Anglican beliefs propelled her to help all those who needed it, both German and Allied soldiers. She was quoted as saying, 'I can't stop while there are lives to be saved'. She is celebrated for saving the lives of soldiers from all sides without distinction and in helping 200 Allied soldiers escape from German-occupied Belgium. She was not arrested for espionage, as many were led to believe, but for treason. She had been recruited by the British Secret Intelligence Service (SIS), although she turned away from her espionage duties in order to help Allied soldiers escape. Despite international pressure for mercy, Edith Cavell, who was 49 at the time of her execution, was shot by a firing squad at dawn on 12 October 1915. Her execution received worldwide condemnation and extensive press coverage. On the night before she was shot she said: 'I have no fear or shrinking. I have seen death so often that it is not strange or fearful.' She further said: 'I thank God for this ten weeks quiet before the end. Life has always been hurried and full of difficulty'. This time of rest has been a great mercy. They have all been very kind to me here. But this I would say, standing as I do in the view of God and eternity. I realise that patriotism is not enough. I must have no hatred or bitterness towards anyone.'

Edith Cavell was born on 4 December 1865 at Swardeston, a village near Norwich, where her father, the Reverend Frederick Cavell, was vicar for 45 years. She was the eldest of four children and was taught to always share with the less fortunate, despite her family's meagre earnings. After a period as a governess, including for a family in Brussels 1900-1905, she trained as a nurse at the London Hospital in Whitechapel under Matron Eva Luckes. In 1907 Edith was recruited by Dr Antoine Depage to be matron of a newly established nursing school by the name of L'ecole Belge d'Infirmières Diplômèes on the Rue de la Culture in Brussels. By 1910 Miss Cavell felt that the profession of nursing had gained sufficient foothold in Belgium to warrant the publishing of a professional journal and therefore launched the nursing journal, L'infirmiere. A year later, she was a training nurse for three hospitals, 24 schools and 13 kindergartens in Belgium. In 1914 she was on a visit to her mother, who then lived in College Road in Norwich, when she heard that Germany had invaded Belgium. She returned at once to Brussels where her clinic and nursing school were taken over by the Red Cross.

In November 1914, after the German occupation of Brussels, Edith Cavell began sheltering British soldiers and funnelling them out of occupied Belgium to the neutral Netherlands." Wounded and derelict British and French soldiers and Belgians and French of military age were hidden from the Germans and provided with false papers by Prince Reginald de Croy at his chateau of Bellignie near Mons From there, they were conducted by various guides to the houses of Edith Cavell, Louis Severin and others in Brussels and furnished by them with money to reach the Dutch frontier and with guides obtained through Phillipe Baucq. This placed Edith Cavell in violation of German military law German authorities became increasingly suspicious of the nurse's actions, which were backed up by her outspokenness. She was arrested on 3 August 1915 and charged with harbouring Allied soldiers. She had been betrayed by Gaston Quien, who was later convicted by a French court as a German collaborator." She was held in St Gilles prison for 10 weeks, the last two in solitary confinement.'7' She made three depositions to the German police, August 8, 18 and 22, admitting that she had been instrumental in conveying about sixty British and fifteen French derelict soldiers and about 100 French and Belgians of military age to the frontier and had sheltered most of them in her house. In her court-martial she was prosecuted for aiding British and French soldiers, in addition to young Belgian men, to cross the border and enter Britain. She admitted her guilt when she signed a statement the day before the trial, thus reaffirming the crime in the presence of all other prisoners and lawyers present in the court at the beginning of the trial Edith Cavell gave the German prosecution a much stronger case against her when she declared that the soldiers she had helped escape thanked her in writing when arriving safely in Britain. This admission proved hard to ignore because it not only confirmed that Edith Cavell had helped the soldiers navigate the Dutch frontier, but it also established that she helped them escape to a country at war with Germany.

As the case stood, the sentence according to German military law was death. Paragraph 58 of the German Military Code says: 'Will be sentenced to death for treason any person who, with the intention of helping the hostile Power, or of causing harm to the German or allied troops, is guilty of one of the crimes of paragraph 90 of the German Penal Code. The case referred to in the above-mentioned paragraph 90 consists of 'Conducting soldiers to the enemy.' Additionally, the penalties according to paragraph 160 of the German Code, in case of war, apply to foreigners as well as Germans. Furthermore, this application of the German law was supported by the First Geneva Convention. While the Convention ordinarily guarantees protection of medical personnel, that protection is forfeit if it is used as cover for any belligerent action. This forfeiture is expressed in article 7 of the 1906 version of the Convention, which was the version in force at the time. Surprisingly from a modern perspective, little was made of the war crime status of her actions; as discussed below, the German authorities instead justified prosecution merely on the basis of the German law and the interests of the German state. The British government said they could do nothing to help her. Sir Horace Rowland of the Foreign Office said, 'I am afraid that it is likely to go hard with Miss Cavell; I am afraid we are powerless'; a sentiment echoed by Lord Robert Cecil, Under-Secretary for Foreign Affairs who advised that 'Any representation by us will do her more harm than good.' The United States however, had not yet joined the war and was in a position to apply diplomatic pressure. Hugh S. Gibson, First

Secretary of the US legation at Brussels, made clear to the German government that executing Edith Cavell would further harm Germany's already damaged reputation Later, he wrote: 'We reminded him (Baron von der Lancken) of the burning of Louvain and the sinking of the Lusitania and told him that this murder would stir all civilized countries with horror and disgust. Count Harrach broke in at this with the remark that he would rather see Miss Cavell shot than have harm come to one of the humblest German soldiers and his only regret was that they had not 'three or four English old women to shoot.' The German civil governor, Baron von der Lancken, is known to have stated that Edith Cavell should be pardoned because of her complete honesty and because she had helped save so many lives, German as well as Allied. However, General von Sauberzweig, the military governor of Brussels, ordered that 'in the interests of the State' the execution of the death penalty against Baucq and Edith Cavell should be carried out immediately, thus denying higher authorities the opportunity to consider clemency. Of the 27 put on trial, five were condemned to death: Edith Cavell, Baucq (an architect in his thirties), Louise Thuliez, Severin and Countess Jeanne de Belleville. Of the five sentenced to death, only Edith Cavell and Baucq were executed. The other three were reprieved.

When in custody, Edith Cavell was questioned in French, but the session was minuted in German. This gave the interrogator the opportunity to misinterpret her answers. Although she may have been misrepresented, she made no attempt to defend herself. Edith Cavell was provided with a defender approved by the German military governor. A previous defender, who was chosen for Edith Cavell by her assistant, Elizabeth Wilkins, was ultimately rejected by the governor.

The night before her execution, she told the Reverend Stirling Gahan, the Anglican chaplain who had been allowed to see her and to give her Holy Communion, 'Patriotism is not enough, I must have no hatred or bitterness towards anyone.' These words are inscribed on her statue in St Martin's Place, near Trafalgar Square in London. Her final words to the German Lutheran prison chaplain, Paul Le Seur, were recorded as, 'Ask Father Gahan to tell my loved ones later on that my soul, as I believe, is safe and that I am glad to die for my country'.

From his sick bed Brand Whitlock, the US minister to Belgium, wrote a personal note on Edith Cavell's behalf to Moritz von Bissing, the governor general of Belgium. Hugh Gibson; Maitre G. de Leval, the legal adviser to the United States legation; and Marquis de Villalobar, the Spanish minister, formed a midnight deputation of appeal for mercy or at least postponement of sentence. Despite these efforts, on 11 October, Baron von der Lancken allowed the execution to proceed. Sixteen men, forming two firing squads, carried out the sentence pronounced on her and on four Belgian men at Tir National 'shooting range' in Schaerbeek, at 6:00 am on 12 October 1915. There are conflicting reports of the details of Edith Cavell's execution. However, according to the eyewitness account of the Reverend Le Seur, who attended Edith Cavell in her final hours, eight soldiers fired at Edith Cavell while the other eight executed Philippe Baucq. There is also a dispute over the sentencing imposed under the German Military Code. Supposedly the death penalty relevant to the offence committed by Edith Cavell was not officially declared until a few hours after her death.

On instructions from the Spanish minister, Belgian women immediately buried her body next to St Gilles Prison. After the War, her body was taken back to Britain for a memorial service at Westminster Abbey and then transferred to Norwich, to be laid to rest at Life's Green. In the months and years following Edith Cavell's death, countless newspaper articles, pamphlets, images and books publicised her story. In Norwich the Eastern Daily Press published a statement:

'ENGLISH LADY EXECUTED IN BRUSSELS The Foreign Office are informed by the United States Ambassador that Miss Edith Cavell, lately head of a large Training School for Nurses at Brussels, who was arrested on the 5th August last, by the German authorities at that place, was executed on the 13th inst [sic; it was the 12th] after sentence of death had been passed on her. It is understood that the charge against Miss Cavell was that she had harboured fugitives, British and French soldiers and Belgians of military age and had assisted them to escape from Belgium in order to join the colours. So far as the Foreign Office are aware, no charge of espionage was brought against her.' Monday's EDP included an editorial stressing Cavell's local connections and that her widowed mother was living in College Road in Norwich. A full report only appeared in the local press on 22 October, ten days after Edith's execution. Did the Germans have the legal right to shoot a citizen of an enemy country in an occupied city? In 1934 The English politician Duff Cooper said, 'If ever a woman was justly executed according to the rules of warfare Nurse Cavell was. She used her position as a nurse to get soldiers back to England. The German soldiers were perfectly entitled to do what they did.' The novelist Rider Haggard noted in his War Diaries as early as 23 October 1915 that her name and portrait were already being used by speakers urging men to enlist and fight the Germans. Two days later he quoted an unnamed American newspaper as saying that 'Emperor William would have done better to lose an entire army corps than to butcher Miss Cavell'. In both Britain and France postcards were issued with slogans such as 'REMEMBER EDITH CAVELL'. [14]

She became an iconic propaganda figure for military recruitment in Britain and to help increase favourable sentiment towards the Allies in the United States. She was a popular icon because of her sex, her nursing profession and her apparently heroic approach to death.' Her execution was represented as an act of German barbarism and moral depravity. News reports shortly following Edith Cavell's execution were found to be only true in part. Even the *American Journal of Nursing* repeated the fictional account of Edith Cavell's execution in which she fainted and fell because of her refusal to wear a blindfold in front of the firing squad. Allegedly, while she lay unconscious, the German commanding officer shot her dead with a revolver. 'Numerous accounts like these stimulated international outrage and general anti-German sentiments.

Along with the invasion of Belgium and the sinking of the *Lusitania,* Edith Cavell's execution was widely publicised in both Britain and North America by Wellington House, the British War Propaganda Bureau. Because of the British government's decision to use Edith Cavell's story as propaganda, she became the most prominent British female casualty of World War I. The combination of heroic appeal and a resonant atrocity-story narrative made Edith Cavell's case one of the most effective in British propaganda of World War I, as well as a factor in enduring post-war anti-German sentiment.

Unlike the rest of the world, the German government thought that they had acted fairly towards Edith Cavell. In a letter, the German Secretary for Foreign Affairs, Arthur Zimmermann, stated: It was a pity that Miss Cavell had to be executed, but it was necessary. She was judged justly. We hope it will not be necessary to have any more executions'.

Their laws do not make distinctions between sexes, the only exception to this rule being that according to legal customs, women in a 'delicate' (probably this means 'pregnant') condition could not be executed; Edith Cavell was not considered delicate From the Germans' perspective, had they released Edith Cavell, there would have been an influx of women partaking in acts against Germany because the women knew they would not be severely punished. It was up to the responsible men to follow their legal duty to Germany and ignore the world's condemnation. The German government also believed that all of the convicted people were thoroughly aware of the nature of their acts. The court paid particular attention to this point, releasing several accused persons because there was doubt as to whether the accused knew that their actions were punishable. The condemned, on the other hand, knew full well what they were doing and the punishment for committing their crimes because 'numerous public proclamations had pointed out the fact that aiding enemies' armies was punishable with death.'

Before the First World War, Edith Cavell was not well known outside nursing circles. This allowed the creation of two different depictions of her in British propaganda, which ignored anything that did not fit this image, including the suggestion that Edith Cavell, during her interrogation, had given information that incriminated others In November 1915 the Foreign Office issued a denial that Edith Cavell had implicated anyone else in her testimony. One image commonly represented was of Edith Cavell as an innocent victim of a ruthless and dishonourable enemy. This view depicted her as innocent of espionage and was most commonly used in various forms of British propaganda, such as postcards and newspaper illustrations during the war. Her story was presented in the British press as a means of fuelling a desire for revenge on the battlefield. These images implied that men must enlist in the armed forces immediately in order to stop the murder of innocent British females. The second representation of Edith Cavell during World War I described her as a serious, reserved, brave and patriotic woman who devoted her life to nursing and died to save others. This portrayal has been illustrated in numerous biographical sources, from personal first-hand experiences of the Red Cross nurse. Pastor Le Seur, the German army chaplain, recalled at the time of her execution, 'I do not believe that Miss Cavell wanted to be a martyr... but she was ready to die for her country Miss Cavell was a very brave woman and a faithful Christian'171 Another account from British chaplain, the

Reverend Mr Gahan, remembers Edith Cavell's words, 'I have no fear or shrinking; I have seen death so often it is not strange, or fearful to me!'' In this interpretation, her stoicism was seen as remarkable for a woman and brought her even greater renown than a man in similar circumstances would have received.

Edith Cavell's remains were returned to Britain after the war and a state funeral was held at Westminster Abbey. On 19 May 1919 her body was reburied at the east side of Norwich Cathedral; a graveside service is still held each October. [15] Following Edith Cavell's death, many memorials were created around the world to remember her. One of the first was the one by Henry Alfred Pegram which was unveiled in October 1918 by Queen Alexandra on the grounds on Norwich Cathedral, near a home for nurses which also bore her name. [16] In the calendar of the Church of England the day appointed for the commemoration of Edith Cavell is 12 October. This is a memorial in her honour rather than formal canonisation.

Footnotes Chapter 4

14 *Norfolk in the First Word War* by Frank Meeres (Phillimore & Co Ltd 2004)

15 The railway van that conveyed her remains from Dover to London is kept as a memorial on the Kent and East Sussex Railway and is usually open to view at Bodiam railway station.

16 This memorial was subsequently moved outside the Cathedral walls. Other memorials include a statue of Edith Cavell at St. Martin's Place adjacent to Trafalgar Square in London. She received part of her education in Peterborough and there is a memorial in Peterborough Cathedral. In Australia there is a marble and stone memorial near The Shrine in Melbourne; an inscription on a war memorial, naming the 35 people executed by the German army in a place called Tir national on the Schaerbeek municipality; a dedication on the war memorial on the grounds of Sacred Trinity Church, Salford, Greater Manchester; Monument to Edith Cavell and Marie Depage in Brussels by Paul Du Bois; a stone memorial statue by Canadian sculptor R. Tait McKenzie in the garden behind the Red Cross National (US) Headquarters, 1730 E Street, NW Washington, DC; in the block south of the Corcoran Gallery of Art and north of the Daughters of the American Revolution building.

Chapter 5

Exploits Of The Escaping Club

A. J. Evans MC and bar

The escape of Second Lieutenant Marcus Kaye RFC *is interesting. The large building (formerly a workhouse) inhabited by the prisoners at Schweidnitz included a sunk rectangular courtyard in which they were permitted to exercise. This courtyard was bounded on one side by the main buildings, on the opposite and one adjacent side by high walls surmounted by barbed wire and on the fourth side by a vertical brick faced embankment, some 30 feet high. The courtyard being sunk, the top of this embankment rose but slightly above the general level of the surrounding ground on that side and from the top of its cliff-like face gardens and allotments sloped gently away from the camp. The buildings, walls and embankment all carried elevated platforms on which the sentries were posted, so that the entire camp was at all times surveyed by the guards. The embankment carried two such platforms, one at each extremity. The sentries thereon could thus look down into the courtyard and observe every movement of the prisoners. These sentries went to and from their posts by permanent ladders reaching from the courtyards to the platforms. In the face of the embankment wall itself was an opening leading to a latrine hollowed out of the earth behind the wall and running up the wall from the latrine, was a six inch air-duct for ventilation; a very necessary measure with the shallow cess-pools usually found in German camps.'*
The sentries were relieved at mid-day. During the morning Kaye paid several visits to the latrine, on each occasion concealing on his person portions of his escape kit which he hid in a previously arranged hiding place within. The last visit was timed for two minutes to twelve, at which time he entered the latrine in his ordinary uniform. At two minutes past the hour, when there were different sentries from those who had seen him enter, Kaye emerged from the latrine dressed in the nondescript clothes of a German workman and with his face sufficiently dirty to fit the part and to prevent recognition; he was now carrying a small bag of tools; odd lumps of metal had to serve, provided they clinked when set down. Kaye then opened his tool bag and selecting a suitable instrument proceeded, very deliberately, to take down, examine, clean and finally replace the last two sections of the pipe. Sentry-go is a boring job and the sentries watched him at his work with mild interest. Having finished the first part of his work, Kaye nodded to the sentry, indicating that he must do the top part of the pipe as well. The sentry nodded back; so Kaye, after collecting his tools, climbed slowly up the ladder. The sentry said something to him as he passed and Kaye grunted a few German words in reply; he was not a very communicative workman! Once again he repeated his operation, dismantling and re-

erecting the pipe at the top and taking some twenty minutes over the job. The sentries were by now quite accustomed to his presence so that, when he had finished his work, it seemed the most natural thing in the world for him to collect his tools and walk off through the allotments.

Escape and Liberation 1940-1945 by A. J. Evans.[17] Evans joined Innes Court OTC 5 August 1914. Transferred to Intelligence Corps, crossed to France August 1914 as Temporary 2nd Lieutenant and took part in the Retreat. Joined Flying Corps in February 1915, observer on 3 Squadron until September 1915; awarded MC for continuing to observe while attacked by German aeroplane at Loos. Pilot on 3 Squadron in spring 1916, taken prisoner on 16 July 1916 after forced landing behind German lines. Escaped from Clausthal camp, recaptured on Dutch frontier. Escaped successfully into Switzerland after eighteen nights' walking. In command of 142 Squadron in Palestine in February 1918. He was captured by the Turks and returned to Egypt at the Armistice. He was awarded a bar to the MC for numerous attempts to escape.

In the early days of the war Fort 9, Ingolstadt, had been a quiet, well-behaved sort of place according to its oldest inmates. But for the six months previous to my arrival before its forbidding gates at the end of 1916, the Germans had collected into it all the naughty boys who had tried to escape from other camps. There were about 150 officer prisoners of different nationalities in the place and at least 130 of these had successfully broken out of other camps and had only been recaught after from three days' to three weeks' temporary freedom. I myself had escaped from Clausthal in the Harz Mountains but had been recaptured on the Dutch frontier after I'd been at large for a few days.

When I arrived at Fort 9, Ingolstadt seventy-five per cent of the prisoners were scheming and working continually to escape again. Escaping and how it should be done, was the most frequent subject of conversation. In fact the camp was nothing less than an escaping club. We pooled our knowledge and each man was ready to help anyone who wished to escape, quite regardless of his own risk or the punishment he might bring upon himself. No one cared twopence for court-martials and nearly everyone in the fort had done considerable spells of solitary confinement. It is scarcely necessary to say that the Germans, having herded some 150 officers with the blackest characters into one camp, took considerable precautions to keep them there. But there were some of the most ingenious people in Fort 9 that I've ever met, particularly among the French and attempts to escape took place at least once a week.

Fort 9 had been built in 1866 after the Austrian wars. There was a wide moat, about fifteen yards broad and five feet deep, round the whole fort and inside the moat the ramparts rose to a height of forty feet. Our living rooms were actually in the ramparts and the barred windows looked down upon the moat, across a grass path along which a number of sentries were posted. It looked as though there were only two possible ways of getting out: to go out the way we'd come in, past three sentries, three gates and a guardhouse; or to swim the moat. It was impossible to tunnel under the moat. It had been tried and the water came into the tunnel as soon as it got below the water level. An aeroplane seemed the only other solution. That was the problem we were up against and however you look at it, it always boiled down to a nasty cold swim or a colossal piece of bluff. We came to the conclusion that we must have more accurate knowledge of the numbers, positions and movements of the sentries on the ramparts and round the moat at night, so we decided that one of us must spend the night out. It would be a rotten job; fifteen hours' wait on a freezing night, for it was now winter. For the first three and last three hours of this time it would be almost impossible to move a muscle without discovery and discovery probably meant getting bayoneted. We cast lots for this job and it fell to a man named Oliphant. I owned I breathed a sigh of relief. There would be two roll calls to be faked, the roll call just before sunset and the early morning one. How was this to be done? Our room was separated from the one next door, which was occupied by Frenchmen, by a three foot thick wall and in the wall was an archway. This archway was boarded up and formed a recess which was used as a hanging cupboard for clothes. Under cover of these clothes we cut a hole in the boarding big enough for a man to slip quickly through, from one room to the other. The planks which we took out could be put back easily and we pasted pictures over the cracks to conceal them.

It was rather difficult work. We had only a heated table knife to cut the first plank with, but later on we managed to steal a saw from a German carpenter who was doing some work in one of the rooms and return it before he missed it. You must remember that there was absolutely no privacy in the fort and a sentry passed the window and probably stared into the room every minute or two. We then rehearsed the faking of the roll calls. One of us pretended to be the German NCO taking the roll. First he tapped at the Frenchman's door and counted the men in the room, shut the door and walked about seven paces to our door, tapped and entered. Between the time he shut the first door till he opened ours only six or eight seconds elapsed, but during these seconds one of the Frenchmen had to slip through the hole, put on a British warm and pretend to be Oliphant; The German NCOs knew every man by sight in every room, but so long as the numbers were correct they often didn't bother to examine our faces. That accounted for the evening roll call. The early morning one was really easier. For several mornings the fellow in bed nearest the hole in our room made a habit of covering his face with the bedclothes. The German NCO soon got used to seeing him like that and if he saw him breathing or moving didn't bother to pull the clothes off his face. So the Frenchman next door had simply to jump out of bed as soon as he had been counted, slip through the hole and into the bed in our room and cover up his face. We practised this until we got it perfect and the rehearsals were great fun.

The next thing to do was to hide Oliphant on the ramparts. Two of us dug a grave for him there while the others kept watch. Then just before the roll call went we buried him and covered him with sods of grass. It was freezing at the time It Was about 4.30 pm when we buried him and he wouldn't be able to return to our room till 8.15 the next morning, when the doors were open. The faking of the evening roll call went off splendidly, but the morning one was a little ticklish, as we couldn't be quite sure which room the NCO would enter first. However, we listened carefully and fixed it all right and when he poked our substitute, who groaned and moved in the rehearsed manner, we nearly died with suppressed laughter. About an hour later Oliphant walked in very cold and hungry but otherwise cheerful. He had had quite a successful night. A bright moon had prevented him from crawling about much, but he had seen enough to show that it would be a pretty difficult job to get through the sentries and swim the moat on a dark night. However, Providence came to our help.

The winter of 1916 was a hard one; and the moat froze over and although the Germans went round in a boat every day and tried to keep the ice broken, they eventually had to give it up. It was difficult to know whether the ice would bear or not, but I tested it as well as I could by throwing stones on to it and decided one morning that I would risk it and make a dash across the moat that evening. A man named Wilkin and Kicq, a little Belgian officer who had accompanied me on my previous attempt to escape, agreed to come with me.

Our plan was to start when the 'Appel' or roll-call bell went at 5 pm, for it got dark soon afterwards and I trusted that this would cover our flight. We had to run down a steep bank on to the ice, about forty yards across the ice and then another two hundred yards or so before we could put a cottage between ourselves and the sentries. There was sure to be some shooting, but we reckoned the men's hands would be very cold, for they would already have been two hours at their posts. Moreover they were only armed with old French rifles, which they handled badly. We arranged with some of the other officers to create a diversion when the roll-call bell went by yelling and throwing stones on to the ice to distract the attention of the two nearest sentries. Our main anxiety was: would the ice bear? I felt confident it would. Wilkin said he was awfully frightened, but would go on with it. Kicq said that if I was confident, so was he. It would be extremely unpleasant if the ice broke for we would be wearing a lot of very heavy clothes. Still, anyone who thinks too much of what may happen will never escape from prison. We filled our rucksacks with rations for a ten days' march and enough solidified alcohol for at least one hot drink a day. We then concealed them and our coats at the jumping-off place.

A few minutes before the bell went we were all three dressed and in our places. It was a bad few minutes. At last it rang and almost immediately I heard laughter and shouting and the sound of stones falling on the ice. We jumped up and bolted over the path and down the slope. I was slightly ahead of the others and when I got to the moat I gave a little jump on to the ice thinking that if it was going to break at all, it would break at the edge instead of in the middle. It didn't break and I shuffled across at good speed. When I was about half-way over I heard furious yells of 'Halt!' behind me, followed by a fair amount of shooting; but I was soon up the bank on the far side and through a few scattered trees. Then I looked back. The others were only just clambering up the bank from the moat and were a good hundred yards behind me. It turned out that instead of taking a little jump on to the ice as I had done they'd stepped carefully on to the edge, which had broken under their weight and they had fallen flat on their faces. Wilkin had somehow got upside down, his heavy rucksack falling over his head, so that he couldn't move, but Kicq had freed himself and pulled Wilkin out.

The covering parties had done their job well. They'd managed to divert the attention of the most formidable sentry until I was well on the ice. He had then noticed me, yelled 'Halt!' loaded his rifle as fast as possible, dropped on one knee, fired and missed. Cold fingers, abuse and some stones hurled at him by the party on the ramparts above had not helped to steady his aim. After one or two shots his rifle jammed. Yells and cheers from the spectators. He tore at the bolt, cursing and swearing and then put up his rifle at the crowd of jeering prisoners above him, but they could see that the bolt hadn't gone home and only yelled louder.

Meanwhile I'd nearly reached the cottage, when I saw a large, four-horse wagon on the main road on my right with a number of civilians by it. They were only about 150 yards away and they started after us, led by a strong, healthy-looking fellow with a cart whip. The going through the snow was heavy, especially with the weight we were carrying; so the carter quickly overtook me and slashed me across the shoulders with his whip. I turned and rushed at him, but he jumped out of my reach. His companions then arrived and I saw, too, some armed soldiers coming on bicycles along the road from the fort. The game was up and the next thing to do was to avoid being shot in the excitement of re-capture. So I beckoned the smallest man and said in German: 'Come here and I'll give myself up to you.' The chap with the whip immediately came forward. 'No, not to you,' I said,' you hit me with that whip.' The little fellow was very pleased, for there was a hundred marks reward for the capture of an officer, so he hung on to my coat-tails as we started back to the fort. I tore up my map and dropped it into a stream as we went.

The scene in the Commandant's office was quite amusing. We were stripped and searched. I had nothing more to hide, but both Kicq and Wilkin had compasses, which they smuggled through with great skill. Kicq's was hidden in the lining of his great coat and Wilkin had his in his handkerchief, which he pulled out of his pocket and waved to show that there was nothing in it. All our food stuffs and clothes were returned to us, except my tin of solidified alcohol. I protested, but in vain I was given a receipt for it and I could have it back at the end of the war. As we left the office I saw it standing almost within my reach and nearly managed to pocket it as I went out. However, I found a friend of mine, a French officer outside and explained to him the position of the tin and suggested that he should go in with a few pals and steal it back for me under the cover of a row. This was the kind of joke that the Frenchmen loved and they were past-masters at it. They were always rushing off to the Commandant's office with frivolous complaints about one thing and another, just for a rag, which never failed to reduce the Commandant and his officers to a state of dithering rage. Within ten minutes I had my solid alcohol back all right and kept my receipt for it as well.

Compasses and maps were of course forbidden, but we managed to get them smuggled out in parcels all the same and watching a German open a parcel in which you knew there was a concealed compass was one of the most exciting things I've ever done.

For the next six weeks life was rather hard. It froze continuously, even in the daytime and at night the thermometer registered more than 27° of frost.

Fuel and light shortage became very serious. We stole wood and coal freely from the Germans and although the sentries had strict orders to shoot at sight anyone seen taking wood, nearly all the wood work in the fort was eventually torn down and burnt.

The Germans didn't allow us much oil for our lamps, so we used to steal the oil out of the lamps in the passage, until the Germans realised that they were being robbed and substituted acetylene for oil. However this didn't deter us, for now, instead of taking the oil out of the lamps, we took the lamps themselves and lamp-stealing became one of the recognised sports of the camp. How it was done has nothing to do with escaping, but was amusing. Outside our living rooms there was a passage seventy yards long, in which were two acetylene lamps. The sentry in the passage had special orders, a loaded rifle and fixed bayonet, to see that these lamps weren't stolen and since the Feldwebel, or sergeant-major, had stuffed up the sentries with horrible stories about our murderous characters, it isn't surprising that each sentry was very keen to prevent us stealing the lamps and leaving him - an isolated German - in total darkness and at our mercy. So whenever a prisoner came out of his room and passed one of the lamps, the sentry would eye him anxiously and get ready to charge at him. The lamps were about thirty yards apart and this is how we got them. One of us would come out, walk to a lamp and stop beneath it. This would unnerve the sentry, who would advance upon him. The prisoner would then take out his watch and look at it by the light of the lamp, as if that were all he had stopped for. Meanwhile a second officer would come quickly out of a room further down the passage and take down the other lamp behind the sentry's back. The sentry would immediately turn and charge with loud yells of 'Halt! Halt!' whereupon the first lamp would also be grabbed, both would be blown out simultaneously and the prisoners would disappear into their respective rooms leaving the passage in total darkness. The amusing part was that this used to happen every night and the sentries knew it was going to happen, but they were quite powerless against tactics of this kind.

At about this time an officer named Medlicott and I learnt that some Frenchmen were trying to escape across the frozen moat by cutting a window-bar in the latrines which overlooked it. The Germans, however, smelt a rat, but though they inspected the bars carefully they couldn't find the cuts which had been artfully sealed up with a mixture of flour and ashes. Then the Feldwebel went round and shook each bar violently in turn until the fourth one came off in his hands and he fell down flat on his back. They then wired up the hole, but Medlicott and I saw a chance of cutting the wire and making another bolt for it about a week later and we took it. We were only at large however for about two hours. The snow on the ground gave our tracks away; we were pursued, surrounded and eventually had to surrender again. This time we had a somewhat hostile reception when we got back to the fort.

They searched us and took away my tin of solidified alcohol again. They recognised it. 'I know how you stole this back' said the senior clerk as he gave me another receipt for it,' but you shan't have it any more.' We both laughed over it! I laughed last, however, as I stole it back again in about a week's time and kept my two receipts for it as well.

It may seem extraordinary that we weren't punished severely for these attempts to escape, but there were no convenient cells in which to punish us. All the cells at Fort 9 were always full and there was a very long waiting list besides.

After this failure I joined some Frenchmen who were making a tunnel. The shaft was sunk in the corner of one of their rooms close under the window and the idea was to come out in the steep bank of the moat on a level with the ice and crawl over on a dark night. It was all very unpleasant. Most of the time one lay in a pool of water and in an extremely confined space and worked in pitch darkness, as the air was so bad that no candle would keep alight. Moreover, when we got close to the frozen surface of the ground it was always a question whether the sentry outside wouldn't put his foot through the tunnel and if he did so whether one would be suffocated or stuck with a bayonet. It was most unpleasant lying there and waiting for him to pass within six inches of your head. All the earth had to be carried in bags along the passage and emptied down the latrines.

Unfortunately, just before the work was finished the thaw set in and it was generally agreed that we couldn't afford to get our clothes wet swimming the moat However, the Frenchmen were undaunted and determined to wade through the moat naked, carrying two bundles of kit sewn in waterproof cloths. The rest of us disliked the idea of being chased naked in the middle of winter carrying two twenty-pound bundles, so we decided to make ourselves diving suits out of mackintoshes. We waterproofed the worn patches of these with candle grease and sewed them up in various places. The Frenchmen would have to fake roll call, so they made most life-like dummies, which breathed when you pulled a string, to put in their beds. Whether this attempt to escape would have been successful I can't say, for, thank Heaven, we never tried it. When we were all ready and the French colonel, who was going first, had stripped naked and greased himself from head to foot, we learnt that the trap door which we had made at the exit of the tunnel couldn't be opened under two hours owing to unexpected roots and stones. We had to put off the attempt for that night and we were unable to make another as the end of the tunnel suddenly fell in and the cavity was noticed by the sentry.

This was practically the end of my residence in Fort 9 for soon after the Germans decided to send the more unruly of us to other camps. We learnt that we were to be transferred to Zorndorf, in East Prussia, an intolerable spot from all accounts and a man named Buckley and myself decided to get off the train at the first opportunity and make another bid for freedom. The train would be taking us directly away from the Swiss frontier, so it behoved us to leave it as soon as possible. We equipped ourselves as well as we could with condensed foods before starting and wore Burberrys to cover our uniforms. Although there were only thirty of us going we had a guard of an officer and fifteen men, which we thought a little excessive. We had two hours' wait at the station and amused ourselves by taking as little notice as possible of the officer's orders, which annoyed him and made him shout. Six of us and a sentry were then packed rather tightly into a second-class carriage. We gave him the corner seat next to the corridor and another sentry marched up and down the corridor outside. Buckley and I took the seats by the window, which we were compelled to keep closed and there was no door in that side of the carriage. The position didn't look very hopeful, for there wasn't much chance of our sentry going to sleep with the other one outside continually looking in. Just before we started the officer came fussing in: he was obviously very anxious and nervous and said he hoped that we would have a comfortable quiet journey and no more trouble. The train started, night fell and the frontier was left further and further behind. We shut our eyes for an hour to try to induce the sentry to go to sleep, but this didn't work.

The carriage was crowded and both racks were full of small luggage and noticing this, I had an idea. I arranged with the others to act in a certain way when the train next went slowly and I gave the word by saying to the sentry, in German: 'Will you have some food? We are going to eat.' Five or ten minutes of tense excitement followed. Suddenly the train began to slow up. I leant across and said to the sentry, 'Will you have some food? We are going to eat.' Immediately everyone in the carriage stood up with one accord and pulled their stuff off the racks. The sentry also stood up, but was almost completely hidden from the window by a confused mass of men and bags. Under cover of this confusion, Buckley and I stood up on our seats. I slipped the strap of my haversack over my shoulder, pushed down the window, put my leg over and jumped into the night. I fell—not very heavily— on the wires at the side of the track and lay still in the dark shadow. Three seconds later Buckley came flying out after me and seemed to take rather a heavy toss. The end of the train wasn't yet past me and we knew there was a man with a rifle in the last carriage; so when Buckley came running along the track calling out to me, I caught him and pulled him into the ditch at the side. The train went by and its tail lights vanished round a corner and apparently no one saw or heard us.

I have not space to say much about our walk to the German-Swiss frontier, about 200 miles away. We only walked by night and lay up in hiding all through the hours of daylight which was, I think, the worst part of the business and wore out our nerves and physical strength far more than the six or seven hours marching at night, for the day seemed intolerably long from 4.30 am to 9.30 pm; seventeen hours - the sun was very hot and there was little shade and we were consumed with impatience to get on. Moreover, we could never be free from anxiety at any moment of those seventeen hours. The strain at night of passing through a village when a few lights still burnt and dogs seemed to wake and bark at us in every house, or of crossing a bridge when one expected to be challenged at any moment never worried me so much as a cart passing or men talking near our daytime hiding places.

We went into hiding at dawn or soon after and when we'd taken off our boots and put on clean socks we would both drop asleep at once. It was a bit of a risk, perhaps one of us ought to have stayed awake, but we took it deliberately since we got great benefit from a sound sleep, while we were still warm from walking. And it was only for about an hour, before we woke again shivering, for the mornings were very cold and we were usually soaked with dew up to our waists. Then we had breakfast - the great moment of the day - and rations were pretty good at first, as we underestimated the time we would take by about four days. But later on we had to help things out with raw potatoes from the fields, which eventually became our mainstay. All day long we were pestered with stinging insects. Our hands and faces became swollen all over and the bites on my feet came up in blisters which broke and left raw places when I put on my boots again.

On the fifteenth day our impatience got the better of us and we started out before it was properly dark and suddenly came upon a man in soldier's uniform scything grass at the side of the road We were filthily dirty and unshaven and must have looked the most villainous tramps; it was stupid of us to have risked being seen; but it would have aroused his suspicion if we'd turned back, so we walked on past him. He looked up and said something we didn't catch. We answered 'Good evening' as usual. But he called after us and then when we took no notice, shouted 'Halt! Halt!' and ran after us with his scythe. We were both too weak to run fast or far and moreover we saw at that moment a man with a gun about fifty yards to our right. There was only one thing to be done and we did it. We turned haughtily and waited for our pursuer and when he was a few yards away Buckley demanded in a voice quivering with indignant German what the devil he meant by shouting at us. He almost dropped his scythe with astonishment, then turned round and went slowly back to his work. Buckley had saved the day.

The end of our march on the following night brought us within fifteen kilometres of the Swiss frontier and we decided to eat the rest of our food and cross the next night. However, I kept back a few small meat lozenges. We learnt the map by heart so as to avoid having to strike matches later on and left all our spare kit behind us in order to travel light for this last lap. But it wasn't to be our last lap.

We were awfully weak by now and made slow progress through the heavy going and about two hours after we'd started a full bright moon rose which made us feel frightfully conspicuous. Moreover, we began to doubt our actual position, for a road we'd expected to find wasn't there. However, we tramped on by compass and reached a village which we hoped was a place named Riedheim, within half a mile of the frontier.

But here we suddenly came on a single line railway which wasn't on our map. We were aghast - we were lost and moreover Buckley was fearfully exhausted for want of food, so we decided to lie up for another night in a thick wood on a hill. The meat lozenges I'd saved now came in very handy and we also managed to find water and some more raw potatoes. Then we slept and when daylight came studied our small scale map and tried to make head or tail of our situation.

We had a good view of the countryside from our position, but could make nothing of it. Perhaps we were already in Switzerland? It was essential to know and it was no good looking for signposts since they'd all been removed within a radius of ten miles of the frontier. I think we were both slightly insane by now from hunger and fatigue; anyhow I decided to take a great risk. I took off my tunic and walking down into the fields asked a girl who was making hay what the name of the village was. It was Riedheim - as I'd originally thought. The railway of course had been made after the map was printed. I don't know what the girl thought of my question and appearance; she gave me a sly look, but went on with her work. I returned to Buckley and when it was quite dark we left our hiding place. We had three quarters of an hour to cross the frontier before the moon rose - and we had to go with the greatest care. For a time we walked bent double and then we went down on our hands and knees, pushing our way through the thick long grass of water meadows. The night was so still surely the swishing of the grass as we moved through it must be audible for hundreds of yards. On and on we went, endlessly it seemed - making for a stream which we had seen from our hill and now knew must be the boundary line. Then the edge of the moon peered at us over the hills. We crawled at top speed now, until Buckley's hand on my heel suddenly brought me to a halt. About fifteen yards ahead was a sentry. He was walking along a footpath on the bank of a stream. He had no rifle and had probably just been relieved. He passed without seeing us. One last spurt and we were in the stream and up the other bank. 'Crawl,' said Buckley. 'Run,' said I and we ran. It was just after midnight when we crossed into Switzerland and freedom on our eighteenth night out.

Footnotes Chapter 5

17   Hodder & Stoughton Ltd London December 1945.

Chapter 6

Inveterate Escapers

Duncan Grinnell-Milne MC DFC and bar

Duncan Grinnell-Milne was commissioned in the Special Reserve Infantry 1914 and seconded to the RFC in July 1915. He served as pilot with 16 Squadron in France until captured on 1 December 1915, escaping from Germany in April 1918. He served with 56 Squadron in France, commanding the Squadron at Armistice and after. After the war he served in Egypt, Palestine, Syria, Sudan and later in Experimental Section at Farnborough. Later he was Assistant Air Attaché, British Embassy, Paris. He retired from the RAF in December 1925. He is the author of 'An Escaper's Log' and 'Fortune of War' (The Bodley Head) and of several other books.

The period of my adventures as a prisoner of war lies between the 1st December 1915 and the end of April 1918; nearly two and a half years. During the whole of that period the thought of escape was uppermost in my mind and therefore I cannot hope to tell you in detail of all the attempts made or of all my adventures. The best I can do is to recount briefly some of my many failures and my final success. I was only nineteen when I was captured, flying; and it seemed tragic enough then to be condemned to that most awful state of things for a young man in war time; inaction. Quite naturally my thoughts turned to escape. My first camp was Mainz; and the first incident to stimulate my imagination occurred on Xmas Eve 1915. Two officers, one British and one French, escaped. They weren't at liberty very long, but the details which slowly trickled through were somehow wildly exciting. They had obtained civilian clothing, German money, maps and a compass; how, I didn't know, but it made me want to find out!

I determined to escape too. I thought about it; I talked about it to one or two kindred spirits. I didn't know a thing of how to get going, but I set out to learn. I had one asset: I could speak German, not really such an asset as it seemed and without wasting much time I started to dig a tunnel. It was a very small tunnel and it had a very long way to go; at least eighty yards. It would have taken many weary months to complete; in fact I was secretly rather glad when the Germans became suspicious and suddenly bundled a few of us who had been connected with it off to another camp.

Weilburg was the name of the new camp; not a bad place, where, under other circumstances, one might have been content to stay for the remainder of the war. But the itch to escape had obtained a firm hold on one or two of us. We were delighted, not with the camp, but with the fact that a tunnel had already been started by some Russians in a disused cellar. Here I had my first experience of making keys and picking locks, for at night the doors leading to the cellar were locked and the Russians had skilfully moulded pass-keys out of soft white-metal spoons. I learnt some valuable lessons from them. But it was far more than a tunnel; it was a conspiracy! After dark, through the passages of the building flitted Russians in long black cloaks, caps pulled down over their eyes, mysterious bundles beneath their arms. In the cellar itself, stumps of candle threw long, distorted shadows, muffled figures like those of Guy Fawkes and his friends, moved as silently as ghosts. At least they tried to be as silent as ghosts, but every now and then someone would trip over a brick or an empty box, or else clumsily drop one of the table-knives used for digging. There would be a crash, a loud clatter, immediately followed by a chorus of hissing and 'shooshing' and hushing, as though one had aroused a nest of angry snakes. The candles would be blown out and we would wait, listening with bated breath, whilst overhead we could hear a sentry passing, coughing and stamping his feet in the cold. At length reassured, we would light up again and cautiously resume work.

Gradually we obtained a bigger proportion of British workers and fewer Russian conspirators; work went on more quickly if less romantically but even so we were doomed to failure. The tunnel was too near the surface; it collapsed beneath a mass of melting snow just before it was finished and we were temporarily heartbroken. But we soon found courage to start again; other schemes were afoot. We were beginning to know the rudiments of the game, of how to make odds and ends of material into rough suits of civilian clothing, of how to get compasses smuggled out from England, or of how to buy very bad maps from a corrupt German guard. A visiting clergyman, who imprudently left his bag unwatched during a church service, gave us the chance to see what an official travelling pass looked like and we banged out many copies on a borrowed typewriter. A little later two of us very nearly escaped in the washing baskets which were carried out of the camp each week. So sure was I of the success of this scheme that on the night when we were to be shut into the baskets I applied a bottle of black hair dye to my red hair. But the baskets were too small and when at dawn we gave up hope I was thankful to think that the hair dye hadn't worked. I should have touched wood. By noon my hair had turned a bright purple and the Germans had a good laugh at my expense. Scheme after scheme went wrong and all I got out of Weilburg was some valuable experience and a few weeks in gaol for helping two other fellows to escape.

The next camp I went to was Friedberg. There, for some three months I worked hard at a number of different plans and at length after many failures three of us tried a new scheme. We were to walk out of the camp in broad daylight, two of us dressed as German officers, the third as a civilian. The supposed civilian, by the way, was my brother, who had recently been captured, also while flying. I cannot go into lengthy details of the slow manufacture of German uniforms - many other prisoners had a hand in it - but I can at least explain that the pre-war Russian overcoat was of much the same colour and cut as the German garment. Of course a good many important alterations were needed; and the remainder of the equipment of caps, badges, shoulder-straps, sword-scabbard, etc, required a vast amount of patient work. However, the main business was wearing the uniform and somehow making it get us past the sentries on the gate. There was a lot of difficulty about this, but providing you had sufficient effrontery it was not impossible, for a large number of visiting commissions from the German War Office, from the Red Cross, from neutrals; had recently inspected the camp. We styled ourselves the Drainage Commission and a very smart trio we were, smart enough to fool the authorities. But no one need ever attempt to explain to me the meaning of 'stage fright.' No actor ever felt as badly as I did on the morning when I led my two drainage friends past the sentries to the gates of Friedberg. After all, in England, nowadays, an actor rarely gets shot or put in prison if he fails to give satisfaction; whereas in our case there was a distinct likelihood of getting shot and a certainty of being gaoled if we were found out. But the great bluff succeeded splendidly. The sentries clicked their heels and saluted as we marched triumphantly out of the camp without any opposition whatsoever; and the only sad thing I have to record is that within five days we had all three been recaptured after long and rather difficult cross-country marches. Naturally we lost all our valuable escaping kit on being recaptured, a very discouraging state of affairs, but something over a month's solitary confinement in the civil prison in the town of Friedberg gave me plenty of time to ponder past adventures and also to plan future attempts. And when at length I was sent off to Fort Zorndorf near the town of Cüstrin, seventy miles east of Berlin, I was impatient to start again.

Life in a fortress isn't too much fun at the best; but the two principal objections to Zorndorf were that it was extremely difficult to get out of and that it lay a very considerable distance from any neutral frontier. In fact the Russian front was as near as anything and whenever Russians escaped or laid plans to escape, they generally made straight for home. Just before I arrived one Russian officer went so far as to make himself a saddle and bridle, intending, so he said, to catch a horse and ride back to Moscow. He actually got out of the fort dressed as a German officer, but he never caught his horse. It was he that was caught, practically at once; the sight of a German officer carrying a set of home-made harness was a trifle too odd!

Zorndorf, like so many old forts, was a sort of five-sided affair, mostly underground, with a few trenches and earthworks on top and a big ditch all round. On the far side of the ditch a thirty-foot wall rose to the level of the surrounding country. There was only one official exit, closely guarded, as, in fact, was the whole camp. When I arrived the few good schemes had already been used up. But the majority of us being there for attempted escapes we went on trying. We talked of, we imagined, we worked at every conceivable scheme, from digging about in the very foundations of the fort for a possible secret passage, to calculating the chances of a man-lifting kite or of a hot-air balloon: and as far as that goes, we must have talked enough hot air to lift a regiment out of the place.

'I first met Captain Hardy [Captain Jocelyn Lee Hardy] at Zorndorf.' (Captain, later Major Jocelyn Lee 'Hoppy' Hardy DSO MC and bar was famed for his courage on the battlefield and repeated escapes from prisoner of war camps. His nickname stems from him losing a leg in combat during the final months of the war. Fitted with an artificial prosthesis, he trained himself to disguise the fact, by walking at a very quick pace, almost completely disguising the notion that he had a wooden leg, but earning him the sobriquet 'Hoppy'). 'He and I racked our brains over many a plot. The first thing we actually tried was a wild dash for freedom from the house of the German Commandant. He used to have us brought out of the fort to his house if we had anything to ask him or to complain about. The house was on the edge of a forest and although close to and in full view of a number of sentries we thought it unlikely that they would fire for fear of hitting the Commandant. On the great day itself the sentries seemed very watchful but only one guard accompanied us and while he was inside the house announcing our arrival we strolled off round the corner, jumped a fence and then sprinted away at full speed into the forest. There were three of us at the start, but the third fellow couldn't run fast enough. He was soon recaptured, unharmed we heard later, but at the time the sounds of shooting and much shouting made us redouble our efforts. Hardy and I ran on, got separated; lost ourselves in the forest and hours afterwards, by an extraordinary chance, found each other in the night miles from anywhere. It was an unpleasant escapade, not even very funny. But then if you want to be really uncomfortable wait for a spell of bad weather in January and having made yourself thoroughly unfit by a few months indoors, preferably in a gaol, put on your thinnest clothing and try an all-night cross-country walk. We met with swamps, dense forest, streams in flood, villages and farms that had to be avoided and the River Oder, which we vainly attempted to cross in a leaky boat. However, allowing for detours, we covered over forty-five miles in fifteen hours!

And in the morning we boarded a train for Berlin! It began to look as though we were on the high-road to success but no, misfortune barred the way. Back at Zorndorf someone had forgotten to tear up a map on which was marked our proposed route. The Germans found it, sent a man ahead of us by rail. We were arrested on the train and brought back to Cüstrin for a little solitary confinement. And when this was over and we were back in the fort, we had to start all over again collecting escaping kit, manufacturing funny-looking civilian clothing, hunting for ever-scarce maps, designing new false police passes; in fact all the lengthy and serious preparation for escape.

As soon as we were ready, Hardy and I with a Belgian officer named

Bastin tried a much more ambitious scheme. It had been worked out by some French officers who had left for another camp. They were responsible for all its brilliant ideas and also, I'm afraid, for its failure. For it depended, at the end, upon a home-made ladder to scale the thirty-foot wall above the ditch; and the ladder was a foot too short! However, we didn't know that when we started. By an ingenious plan, also worked out by the French and involving being locked up in the camp chapel all night, we got out on top of the fort before daybreak and carrying our kit and the ladder in sections, we crept around the trenches under the very noses of the sentries, eventually sliding down a long slope into the ditch. There, behind a wall, we built up the ladder and waited for dawn. We had really succeeded wonderfully well till then; there had been a flock of sentries about, but we had dodged them all, greatly assisted by deep snow and the fact that we were wearing white clothing. The white clothing, covering us literally from head to foot, was made up of various odds and ends, but I remember that it consisted in part of female nightgowns, purchased for us by a German guard; heaven knows what he thought we were going to do with them! Yes, it was a splendid scheme, but the ladder was too short! And the wall was covered with ice so that one couldn't get a grip to pull oneself up from the top of the ladder. We were caught in the ditch. [18]

Three months' solitary confinement this time, in Cüstrin Citadel, then back to Zorndorf for further vain attempts and more hard work collecting kit. I won't say that we ever gave up hope; but the outlook was becoming pretty desperate, when suddenly after a total of ten months in the fort, I was packed off to Ströhen Moor, a place west of Hanover and only about one hundred miles from the Dutch frontier. Ströhen was quite the funniest camp I was ever in. To begin with, it was all-British; no Allies. Secondly it was notoriously unhealthy, which made everyone much more irresponsible, discontented and ready to annoy the guards in any way possible. Also it was, at the start, a very easy camp to escape from; people walked out of it with but little trouble. Several who escaped reached the frontier; one or two successfully crossed it. But all the easiest schemes were soon exploited; the Germans became thoroughly alarmed and the mesh of the wire surrounding the camp seemed to grow finer each day. When I arrived it was time to think of something serious. Yet only a day after my arrival I was taken into a scheme which, for simplicity, craziness and also, likelihood of success, was hard to beat. It was proposed to charge one of the small side gates of the camp with a 'battering-ram' at dusk. The lock was believed to be quite weak and the momentum of our charge would, it was thought, break the lock and carry us on into outer darkness; while the yells of a gang of accomplices in the camp would distract the attention of the sentries. The 'battering-ram' was an iron bar; part of a gymnastic bar erected in the camp by the Germans and about six men were to carry it during the charge. I applied for a position at the tail-end! But I had come into the scheme rather late and there were already quite a number of applicants for the post of honour. Another job was found for me; a nastier one. There were two rows of wire at Ströhen: one row, tall, close-meshed, surmounted by barbed wire ; the other, the inner row, a fence some three or four feet high, designed to keep us away from the outer row. The space between was called the 'neutral zone'; anyone found inside it got shot! Wherever there was a gate in the outer wire fence, there was naturally a smaller gate in the inner one; and it was my job to open this small gate, at the crucial moment, so as to let the 'battering-ram' party go through at speed. I also had to watch the sentries, lest they should smell a rat; meaning me!

On the evening of the appointed day, the gallant party assembled behind a nearby hut; iron bar, rucksacks, escaping kit and all, in readiness. As it grew dark I commenced pacing up and down near the wire, trying to look happy, with an eye on the sentry. Presently, when no Germans were looking, I gave the signal to 'stand by.' Then I strolled up to the small gate, unlatched it and pulled it open. It squeaked horribly, but I couldn't let go or it would have swung to and I had already waved and whistled for the charging-party to start. I couldn't see much in the dark, but I heard a scuffling sound as they got under way; and a second later they came thundering past. I have a recollection of feeling at that moment exactly like an old man at a level-crossing holding open the gates for an express to go by and the next moment the express was derailed and I was left looking stupidly at the accident.

There was a tremendous crash as the front man of the party hit the gate. In the darkness he had missed the lock with the end of the ram and it was his face that charged the framework. But in spite of the five strong men behind him, his face wasn't hard enough to push down the obstruction and he let forth a yell that must have curdled the blood of all the sentries round the camp. The iron bar was immediately dropped with a loud clang and the party having picked itself up made off at top speed in the direction of the huts. I fancy I was rather dazed at the rapidity of these happenings, for I stood for a moment, still holding the little gate open, gaping at the 'battering-ram' on the ground, until a loud report close behind brought me suddenly to my senses and I just managed to dodge into a hut before the infuriated guards came streaming into the camp, ready to start the inevitable search.

And not long afterwards, when numerous attempts had driven the Commandant to the verge of insanity, a properly organized search for escaping kit was made with the help of detectives from Berlin. We all felt very sorry for those poor detectives! From the time they entered the camp to the time they left, the unfortunate men were given no peace. Impeded at every turn, they were harried from one room to another; contraband captured in one hut was recaptured by the prisoners in the next. On leaving, surrounded by a band of cheering British officers, several of them complained that their pockets had been picked; their identity cards and police papers stolen. And one wretched man walked out with a notice pinned to his coat-tail: 'You know my methods, Watson!' Next day more prisoners escaped.

My brother turned up at Ströhen, fresh from gaol after an escape which had brought him close to the Dutch frontier. Together we started to work out a new and fairly ingenious scheme. We couldn't get material for German officers' uniforms (and in any case very few officers came into the camp) so we decided to dress me up as a German soldier and let me escort a couple of prisoners, my brother and another man, out of one of the main gates. The manufacture of the German uniform out of spare bits and scraps of clothing wasn't too difficult, but the rifle took weeks to make. We hunted for many days, in and around and under the huts, before finding a suitable piece of wood out of which to carve the stock; a bar wrenched from a cooking range formed the barrel. Tin cans were cut up to make the breech mechanism. It was a masterpiece when it was finished. I believe it was put in a German war-museum later; at any rate the odd pieces of scrap-iron, wood and tin were faked up so that it would stand a really close inspection.

The party was eventually increased to five prisoners under my supposed command. They were disguised as British orderlies, of whom there were a large number at Ströhen and who were frequently employed in bringing food and parcels from the station. In our case, we put all our kit into a big sack, labelled it for another camp as though it were being sent after a departed officer and loaded it on to a wheelbarrow. The scheme for getting out of the camp, first unlocking and passing through an inner gate in full view of the Germans, was pretty complicated and required a great deal of preparation. In addition to the German uniform and rifle we had to make forged passes, false keys, etc. In fact there was so much to think of that we felt sure of forgetting some small but vital detail. But everything worked out remarkably well. I admit that I felt like the world's biggest fool when I collected my orderlies, yelled commands at them in German, herded them past the sentry and marched out of the gate, wheelbarrow and all felt that everyone in and about the camp, Germans included, was looking and laughing at me! But we got out all right, the whole lot of us. And then it went wrong! My brother was recognized. It wasn't his fault; he'd been in gaol so long that all the guards knew him well by sight. And once we were stopped, we knew it was all up.

I did about nine weeks 'solitary' that time, followed by a couple of weeks hospital, an attempt to cut the wire, some more gaol ; and then off to Neunkirchen, in the Saar district, a nasty little camp in the middle of the town. We lived in a small theatre, over eighty of us in one room, which made escape practically essential. Exercise was what we chiefly needed and we got all we wanted in the digging of a superb tunnel beneath the stage. This time we had almost every advantage and if that tunnel had ever been completed a very large number would have left the camp. We spent all our spare time manufacturing compasses, copying maps, printing false papers and making a sort of escapers' phrase-book in German; all so as to enable between forty and fifty prisoners to escape. The tunnel itself was fitted with electric light; rigged up with the help of electric torches bought from the Germans and an electric buzzer to warn the workers of the approach of danger. A great pity it didn't work! Rain spoilt it and bad drainage. For more than a month we fought the rising flood, until everything in the camp was wet and muddy and the water began to overflow into our dormitory. Then, rather naturally, the Germans suspected something.

Weeks passed in the planning of fresh attempts and after one or two short stretches in gaol I was beginning to plan something desperate, so as at least to be sent away from Neunkirchen, when I had a stroke of good luck. An exchange of prisoners had been taking place for some time between England and Germany. Officers and men of both nations who had been captured early in the war were being sent to Holland, where they were given complete liberty but forbidden to return to their respective countries. This plan, essential for the health of the prisoners, of course meant abandoning all idea of taking any further part in the war. A few of us who still thought we would eventually escape refused the exchange and when my turn came, I told the authorities of my intention to stay in Germany; though not, of course, of my reasons. Then came the good luck. I was sent with the other prisoners to a camp at Aachen. There my refusal was to be officially accepted and I was to be sent back to a camp in the interior; one of the authorities hinted darkly at Fort Zorndorf!

Now the north-western side of the town of Aachen is less than five miles from the nearest point of the Dutch frontier, so that at a glance an escape looks remarkably easy. But there were several things that made it difficult. We found that the camp was in the south-eastern part of the town and the thickly populated outskirts would have to be cleared before one could turn west towards the frontier. There were three of us intending to escape and from our rather sketchy maps it was plain that we would have to march fifteen to twenty miles in all and at top speed. That was the real difficulty; time. We found out that after one day and one night the formalities would be completed; then we should be sent to another camp.

On the morning of our arrival we started desperately searching for an exit. Never before had it been necessary, or possible for that matter, to get out of a camp within twenty-four hours of arrival. Never had it been possible or so absolutely essential to reach the frontier and cross it in one short night. For with Holland so close it would be simple for the Germans, once warned of our escape, to guard every inch of the small sector at which we were bound to aim. A daylight attempt was impossible; we had to leave after dark and be in Holland before dawn. It seemed utterly hopeless. The camp was small, closely guarded; we knew nothing of its routine or even of its topography; we had practically no kit. After roll-call that morning, we had a total of eighteen hours daylight and darkness, in which to escape and make good.

Round that small camp we marched innumerable times; searched the building in which we were housed, searched the yard, searched the palisade and the main gate for weak spots; searched everything with a horrible feeling that we were attempting the impossible.

And yet by 9.30 that night two of us were out of the camp. The third man, observed by a watchful sentry, had been unable to follow. But the two of us had left unobserved, neatly, efficiently, but unromantically enough, through a small, almost invisible, ventilating shaft in the camp lavatory; thence through another lavatory (used by the Germans) to a wire fence. Hurriedly, but as silently as possible, we tore our way under the wire, crawled past a couple of sentries and crept out into an open field. Then under cover of a hedge we made our way cautiously to a road leading through the suburbs to the country east of Aache. The first great difficulty was surmounted: we had cleared out of the camp within the specified time. Now the second great obstacle faced us: to reach and cross the frontier before dawn. The suburbs were difficult enough to clear; we never seemed to reach open country. There were villages, factories, coal mines to be avoided all along our route and in the intervals, densely wooded hills where we wandered about, our maps useless and only a rough compass course to guide us. I had a feeling that we were still alarmingly close to the camp, that we were being followed, that we should never reach the frontier before dawn. It was generally agreed among escapers that the only safe thing to do was to spend a night or two approaching the frontier and practically crawl the last few miles to the border. But here we were, marching along at our best pace, with no more than the faintest idea of our position. As we gradually turned from east to north and north-west, the country did open up a little but our maps became even vaguer.

The hours passed. There were fewer houses, but nevertheless we kept on blundering into obstacles: well-fenced farms, the outskirts of villages. And then as we hurried on beneath a dark and raining sky, tired, muddy, wet through from wading streams, our clothing torn to rags, we began to encounter obstacles of a different sort. All the woods were crossed by barbed wire fences; farmhouses contained wakeful men; we heard the click of rifle-bolts; shadowy silhouettes showed faintly on the skyline. We were close! But our maps were nearly useless; only memory of the Dutch frontier studied during over two years helped us; that and a compass course. The obstacles and unknown features of the country delayed us terribly. We had to make wide detours; once we had to retrace our steps after nearly bumping into a sentry. Dawn came suddenly out of a grey, hopeless sky. We had reached the end of the time limit set in the camp on the previous day. In the first light we hurried on, crawled through hedges, skirted open fields and in desperation finally ran a hundred yards to find cover in a bramble bush. There we rested, stared at our maps, studied the features of the country and at length ascertained our exact position. We had succeeded! We had won the race. We stood up on the Dutch frontier - free!

Footnotes Chapter

18   Hardy made twelve escape attempts from PoW camps succeeding in actually escaping on 5 separate occasions. In early 1915 he attempted to escape from Halle Camp near Leipzig by breaking through a brick wall into an adjacent ammunition factory. After 5 months work the project proved impracticable. In the summer of 1915 he was transferred to Augustabad Camp near Neu Brandenburg and after being there 10 days he managed to slip away from a bathing party outside the camp, together with a Russian officer. After a difficult journey they covered the 50 miles to the Baltic coast. They had to swim a river, were nearly recaptured once, but eventually reached Stralsund. They nearly managed to get the crew of a Swedish schooner there to give them passage, but were arrested at the last moment. Hardy was returned to Halle and joined an unsuccessful attempt with a group of Russian officers to break down a wall. He then made a solo escape attempt by picking locks and breaking through a skylight before sliding down a rope onto the street. From here he slipped into the rain and the darkness. He spoke enough German to make his way by train to Bremen. Here, broken down by cold and hunger, the Germans recaptured him. He was then transferred to Magdeburg, where he escaped with a Belgian officer using 'subterfuge, audacity and good fortune'. They reached Berlin by train and went on to Stralsund. From there they crossed to the island of Rügen, but were arrested before they could find a fishing boat to take them to Sweden. His next PoW camp was Fort Zorndorf where he made several unsuccessful escape attempts.

Chapter 7

Billy Bishop vc

Captain Billy Bishop RFC watched the first yellow streaks of dawn light up the dark sky ahead of him as he flew across the German lines. A cool wind blew against his cheeks as he pressed on in his solitary blue-nosed Nieuport a few hundred feet above the sleeping hordes of grey-clad German soldiers. As his eyes searched the crater-marked, muddy battlefields around him, Bishop felt the tingling muscles of his empty stomach involuntarily tensing in eager anticipation of the combat that lay ahead. In his lone Nieuport, Billy Bishop was going to take on an entire German airfield single-handed!
Paul Clifton, writing in *RAF Flying Review*, December 1957. During the First World War, just a handful of pilots became the top-scoring aces in the cut-and-thrust single-handed air fighting over the Western Front. These great aces included, among others, Germany's Manfred von Richthofen, who was credited by the Germans with shooting down 80 aircraft; France's Rene Fonck, who destroyed 75; and Edward Mannock, who bagged 73. Canada's Billy Bishop, who shot down a total of 72 air victories, including two balloons, 52 and two shared 'destroyed' with 16 'out of control' was thus one of the top-scoring aces on both sides in the First World War.

Captain William Avery 'Billy' Bishop, an aggressive Canadian who enjoyed every minute of the exciting sport of hunting German aircraft, had been turning his daring plan over in his mind for many days. The idea he had been pondering was to attack a German airfield when all aircraft were on the ground. Dawn, he concluded, was the obvious choice of time. He would surprise the German aircraft just as they were preparing to get airborne and his plan was to shoot each German aircraft down as it took off to attack him. Now, as he pressed still deeper into enemy territory, he was giving up his day off, 2 June 1917 to put his highly original plan into practice. But when, at length, Bishop reached the airfield he had selected as his target, he was bitterly disappointed: the grass field was completely deserted. He could see no sign of either German soldiers or their machines. Terribly depressed, he consoled himself with the thought that he could still make his surprise attack on another day. Suddenly, to his joy, as he peered through the early morning light, he made out the low shapes of enemy hangars a short distance away. Another German airfield was immediately ahead!

When he reached this airfield, he saw that he had surprised seven German machines on the ground. Evidently, they were just preparing to take off on their dawn patrol; for, as he flew his little Nieuport about 300 feet above the dew-covered grass, he noticed that several of the German machines had their engines revving. Groups of German mechanics were standing beside their machines; and near them were several enemy Archie nests. In spite of the far bigger odds that faced him, Bishop unhesitatingly pushed down the nose of his Nieuport. Racing low above the grass, he raked the German machines. As he flashed past a mere 50 feet above them, Bishop glimpsed the startled faces of the German pilots, turned up in terror to watch him. Bishop saw at least one stiff-backed figure fall as he watched the mechanics scatter away from his deadly stream of bullets. Suddenly, every muscle in Bishop's body tensed as he heard the staccato chatter of machine-guns firing at him from the ground. Glancing rapidly from side to side, Bishop was horrified to see that ugly patterns of bullet holes had already been ripped in the fabric of his mainplanes. The enemy ground fire, he grimly reflected, was uncomfortably accurate. However, he dared not fly away from the airfield; for, if he wanted to live, he had got to shoot down every German aircraft as it rose to kill him. Suddenly, Bishop saw one of the German machines begin to take off. With bullets whining all around him, Bishop put his Nieuport into a shallow dive and raced after the German machine. The German was now hovering just above the ground. Coolly, Bishop took aim. He saw the enemy machine rise to fill his sight. Then he pressed his gun lever. He saw the German slither sideways. Finally, the machine dropped sickeningly and then crashed into the ground. Bishop had chalked up Number One.

He then saw another German aircraft flying low above the ground. Heavily outnumbered, Bishop could not afford to waste time by closing. He took careful aim and fired from where he was. Unforgettably, Bishop glimpsed the taut white face of the German pilot as he turned to watch his opponent's stream of bullets streaking towards him. At almost the same instant, the German machine crashed headlong into some trees. Bishop had accounted for Number Two but he still had heavy opposition to face. Now, as the Canadian turned back towards the airfield, his eyes were greeted by the sight that he had feared most of all; a situation which, he had previously calculated, he would not be able to defeat. The sight which caused Bishop such dismay was the spectacle of two German machines taking off at the same time; heading in slightly different directions. Since he had worked out no solution to this problem when he had been planning his lone sortie, Bishop had decided that he would fly home if this baffling situation should occur; and now, faced with what seemed an impossible task, he began to climb away. But only one enemy aircraft came after him. Glancing back, Bishop saw that this German was catching him up. The Canadian turned to face his opponent and opened fire. The two aircraft flew warily around one another - each seeking to inflict the death-blow. In a flash, Bishop saw his opening. Taking rapid aim, he fired a short burst and sent his adversary crashing into a field. Bishop had chalked up Number Three.

Immediately, he turned to take on the fourth German machine, which was now flying towards him. But, he quietly reflected, he was now in an extremely tight spot: he had used up almost all of his ammunition, yet there was no apparent end to the stream of German machines still coming up to attack him. However, Bishop had no choice: this latest German assailant had him cold. Stubbornly, Bishop dashed at the enemy and emptied his last drum into him. Fortunately, at this point, the German flew off. Now completely unarmed, Bishop sensibly started to fly home. Suddenly, however, as his eyes searched the sky around him, Bishop looked up at a terrifying sight. To his dismay, he saw four German scouts flying immediately above him! Alone and unarmed and deep inside enemy territory, Bishop knew he was no match for such a deadly quartet. Eventually he managed to give them the slip without being attacked. He finally landed back at base, considerably shaken. However, characteristic of the luck that stayed with him throughout his air fighting career, Bishop found that no bullet had passed closer than a couple of feet from where he sat. It was one of the most audacious lone air exploits of the First World War. Not surprisingly, in recognition of his incredible valour, Bishop was subsequently awarded a VC.

The fearless fighting spirit that so conspicuously earned a VC for 'Billy' Bishop, Canada's most famous air ace of World War One, was characteristic of the aggressiveness which drove this plucky fighter pilot throughout his career on the Western Front.

Bishop was born in Owen Sound, Ontario on 8 February 1894, the second of three children born to William A. and Margaret Bishop. His father, a lawyer and graduate of Osgoode Hall Law School in Toronto, was the Registrar of Grey County. Attending Owen Sound Collegiate and Vocational Institute, Bishop earned the reputation of a fighter, defending himself and others easily against bullies. He avoided team sports, preferring solitary pursuits such as swimming, horse riding and shooting. Bishop was less successful at his studies; he would abandon any subject he could not easily master and was often absent from class. At 15 Bishop had his first experience with aviation; he built an aircraft out of cardboard, wood crates and string and 'flew' off the roof of his three-story house. He was dug, unharmed, out of the wreckage by his sister. In 1914, at the age of 20, Billy Bishop entered the Royal Military College of Canada (RMC) in Kingston, Ontario, where his brother Worth had graduated in 1903. At RMC, Bishop was known as 'Bish' and 'Bill'. Bishop failed his first year at RMC, having been caught cheating. When the First World War broke out later that year, Bishop left RMC and joined the Mississauga Horse cavalry regiment. He was commissioned as an officer but was ill with pneumonia when the regiment was sent overseas. After recovering, he was transferred to the 8th Canadian Mounted Rifles, a mounted infantry unit, then stationed in London, Ontario. Bishop showed a natural ability with a gun and excelled on the firing range. His seemingly 'super-human' eyesight allowed him to put bullets in a target placed so far away others saw only a dot. They left Canada for England on 6 June 1915 on board the requisitioned cattle ship Caledonia. On 21 June, off the coast of Ireland, the ship's convoy came under attack by U-boats. Two ships were sunk and 300 Canadians died, but Bishop's ship remained unharmed, arriving in Plymouth Harbour on 23 June.

Bishop quickly became frustrated with the mud of the trenches and the lack of action. In July 1915, after watching an RFC aircraft return from a mission, Bishop said '...it's clean up there! I'll bet you don't get any mud or horse shit on you up there. If you die, at least it would be a clean death.' He transferred to the RFC and as there were no spots available for pilots in the flight school, he chose to be an observer. On 1 September he reported to 21 (Training) Squadron at Netheravon for elementary air instruction. The first aircraft he trained in was the Avro 504, flown by Roger Neville. Bishop was adept at taking aerial photographs and was soon in charge of training other observers with the camera. The squadron was ordered to France in January 1916. It arrived at Boisdinghem airfield, near Saint-Omer equipped with R.E.7 reconnaissance aircraft. Bishop's first combat sortie was as an aerial spotter for British artillery. At first, the aircraft would not get airborne until they had offloaded their bomb load and machine guns. Bishop and pilot Neville flew over German lines near Boisdinghem and when the German howitzer was found, they relayed co-ordinates to the British, who then bombarded and destroyed the target. In the following months, Bishop flew on reconnaissance and bombing flights, but never fired his machine guns on an enemy aircraft. During one takeoff in April 1916, Bishop's aircraft experienced an engine failure and he badly injured his knee. The injury was aggravated while on leave in London in May 1916 and Bishop was admitted to the hospital in Bryanston Square, London. While there he met and befriended socialite Lady St. Helier, who was a friend to both Winston Churchill and Secretary for Air Lord Hugh Cecil. When his father suffered a small stroke, St. Helier arranged for Bishop to recuperate in Canada, thereby missing the Battle of the Somme.

Bishop returned to England in September 1916 and with the influence of St. Helier, was accepted for training as a pilot at the Central Flying School at Upavon on Salisbury Plain. His first solo flight was in a Maurice Farman 'Shorthorn'. In November 1916 after receiving his wings, Bishop was attached to 37 Squadron RFC at Sutton's Farm, Essex flying the B.E.2c. Bishop disliked the flying at night over London, searching for German airships and he soon requested a transfer to France. On 17 March 1917 Bishop arrived at 60 Squadron at Filescamp Farm near Arras, where he flew the Nieuport 17 fighter. At that time, the average life expectancy of a new pilot in that sector was 11 days and German aces were shooting down British aircraft 5 to 1. Bishop's first patrol on 22 March was less than successful. He had trouble controlling his run-down aircraft, was nearly shot down by anti-aircraft fire and became separated from his group. On 24 March, after crash landing his aircraft during a practice flight in front of General John Higgins, Bishop was ordered to return to flight school at Upavon. But before he could leave, Major Alan Scott, new commander of 60 Squadron, convinced Higgins to let him stay until a replacement arrived. The next day Bishop claimed his first victory when his was one of four Nieuports that engaged three Albatros D.III Scouts near St Leger but his engine failed in the process. He landed in No Man's Land 300 yards from the German front line. After running to the Allied trenches, Bishop spent the night on the ground in a rainstorm. There Bishop wrote a letter home, starting: 'I am writing this from a dugout 300 yards from our front line, after the most exciting adventure of my life.' General Higgins personally congratulated Bishop and rescinded his order to return to flight school. On 30 March 1917 Bishop was named a flight commander. The next day he scored his second victory. Bishop, in addition to the usual patrols with his squadron comrades, soon flew many unofficial 'lone-wolf' flights deep into enemy territory, with the blessing of Major Scott. As a result, his total of enemy aircraft shot down increased rapidly. On 8 April he scored his fifth victory and became an ace. To celebrate, Bishop's mechanic painted the aircraft's nose blue, the mark of an ace.

Captain Albert Ball, at that time the Empire's highest scoring ace, had had a red spinner fitted.

Bishop's no-hold-barred style of flying always had him 'at the front of the pack,' leading his pilots into battle over hostile territory. Bishop soon realized that this could eventually see him shot down; after one patrol, a mechanic counted 210 bullet holes in his aircraft. His new method of using the surprise attack proved successful; he claimed twelve aircraft in April alone, earning the Military Cross and a promotion to Captain for his participation at the Battle of Vimy Ridge. The successes of Bishop and his blue-nosed aircraft were noticed on the German side and they began referring to him as 'Hell's Handmaiden'. Oberleutnant Ernst Udet, who accumulated 62 victories to make him the second top scoring ace behind Manfred Freiherr von Richthofen, called him 'the greatest English scouting ace' and one Jasta had a bounty on his head. On 30 April Bishop survived an encounter with Jasta 11 and Manfred von Richthofen, the Red Baron. In May Bishop was awarded the Distinguished Service Order for shooting down two aircraft while being attacked by four others.

In truth, stocky, sandy-haired Billy Bishop was a warm-hearted extrovert who had a great capacity for friendship and laughter, yet his determination to destroy Germans eventually became an obsession. At first, though, he looked on shooting down the enemy as a sport. Said Bishop, referring to this period: 'To me it was not a business or a profession, but just a wonderful game. To bring down a machine did not seem to me to be killing a man; it was more as if I was just destroying a mechanical target...' However, the destruction of opponents later came to mean much more to him than a mere sport. Ultimately, the desire to raise his total of kills to a record score became an all-consuming ambition that dominated his entire life. Referring to this later relentless period, Bishop said: 'I had become very ambitious and was hoping to get a large number of machines officially credited to me... With this object in view, I planned many little expeditions of my own and with the use of great patience, I was very successful in one or two.' The truth is that, in his final days on the Western Front, Billy Bishop lived just to destroy the enemy.

Because of his insatiable aggressiveness. Bishop sometimes hunted enemy aircraft for as many as seven-and-a-half hours a day. Altogether, he took part in more than 200 combats - usually fought alone, over enemy territory and against greater odds. As a result, he was finally credited officially with shooting down no fewer than 72 enemy aircraft. His reward for his brilliant successes was that, ultimately, he was privileged to wear, beneath the wings on his left breast, the ribbons and rosettes of not only a VC, but also those of a DSO and Bar, MC and DFC. He was also mentioned in despatches. In addition, he received a Légion d'honneur and a Croix de Guerre with Palm; and by the end of the First World War, he had risen from Lieutenant to become a Staff Lieutenant Colonel on the Canadian General Staff.

Bishop was never satisfied with a day's air fighting unless he was able to add at least one fresh kill to his bag. On one occasion, he went up six times in one day without scoring a single confirmed victory. By evening, the fabric of Bishop's machine was ripped with bullet holes and his port aileron was damaged. Sensibly, Bishop's mechanic strongly urged his irrepressible pilot to ground his battered Nieuport for repairs. But Bishop would not hear of it. Late in the evening, Bishop stubbornly took off for the seventh time that day, determined to add at least one more German scalp to his already impressive total. Doggedly, Bishop searched the evening sky, looking for Germans. Eventually, at 5,000 feet over the German lines, near Armentieres, he spotted a silver Albatros far below. Joyfully, he pounced on it. However, the Canadian pilot had unsuspectingly fallen into a trap. Five more Albatrosses, which had been hiding in the clouds, waiting for just such an opportunity, dived on Bishop's lone Nieuport. Determined to get at least one ' kill,' Bishop immediately got on the tail of the decoy aircraft and sent it crashing. Then he turned to face the remaining five Albatrosses that now surrounded his lone machine. Aggressively taking the initiative, Bishop flew straight towards the leader as the German attempted to make a broadside attack on his Nieuport. Bishop stubbornly held to his course as the German plunged head-on at him. The Canadian did not touch his gun lever. He just kept pressing on. Finally, just as the two machines seemed about to crash into one another, the German leader broke. He went into a steep dive. As Bishop glanced down, he saw him flick into a spin. Finally, the German crashed into a tree. The remaining four Albatrosses now fled from Bishop's lone Nieuport.

Once again determinedly seizing the initiative, Billy got on to the tail of a fleeing Albatros and fired. Then his gun jammed. Now Bishop was not only, in effect, unarmed, but also, because of his damaged aileron, he was having difficulty in controlling his machine. However, he was still not satisfied with his achievements for the day. Boldly, he opened his throttle wide. His battered Nieuport, now highly unstable, shuddered dangerously. Handling his vibrating aircraft with great skill, Bishop coolly brought his badly damaged Nieuport right up alongside the German machine. The Canadian glanced at the harassed face of the German pilot. His machine was even more badly crippled than Bishop's little Nieuport. The starboard wing of the Albatros, Bishop noticed, was badly ripped; and many struts, he also saw, were severed. The Albatros was skidding badly. Inch by inch, Bishop edged his battered Nieuport closer to the crippled Albatros. Eventually, he got his port wing-tip right underneath the starboard wing-tip of the Albatros. Then, violently, he slammed on hard starboard rudder. Bishop heard a loud ripping of fabric and a ghastly crunching of wood, as his little Nieuport went into a wild skidding turn. He felt the stick wobble dangerously in his hand. His whole aircraft was juddering terribly. However, as he glanced rapidly over the side of his cockpit, he glimpsed a sight which gave him immense satisfaction. Looking down, he watched the battered Albatros slither towards the earth, fluttering violently. Then he saw it crash. Billy Bishop flew his battered aircraft home. He was satisfied with his day's work at last.

Billy Bishop's determination to keep on pushing his personal score continually higher kept driving him on right up until his last flight over the Western Front. On his last day in action, highly annoyed at having his ambition thwarted by being ordered to return to office duty, Bishop went up to seek out Germans for the last time. To his joy, when he reached the lines near Ypres, he saw three new Pfalz fighters. Though, as usual, Bishop was flying alone, he immediately attacked the nearest and sent it crashing in flames.

Now, as he had anticipated, he watched the remaining two Germans turn to attack him. But then, to his astonishment, he saw an additional two German fighters dive on him from out of the clouds. He had not bargained for the extra opposition. However, he was not only undeterred - he was also jubilant: odds of four to one against were nothing new to him and the extra machines now provided him with the opportunity to chalk up the additional victories he was seeking. As he dodged and twisted his lone machine, Bishop coolly watched two enemy machines that were circling him, desperately trying to get on his tail. Then, in a flash, Bishop saw his opportunity. As the two machines turned towards him, he dived between them. Thrown into a state of complete confusion, the two Germans crashed into one another. Both fluttered down and one of them burst into flames.

Obviously terrified by the slaughter they had just witnessed, achieved against far greater odds, the remaining two German machines immediately climbed away in alarm. But Bishop was determined not to let this last opportunity for additional victories get away unchallenged. Aggressively, he gave chase. Racing fast after one fleeing German aircraft, he opened fire at 200 yards. The enemy went into an uncontrollable spin and crashed. To his intense annoyance, Bishop watched the remaining German escape by zooming into a cloud. However, the Canadian's lust for fresh German blood was not yet satisfied and he still had some ammunition left. Alertly, he searched the sky for further opponents; and finally, near Neuve Eglise, he came across a two-seater. Calculatingly, he flew up from behind and underneath the enemy machine and then attacked. Taken completely by surprise, the unsuspecting two-seater burst into flames and crashed. This further kill brought Bishop's total for his last day in action to five enemy machines destroyed in two hours!

Accuracy in shooting, Bishop himself believed, was the principal factor which contributed to his outstanding success in the art of shooting down German aircraft. 'I... learned that the most important thing in fighting was the shooting,' he said. Not surprisingly, because of his belief in the value of good marksmanship, Bishop was continuously practising his shooting. When he was first getting the feel of the Nieuport, for example, he collected, from the mess cook, all the old tin cans he could lay his hands on. Then he took up his collection of tins in a sack and at 10,000 feet, tossed them over the side. As the floating tins drifted through the sky, blown by the breeze, Bishop chased each in turn and fired a burst to destroy it. By the time he had shattered all of his tins, he not only felt quite at home in the Nieuport, but, more important, he had also improved his marksmanship enormously.

Employment of the best tactics in air fighting was, Bishop believed, the second most important factor which contributed to his success as an air fighter. On one occasion he saw a single enemy scout flying at a great altitude above him and coolly he planned its carefully premeditated destruction. Calculatingly, he positioned himself between the enemy machine and the sun - to take the enemy completely by surprise; and finally, he attained the superior altitude he wanted. Then, diving at great speed, Bishop managed to slip underneath the German aircraft without being seen.

Now, as he flew along right underneath the enemy he could plainly see the black crosses on the undersurfaces of both mainplanes. Gradually, he crept closer. He had to use great self-control to restrain himself from firing too soon. But, eventually, he got to within 20 yards of the enemy machine. He was in precisely the correct position. Carefully, he picked the exact spot where he knew the German pilot was sitting. Then he fired. Calmly, he watched just 20 tracer bullets streak into the precise spot where the pilot's seat was located. Instantly, he saw the German machine lurch to one side. In a flash; he skidded his own machine in the opposite direction in order to avoid being hit by the falling aircraft. Then, to his great joy, he watched smoke begin to pour from the German aircraft.

The third and least important, of Bishop's secrets of success, in the great ace's view, was the ability to fly an aircraft competently. Said Bishop: 'To be able to fight well, a pilot must be able to have absolute control over his machine... When the fight comes along he...can devote all his time to fighting the other fellow, the flying part of it coming instinctively.' Significantly, though, he added: 'I put aerial gunnery down as the most important factor in fighting in the air.'

When he was a boy in Canada, Billy Bishop learned to shoot in the backwoods around Owen Sound, Ontario, where he was born. Later, at the Royal Military College, Kingston where he was a cadet when war broke out, young Billy could ride any horse that could be saddled and he was also a superb rifle shot. The basis for his brilliant air fighting career had already been laid.

After Billy had finished his three years at the RMC, he was sent to England as a Lieutenant. One day, as he was slopping around in sticky mud during manoeuvres he suddenly saw a trim little aircraft appear from out of the depressing drizzle. 'It landed unhesitatingly in a nearby field as if scorning to brush its wings against so sordid a landscape,' wrote Bishop in Winged Warfare, his autobiography of his air fighting adventures, 'then away again up into the clean grey mists.' He added, ' How long I stood there gazing into the distance I do not know, but when I turned to slog my way back through the mud my mind was made up...I was going to meet the enemy in the air.'

On his next weekend in London, Billy bumped into a couple of Englishmen who had recently transferred to the RFC. Bishop asked them how one got into the Flying Corps. The two Englishmen advised him to go to the War Office and see Lord Hugh Cecil. Accordingly, Bishop stayed over until Monday morning and called on Cecil at the War House. Sure enough, the RFC would be glad to accept him, the Canadian was delighted to learn from Lord Cecil; however, it would be easier to get in as an observer. Though Billy had set his heart on becoming a pilot, he saw his opportunity at least to get into the Flying Corps, so he volunteered as an observer.

Bishop spent four months in France as an observer. ('How I longed during all that time for a fight in the air!') No real opportunities for action came, however. Finally, Billy's pilot crash-landed and the Canadian injured one knee. He was sent back to England to receive proper medical attention. While in England, he determinedly kept hammering away to be accepted for pilot training; and finally, after passing the necessary medical examinations (which included being spun sharply round in a swivel chair, then being suddenly instructed to spring to attention) he was sent to be trained as a pilot.

Like several other famous air aces, Billy Bishop at first found great difficulty in learning to fly. On his first solo in a Maurice Farman (which he knew disrespectfully as the 'Rumpty') he made, first of all, a perfect landing 40 feet above the ground; then, after he had put his nose down, he made another three-pointer - this time a mere eight feet up ! When he had logged no more than 15 hours' solo, he was sent to guard the mouth of the Thames against Zeppelins. The trouble was that he never saw any Zepps and the determined young Billy still longed for action as a fighter pilot.

Eventually, he got the chance he had been seeking: he was sent to France to fly the latest type of Nieuport. When Billy returned from his second flight in a Nieuport he completely wrote off the machine in a bad crash-landing; and for once, he was out of luck - for it so happened that the Wing Commander had been watching the whole unfortunate incident. When the Wingco afterwards had Billy on the carpet, he threatened to send him back to the Pilots' Pool. Billy used all of his considerable charm and eloquence and finally persuaded the Wing Commander to give him another chance. A few days later, in his first real fight in the air, Bishop scored his first victory and his colleagues in the RFC soon came to realise that the enthusiastic Canadian was a fighter pilot of quite exceptional calibre.

In July 1917 60 Squadron received new Royal Aircraft Factory S.E.5s, a faster more powerful aircraft with better pilot visibility. In August 1917 Bishop passed the late Albert Ball in victories to become (temporarily) the highest scoring ace in the RFC and the third top ace of WW1, second only to René Fonck and third to the Red Baron. Soon after he was informed he had won the Victoria Cross for his June attack on the German aerodrome. Bishop returned home to Canada in 1917 where he was acclaimed a hero and helped boost the morale of the Canadian public, who were growing tired of the war. On 17 October 1917 at Timothy Eaton Memorial Church in Toronto, he married his longtime fiancée, Margaret Burden, a granddaughter of Timothy Eaton and sister of ace Henry John Burden. After the wedding he was assigned to the British War Mission in Washington DC to help the Americans build an air force. While stationed there he wrote his autobiography entitled *Winged Warfare*.

Upon his return to England in April 1918, Bishop was promoted to Major and given command of 85 Squadron, the 'Flying Foxes'. This was a newly formed squadron and Bishop was given the freedom to choose many of the pilots. The squadron was equipped with SE5a scouts and left for Petit Synthe, France on 22 May 1918. On 27 May, after familiarizing himself with the area and the opposition, Bishop took a solo flight to the Front. He destroyed a German observation aircraft in his first combat since August 1917 and followed with two more the next day. From 30 May to 1 June Bishop destroyed six more aircraft, including German ace Paul Billik, bringing his score to 59 and reclaiming his top scoring ace title from James McCudden, who had claimed it while Bishop was in Canada and was now the leading Allied ace. The Canadian government was becoming increasingly worried about the effect on morale if Bishop were to be killed, so on 18 June he was ordered to return to England to help organize the new Canadian Flying Corps. Bishop was not pleased with the order coming so soon after his return to France. He wrote to his wife: 'I've never been so furious in my life.' The order specified that he was to leave France by noon on 19 June. On that morning, Bishop decided to fly one last solo patrol. In just 15 minutes of combat he added another five victories to his total. He claimed to have destroyed two Pfalz D.IIIa scouts, caused another two to collide with each other and shot down a German reconnaissance aircraft.

On 5 August, Bishop was promoted to Lieutenant-Colonel and was given the post of 'Officer Commanding-designate of the Canadian Air Force Section of the

General Staff, Headquarters Overseas Military Forces of Canada.' He was on board a ship returning from a reporting visit to Canada when news of the armistice arrived. Bishop was discharged from the Canadian Expeditionary Force on 31 December and returned to Canada.

After the war, Bishop established a short-lived passenger air service with fellow ace Lieutenant Colonel William 'Billy' Barker VC DSO* MC** (who had 53 victories [19]) but after legal and financial problems and a serious crash, the partnership and company was dissolved. In 1921 Bishop and his family moved to Britain, where he was quite successful. In 1928 he was the guest of honour at a gathering of German air aces in Berlin and was made an Honorary Member of the Association. However, the family's wealth was wiped out in the crash of 1929 and they had to return to Canada. There Bishop was offered a vice-presidency of McColl Frontenac Oil Company.

In 1938, Bishop was made an Honorary Air Marshal of the Royal Canadian Air Force (RCAF) and placed in charge of recruitment. He was so successful in this role that they had to turn many applicants away. He created a system for training pilots across Canada and became instrumental in setting up and promoting the British Commonwealth Air Training Plan, which trained over 167,000 airmen in Canada during the Second World War. In 1942 he appeared as himself in the film *Captains of the Clouds,* a Hollywood tribute to the RCAF.

During World War Two Air Marshal W. A. Bishop took charge of recruiting for the RCAF and received a CB for his distinguished services. A proud moment was when he pinned pilot's wings on the breast of his son, W. A. Bishop, Jr. who would go on to become a Spitfire pilot and served with 401 Squadron RCAF in 1944. By 1944 the stress of the war had taken a serious toll on Bishop's health and he resigned his post in the RCAF to return to private enterprise in Montreal, before retiring in 1952. His son later commented that he looked 70 years old on his 50th birthday in 1944. However, Bishop remained active in the aviation world, predicting the phenomenal growth of commercial aviation postwar. His efforts to bring some organization to the nascent field led to the formation of the International Civil Aviation Organization (ICAO) in Montreal. He wrote a second book at this time, *Winged Peace,* advocating international control of global air power.

With the outbreak of the Korean War, Bishop again offered to return to his recruitment role, but he was in poor health and was politely refused by the RCAF. Air Marshal W. A. Bishop died in his sleep on 11 September 1956 aged 62 while wintering in Palm Beach, Florida. He is buried in Greenwood Cemetery in Owen Sound, Ontario.

Footnotes Chapter 7

19 Major William G. Barker DSO MC, attached to 201 Squadron RFC was flying alone on the early morning of 27 October 1918. Barker had shot down a German two-seater when he was attacked and wounded in the right thigh by a Fokker D.VII. Barker's Sopwith 7F.1 Snipe lost height in a spin; in the course of the next few minutes he passed through successive layers of a large German formation, being attacked on four separate occasions by groups of at least a dozen Fokker scouts. Before he finally managed to bring his damaged Snipe down for a successful forced landing, Barker had been wounded twice more (in the left thigh and the left elbow); had lost consciousness twice and twice recovered and regained control of his aircraft; and had shot down three more enemy aircraft. This epic engagement led to the award of the Victoria Cross.

Chapter 8

The King of the Fighter Aces

'Of no military use.' That was the label borne by a British national returned to England from Turkey in June 1915. When Turkey had declared war on Britain in November 1914 she had interned all British people in her borders. One, in particular, had made himself a troublesome prisoner and when the opportunity came to exchange internees on medical grounds the Turks were only too pleased to rid themselves of this character. It seemed to them that his blind left eye made him quite useless in a military capacity. But no doubt the Turks would have borne with this man a little longer if they had known that he was later to personally destroy the equivalent of several squadrons of German aircraft. He was to be officially credited with 73 victories - more than any other British fighter pilot before or since. He was a man whose name was to shine above those of Ball, Bishop and McCudden. His name was Major Edward Mannock VC DSO MC. The immortal Mick Mannock.

It is an afternoon early in August 1917 Mannock, by this time an acting Captain and Flight Commander, has just landed at a field in France with his Flight. But, within minutes, Mannock is streaking across the field once more in a hurried take-off. Those on the ground wonder what he has seen. Then, in the east, they spot a black Albatros approaching low down, intent on attacking British observation balloons. Now Mannock in his Nieuport is airborne and flying straight towards the German. The Albatros pilot sees him coming and turns away, relying on his superior speed to escape the Nieuport's attentions.

Both aircraft are now at 1,000 feet and Mannock is 100 yards behind the German. From this range he opens fire - accurate shots which whine all around the Albatros. The German pilot is compelled to twist and turn to try and upset Mannock's deadly aim. Every time he flies straight, even for a few seconds, the bullets are flying past him again. Now Mannock holds the advantage. The German dare not fly straight and so cannot make use of his superior speed. Realising that there is no escape, he turns to do battle with Mannock. Mannock sees his opportunity. Promptly he dives and zooms up under the Albatros and one short burst is enough to send the German crashing just behind British lines. The German was the redoubtable von Bartrap, Iron Cross, one of the Luftwaffe's crack pilots. The engagement had lasted only four and a half minutes. The battle had been witnessed by British troops in the trenches along the whole front and

Mannock was given a great ovation later when he went to salvage the Albatros.
This was Mannock at the height of his career - a career which was to make him
Britain's greatest fighter pilot. Yet this was a man who, despite a natural
aptitude for flying, had great difficulty in learning to land! And when he joined
his first operational Squadron he was believed to be too frightened to fight the
enemy. Mannock himself admitted that he was frightened. But he was to conquer
his fear. Mannock's was no simple character...

**Vernon Smythe writing in *RAF Flying Review,* December 1958. Major
Edward 'Mick' Mannock of Nos. 40, 74 and 85 Squadrons RFC was
Britain's most successful fighter pilot in the First World War. He also
gained a reputation for ruthless hatred of his German adversaries,
delighting in burning them to death. Mannock went into combat on the
Western Front on three separate combat tours. Although initially a
social misfit suspected of cowardice in his first assignment to 40
Squadron, he began to accumulate victories. He took on the highly
hazardous task of balloon busting for his first aerial victory and by
dogged concentration on his gunnery skills, tallied 15 victories by the
end of his first combat tour. After two months back in England, he
returned to France as a Flight Commander in the fledgling 74
Squadron. He amassed 36 more victories between 12 April and 17 June
1918. His official score of enemy aircraft destroyed stands at 73 but his
actual total is unknown.**

Edward Corringham 'Mick' Mannock had humble beginnings and enjoyed
none of the social and educational advantages of many of his colleagues in
the RFC and RAF. The second son of Edward Mannock, a Scottish corporal
in the Royal Scots regiment and his English wife, Julia, he was born on 24
May 1887 probably in Ballincollig, County Cork, Ireland, although
Aldershot and Preston Barracks in Brighton have also been claimed. The
family was constantly on the move. As a child Mick lived in England,
Scotland, Ireland and India. While in India, in 1897, Mannock developed
amoebic infestation which rendered him temporarily blind. Legend has it
that it left him with permanently impaired vision in his left eye; however
accounts written by former comrades discount any such impairment. His
father, a hard-drinking, brutal man, returned from the Boer War when
Edward was thirteen years old and he deserted his wife and four children.
Mick, who had suffered from his father's drunken rages, revealed later that
he was pleased when he heard that his father had left the family home.
However, the family were now very poor and Mick had to abandon his
schooling at the earliest opportunity in order to bring in some much needed
money. He had educated himself, more or less, was a profound reader and
very fond of music, having taught himself to play the violin.

After a series of menial jobs, first as a messenger boy and later as a
barber's assistant, Mick was determined to better himself and found work
as a telephone engineer in the National Telephone Company in
Wellingborough, Northamptonshire in 1911. He was quiet and reserved.
He was always a great idealist and his early hardships had given him a

great compassion and love of his fellow men - especially the underdog. Mannock hated snobbery and sham. He believed that Prussianism meant a threat to the progress towards a better world which he felt would emerge from the chaos and industrial slavery of the Nineteenth Century. He became interested in politics and as a young man became a committed socialist. In 1913 he became the Secretary of the Wellingborough Independent Labour Party. Jim Eyles, a close friend later said that: 'Mick told everyone he met that every man should prepare himself for the new age. The downtrodden of the world were about to get their chance at last; it was a duty for men to make the best of this opportunity for which the up-and-coming leaders of the new ideas had suffered so much.' Mick spoke at political meetings and Jim Eyes later remarked how surprised he was that this young man 'who had been dragged up in the most awful squalor, could match wits with these high-born and well-educated classes.'

In February 1914 the National Telephone Company sent Mannock to work in Constantinople in Turkey. When war was declared on 4 August, he attempted to get back to England. Turkey had formed a defence alliance with Germany and Mannock realised that he was in danger. However, before he could arrange transport, he was arrested by the Turkish authorities and put into a concentration camp. Several attempts at escape resulted in long periods of solitary-confinement in a six feet cage and his health rapidly declined. Near death Mannock was allowed to leave for England in April 1915. As soon as he landed in England he rejoined the RAMC Territorial Unit he had belonged to before going to Turkey. He was soon promoted to the rank of sergeant-major, but his health was poor and the army considered him unfit for military duties but he applied for a commission in the Royal Engineers in March 1916. As he told his CO: 'I can't serve in this unit with a clear conscience. I don't want to nurse sick and wounded Huns; I want to fight them first. We've got to win this war.'

He managed to obtain a transfer to the Royal Engineers as an officer cadet. Although he had very little formal schooling, Mick found he could compete with his well educated companions and was not long before he achieved the rank of Second Lieutenant. In the summer of 1916 Mannock began reading in the newspapers about the exploits of Captain Ball VC, Britain's leading flying ace. Ball, who was not yet twenty years old, had already shot down eleven German aircraft. Mannock was enthralled. He read all about Ball's air combats in the papers and decided that he, too, would fight in the air. As soon as he was granted his commission in the Royal Engineers he applied for a transfer to the RFC in August 1916. Then came the first big snag. He knew his defective eye would disqualify him from flying, so he arrived at the medical examination room well before the Medical Officer was due, so as to memorize the letters on the test card. To his dismay the MO turned up a couple of minutes later. 'Are your eyes good?' he asked. 'Of course,' replied Mannock. The doctor covered Mannock's left eye first and in reading off the letters with his right eye he managed to finish memorizing them, so that when his right eye was covered he repeated them from memory and passed! He transferred to the

RFC and was sent to the School of Military Aeronautics in Reading. He was now nearly 29 years old and was in deadly earnest about the war. Mannock had a natural aptitude for flying. Captain Chapman, one of the men responsible for training Mick, later reported that: 'He made his first solo flight with but a few hours' instruction, for he seemed to master the rudiments of flying with his first hour in the air and from then on threw the machine about how he pleased.' Despite his blind eye he was never to be surprised in the air and time and time again surprised the enemy. In two flights in 40 and 74 Squadrons which he commanded, over 80 victories were gained for the loss of only two pilots - another all-time record.

His friends are agreed that this tall Irishman - he was over six feet in height - with his blue eyes and dark hair, his charming smile and infectious laugh, was an outstanding personality. His speech had a very slight Irish intonation. He was reserved to the point of shyness at first, but his boyish high spirits would emerge when he had made friends and he was a great favourite with the fair sex.

After courses in flying and gunnery Mannock was appointed Flying Officer on probation on 1 February 1917 and went for his final course to the Joyce Green Reserve Squadron near Dartford. It was here that he first met James McCudden, then a Captain, who was a flying instructor during his three months' Rest and Home Service. McCudden, who was later to become one of Britain's leading flying aces, was another instructor who was impressed with Mick Mannock's skills as a pilot. The two men became close friends. During his first solo in an Airco DH.2 pusher biplane, Mannock got into a spin at 1,000 feet and recovered, but got in trouble with his commanding officer, Major Keith Caldwell, who suspected him of showboating. But he soon got on well with the major, Caldwell describing him as 'very reserved, inclined towards a strong temper, but very patient and somewhat difficult to arouse'.

In March 1917 it was decided that Mannock was ready to be sent to the Western Front. He arrived at St. Omer on 6 April and joined 40 Squadron - his first operational squadron - the unit being equipped at that time with Nieuport scouts. The Nieuport 17 was a French-built scout that by 1917 was outclassed in most respects by the latest German fighters. Initially, Mannock's reserved, working class manner and political opinions upset the other pilots, the majority of whom were well-heeled upper-middle-class, ex-public schoolboys. On his first night, Mannock inadvertently sat down in an empty chair, a chair which a newly fallen flier had occupied until that day.

Lieutenant Lionel Blaxland later recalled his first impression of Mannock: 'He was different. His manner, speech and familiarity were not liked. New men usually took their time and listened to the more experienced hands; Mannock was the complete opposite. He offered ideas about everything: how the war was going, how it should be fought, the role of scout pilots, what was wrong or right with our machines. Most men in his position, by that I mean a man with his background, would have shut up.'

Soon after arriving in France, Mannock heard the news that Albert Ball, the man whose example had inspired him to join the Royal Flying Corps, had been shot down and killed. The same day, Captain Nixon, Mannock's patrol leader, was also killed during a mission to destroy German observation balloons.

At first Mannock was unsuccessful in action. He could fly an aircraft superbly but he found landing difficult. Also, his shooting was poor. In addition to this he was bewildered in his first 'dog-fight' - being unable to distinguish friend from foe. So he preferred to master the technique of air fighting first, rather than to be reckless. And so it came about that some of the other pilots said he was suffering from cold feet and even suggested that he was 'yellow.' He afterwards admitted to a flight commander that he had been very frightened at first, but had conquered his fear - the real quality of a brave man. He also realised that good shooting was essential and he put in much time sighting his guns and practising on a ground target. This was interpreted by his critics as putting on an act of keenness to cloak 'cold feet.' He needed a victory to give him confidence.

He shot down a balloon on 7 May. Mannock had one very unpleasant experience, on 9 May. He was out alone at 16,000 feet when he was attacked by three enemy planes. At the critical moment his gun jammed and his engine failed. He dived and spun and zigzagged away, with the barking of the enemy's guns behind him. At 3,000 feet his engine started again and he turned and climbed to 12,000 feet. Then he sighted another German plane, but so shattered was his nerve after his recent experience that - as he said himself - he hadn't the pluck to face him and he turned away and landed at the aerodrome with his knees shaking.

It was on 7 June 1917 while escorting two-seater machines engaged on a photographic mission that he gained his first official victory. A brightly coloured Albatros dived to attack the leading two-seater. But Mannock's keen eye had spotted the enemy and even as the German dived steeply on his intended victim, Mannock swooped like a hawk. It was a near thing. But before the Albatros reached his prey, Mannock's Nieuport was on his tail - ten yards behind him - and a short, accurate burst of 30 rounds sent the enemy straight down.

Before he could add to his total he received a wound to the head during a dogfight with two German pilots. Mannock was sent back to England to recover. He became phobic about burning to death in midair and was deeply affected by the men he was killing. Later, in his diary he recorded visiting the site where one of his victims had crashed near the front-line: 'The journey to the trenches was rather nauseating - dead men's legs sticking through the sides with puttees and boots still on - bits of bones and skulls with the hair peeling off and tons of equipment and clothing lying about. This sort of thing, together with the strong graveyard stench and the dead and mangled body of the pilot combined to upset me for a few days.'

Mannock was especially upset when he saw one of his victims catch fire on its way to the ground. From that date on, Mick Mannock always carried a revolver with him in his cockpit. As he told his friend Lieutenant

MacLanachan or 'McScotch' as he was known on 40 Squadron: 'The other fellows all laugh at me for carrying a revolver. They think I'm going to shoot down a machine with it, but they're wrong. The reason I bought it was to finish myself as soon as I see the first signs of flames.'

Mannock's fear of fire was made worse by the British High Command's decision not to allow pilots in the Royal Flying Corps to carry parachutes. Mannock believed it was unfair to deny British airman to right to have parachutes when German pilots had been using them successfully for several months. He was especially angry about the main reason given for this decision: 'It is the opinion of the board that the presence of such an apparatus might impair the fighting spirit of pilots and cause them to abandon machines which might otherwise be capable of returning to base for repair.'

The stresses of combat began to tell on him. He also became ill with a lingering case of influenza and when ordered home on leave, he wept. Mick went to stay with his mother but was dismayed to find that his mother, like his father, was now an alcoholic. He also discovered that his sister, Jessie, was working as a prostitute in Birmingham. Upset by the state of his family, Mick was anxious to get back to France and desperately short of trained pilots the RFC agreed that he could return to duty.

After returning to France in July, Mannock quickly developed a reputation as one of the most talented pilots in the RFC. Bit by bit - his score mounted. He not only conquered himself but proved his prowess as an air fighter. He realised that air-fighting was a science and he became a master of deflection shooting. In the first two weeks after arriving back at the Western Front he won four dogfights in his S.E.5a. This gave him new confidence and on 12 August he shot down and captured Leutnant Joachim von Bertrab of Jasta 30. Ironically, Bertrab had shot down five enemy aircraft and was trying to shoot down a balloon. Four days later Mannock shot down four aircraft in a day. The following morning he added two more victories to his total. After one kill, he coldly described it. 'I was only ten yards away from him - on top so I couldn't miss. A beautifully coloured insect he was - red, blue, green and yellow. I let him have 60 rounds, so there wasn't much left of him.'

On 17 September he was awarded the Military Cross for driving off several enemy aircraft while destroying three German observation balloons. The following month he was awarded a bar to his Military Cross. The official citation read: 'He attacked a formation of five enemy machines single-handed and shot one down out of control; while engaged with an enemy machine, he was attacked by two others, one of which he forced down to the ground.'

The Mannock legend had begun. Lieutenant MacLanachan, writes of him at this time: 'Encouraged now by initial successes, Mannock spent much time in the air. In the evenings, shunning the mess, he frequently went off alone. Several times I saw him walking away without having changed his flying boots and a wave of sympathy would sweep over me. At other times, meeting the steely challenge of his piercing blue eyes and reading in them the mental turmoil that was going on within him, I became afraid of him. Mannock felt things much more keenly than the rest of us. He had shown that he could kill, not instinctively but with deliberation; not for hatred, but for an ideal.'

It was about this time that Mannock revealed another aspect of his character. He was induced to play his violin in the mess. It was a welcome change from the few gramophone records they had at this time. 'McScotch' describes one such occasion as follows: 'On watching Mick's expressive face as he successfully accomplished the difficult 'double-stopping ' passages in Schubert's famous *Caprice*, I was amazed at the emotional splendour of his playing. Mick had the soul of an idealist, one that can endure agonies of mind and body for his ideals, can kill for his beliefs. He told us all this in his playing.'

On 22 July 1917 Mannock was awarded the Military Cross and promoted to Acting Captain and Flight Commander. As flight commander he was able to introduce a new approach to combat flying. Mannock believed that the 'days of the lone fighter was past and air fighting was now a matter for co-ordinated and planned fighting units which could inflict maximum damage and minimum losses.' By now Mannock's former critics were glad to come out with him on patrol, knowing he was never taken by surprise and that no planes escorted by him were ever successfully attacked. One afternoon Mannock landed much too fast and ran into a haystack. As he sat in his cockpit, holding his hands to his face, another pilot rushed up to him and said, 'I say, that was a damned silly thing to do! Didn't you see it?'

'No. That's the tragedy of it, old boy,' said Mannock, 'I can't see that side. I thought at first the other eye was done in as well, but I can still see out of it.'

On 14 October he was awarded a bar to his MC and soon after that he was granted leave. By now he had developed the technique that was transforming the era of the lone fighter, like Ball, Bishop and - in a certain degree - McCudden, into that of the formation attack. His score grew rapidly; he was possessed by a bitter and ruthless hatred of the enemy uncommon among his contemporaries and showed no mercy to any German airman. His care of the pilots under his command, however, was irreproachable and he has been judged the greatest patrol leader of any combatant air force. He took the greatest pains to plan every sortie in detail and shepherded less experienced pilots until they gained skill and confidence, often insisting on crediting them with victories to which he was rightfully entitled. His patrols were never on any occasion attacked by surprise.

Quite early in his period of service in 40 Squadron he developed an obsession that he would eventually be shot down in flames. It was one day after two of the pilots had been killed, that 'McScotch' decided to load his drums with some incendiary ammunition to make sure of his next enemy plane, knowing that the Germans always used it against us. Mannock - on learning of this from the mechanics - tried to dissuade him, saying: 'Do you mean to say, Mac that you would coolly fire that muck into a fellow creature - or into his petrol tank - knowing what it would mean?' The other did not reply, so he went on, 'If you won't chuck it for humanity, will you for me? Because that's the way they're going to get me in the end. Flames and finish. I'm never going to have it said that my own right hand ever used the same dirty weapons...They'll never be able to get you, but as sure as I'm talking to you now, that's the way they're going to finish me.'

Mannock finally left 40 Squadron on 2 January 1918 for England to take enforced leave, cheered by the whole Squadron, who had lined the road to see him off. He now had 23 victories to his credit. His modesty, generosity and unselfishness, as well as his courage had won the affection of all the Squadron. After a month's leave he was posted to Biggin Hill. This did not satisfy him as he wanted to get back and fight. In February he managed to get an appointment as Flight Commander to 74 Training Squadron - flying S.E.5s - at London Colney. Group Captain Ira Jones - who was a pupil there then - gives this impression of Mick Mannock: 'His tall lean figure, his weather-beaten face, with its deep-set Celtic blue eyes ; his unruly dark brown hair; his modesty appealed to me and immediately, like all the other pupils, I came under his spell. He had a dominating personality. Whatever he said or did, compelled attention. It was obvious he was a born leader of men.' His lectures on air fighting instilled into his listeners the offensive spirit which stood them in such good stead later.

The newly-formed 74 Fighter Squadron left for France at the beginning of April under the command of Major Keith Caldwell, a New Zealander (known to his friends as 'Grid' because he referred to all planes as grids). He was a well known air fighter and leader. Mannock, in speaking of him to the pilots, said: 'He (Caldwell) is the bravest man in the Air Force and he'll frighten the life out of you when he leads the patrol! In his three months with the unit Mannock added 36 to his score. He was an excellent patrol leader; he took a very protective attitude toward his fliers and lectured them on survival and success. 'Sight your own guns,' he told them, 'The armourer doesn't have to do the fighting.'

On 12 April Major Caldwell came into the mess at breakfast time and read out to the assembled officers Haig's famous 'Backs to the wall' order to the British Army. The grim silence was immediately broken by Mannock, who jumped up and said: 'They're going to get it now! And they won't have more than half an hour to wait for it. Come on ' A ' Flight; we take off at 8.25!'

The first two victories for 74 Squadron were gained by Mannock, who insisted that one should be credited to his flight. That day the Squadron shot down five enemy planes without loss. The combination of 'Grid' Caldwell and Mannock resulted in the astonishing record for 74 Squadron in the last eight months of the war, of 223 victories for the loss of only fifteen pilots and Mannock's flight only lost one.

His reputation was such, at this time, that, he was frequently called upon to give lectures on air-fighting and tactics to other squadrons. During the ten weeks active service in 74 Squadron he had added a further 40 victories to his score. He was awarded the DSO on 24 May, a bar to it on June 7 and a second bar on 3 July.

His hatred of the Germans grew; 'I sent one of them to Hell in flames today ... I wish Kaiser Bill could have seen him sizzle.' Once, he forced a German two-seater to crash. Most pilots would have been satisfied with that, but not Mick. He repeatedly machine-gunned the helpless crew. When his squadron mate questioned this behaviour, Mannock explained 'The swines are better dead - no prisoners.' Another time he pursued a silver Pfalz scout; the two aircraft rolled, dived, looped and fired their guns. Eventually Mannock got the better of his opponent and the German started twisting and turning as it fell toward a certain crash. Mannock stayed on it, firing away, 'a really remarkable exhibition of cruel, calculated Hun-strafing' another pilot called it. On this day, Mannock shot down four aircraft. He delightedly announced to the mess hall, 'Flamerinoes - four! Sizzle sizzle wonk!' Van Ira, a South African flier on 74 Squadron commented on Mannock's success: 'Four in one day! What is the secret? Undoubtedly the gift of accurate shooting, combined with the determination to get to close quarters before firing. It's an amazing gift, for no pilot in France goes nearer to a Hun before firing than Caldwell, but he only gets one down here and there, in spite of the fact that his tracer bullets appear to be going through his opponent's body'.

Mannock was deeply affected by the number of men he was killing. In his diary, he recorded visiting the site where one of his victims had crashed near the front-line: 'The journey to the trenches was rather nauseating - dead men's legs sticking through the sides with puttees and boots still on - bits of bones and skulls with the hair peeling off and tons of equipment and clothing lying about. This sort of thing, together with the strong graveyard stench and the dead and mangled body of the pilot combined to upset me for a few days.'

Mannock became especially upset when he saw one of his victims catch fire on its way to the ground. His fear of 'flamerinoes' meant that from that date on, he always carried a revolver with him in his cockpit. As he told his friend Lieutenant MacLanachan, 'The other fellows all laugh at me for carrying a revolver. They think I'm going to shoot down a machine with it, but they're wrong. The reason I bought it was to finish myself as soon as I see the first signs of flames. They'll never burn me.'

His aircraft was once set alight but he managed to extinguish it by diving. On landing he told the mechanic to put more tracers into his ammunition, remarking, 'I'll give 'em set me alight!

On 18 June Mannock went on a fortnight's leave and was promoted Acting Major and to Command 85 Squadron at their request. On starting his third tour of duty in July, as CO of 85 Squadron, he confided his mortal fears to a friend, worried that three was an unlucky number. He became obsessed with neatness and order; his hair, his medals, his boots, everything had to be 'just so.' He soon re-organized the Squadron and led 85 on several very successful operations. One officer said of him about this time: 'He treated everyone alike. He had no use for slackers, but until he found them hopeless he gave them endless encouragement. When he caught a member of his flight deliberately leaving his formation, as on one occasion, after he had given the signal ' Prepare to attack,' his anger was such that the coward was lucky to escape with his life.'

The news of McCudden's death on 9 July 1918 came as a great shock to him. He had had a bad dose of flu on his last leave, much of which he had spent with McCudden and his friends had been much troubled by his obsession that he would be killed on his return to France. By now Mannock should have been having a well earned rest as he was living on his nerves. One moment he was gay and light-hearted and the next, almost depressed. His bitterness against the Germans had mellowed somewhat. He knew their defeat was certain now. One evening - alone with Ira 'Taffy' Jones - he said with a weary smile, 'I don't feel I shall last much longer.' Then suddenly, placing both hands on the other's shoulders, he said: 'Taffy old lad, if I am killed I shall be in good company. I feel I have done my duty.' Then, in a tone of banter, but with sadness in his voice, 'You watch yourself, Taffy; you're getting reckless. Don't go following any Huns too low or you'll join the ' sizzle brigade ' with me!'

'Now you're getting morbid Mick' said Jones.

'No, not morbid, just a premonition.'

In July 1918 Mannock scored nine more victories. He had now overtaken Albert Ball's total of forty-four kills and on 20 July he shot down a Albatros giving him fifty-eight victories, one more than the British record held by James McCudden. By now, his phobias had spread to include excessive tidiness. He also had presentiments of his coming end. On 20 July, at a farewell luncheon for his friend 'Noisy Lewis', Mannock took their mutual friend and fellow ace George McElroy aside to counsel him on the deadly hazards of following a German victim down within range of ground fire. When he shot down an aircraft on 22 July, a friend congratulated Mannock. 'They'll have the red carpet out for you after the war, Mick.' But Mannock glumly replied, 'There won't be any 'after the war' for me.'

With 85 Mannock raised his score to 73 by 26 July. At dawn on 26 July Mannock entered the mess and played his favourite gramophone record, Londonderry Air, a thing he frequently did before dawn patrol. Then he took off with Lieutenant Donald C. Inglis, a newcomer to the Squadron who had yet to shoot down an enemy aircraft. In typical fashion, Mannock was taking him up to give him the benefit of his experience. As usual on such occasions, he flew at 30 to 40 feet from the ground, first up on one wing tip and then on the other, never straight for more than a few seconds. Suddenly he turned for home full out and climbing.

He had evidently sighted an enemy, though Inglis couldn't see anything. It was an LVG. Then, a quick turn and a dive and Mannock's gun was firing. As Mannock pulled up, Inglis found the German right in his sights and gave him another burst and the two-seater went down in flames behind the German front-lines. Then Mannock did the thing he had always warned others never to do; he followed the blazing enemy aircraft down until it crashed. They were now at 200 feet. Mannock then turned for home,

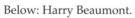
Left: J. R. Ackerley.

Below: Harry Beaumont.

Above: Nurse Edith Cavell.

Right: A. J. Evans MC and bar.

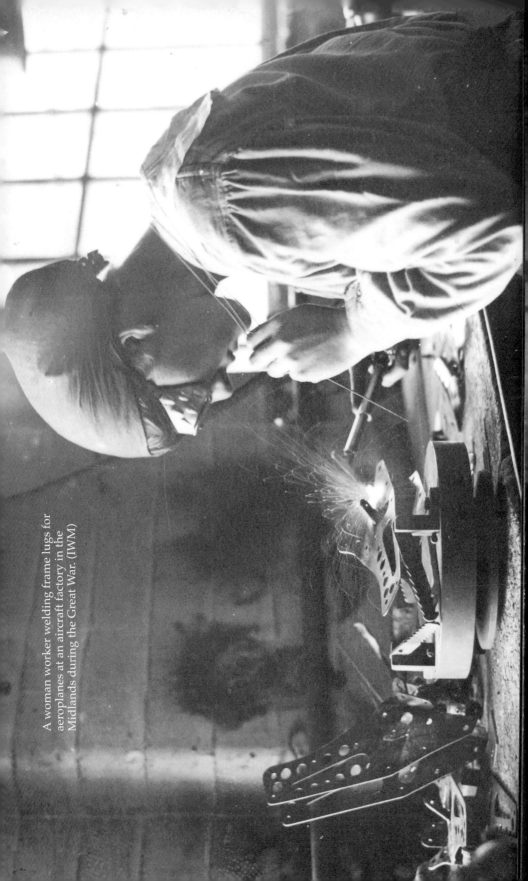

A woman worker welding frame lugs for aeroplanes at an aircraft factory in the Midlands during the Great War. (IWM)

Lewis guns and ammunition being issued to observers on 22 Squadron at Vert Galland on 1 April 1918, the day that the RAF came into being as an independent service. (IWM)

A single-seat B.E.12b armed with a single Lewis gun above the upper wing and also carries two 112lb bombs. Thirty six of these aircraft were used for Home Defence duties in 1917-18. (IWM)

Lieutenant (later Major) H. D. Harvey-Kelly reclines by a haystack in a field at Lythe near Whitby, Yorkshire, in June 1914 during a stop on 2 Squadron's flight south from Montrose. In this aircraft, BE2a No.347, Harvey-Kelly became the first RFC pilot to land in France after the outbreak of war. He subsequently commanded 19 Squadron. Flying a Spad SVII he was shot down by Kurt Wolff of Jasta 11 on, 29 April 1917 and died of wounds three days later.

Left: Duncan Grinnell-Milne.

Below: Edward McKeever – 'Two-Seater Ace'.

Above left: Major Edward 'Mick' Mannock VC DSO was an outstanding patrol leader and tactician and was officially credited with 73 victories, making him the top-scoring British fighter pilot of the war. He was killed on 26 July 1918, while commanding 85 Squadron, his aircraft being shot down in flames by ground fire. His VC was awarded posthumously in 1919.

Above right: Major (later Air Marshal) W. A. 'Billy' Bishop, VC DSO MC DFC. Officially credited with seventy-two victories, Bishop, a Canadian, was the second highest-scoring fighter pilot in the RFC and RAF during the First World War. On 2 June 1917 he carried out a single-handed attack on the German aerodrome at Estourmel at dawn and he shot down three of the aircraft which came up to engage him. The action earned Bishop the Victoria Cross.

S.E.5as of 85 Squadron at St. Omer on 21 June 1918. (IWM)

The Sopwith 2F.1 Camel armed with a single Vickers fixed gun on the fuselage and a Lewis gun mounted above the centre section of the upper wing. (IWM)

One of the first production batches of Bristol Fighters (F.2Bs) in England, probably in 1917.

Left: Second Lieutenant (later Captain) Albert Ball VC shortly after he had obtained his Royal Aero Club Pilot's Certificate in October 1915. With at least 44 victories to his credit, Ball was killed on 7 May 1917 while serving with No.56 Squadron. The Germans claimed that he was shot down by Lothar von Richthofen of Jasta 11 but the exact circumstances of his death still remain unresolved.

Below: Albert Ball in the cockpit of his personally modified S.E.5 A4850 at London Colney airfield in March 1917 with 56 Squadron. It was in this machine, further modified, that he died, on 7 May 1917.

Major (later Air Vice-Marshal) Raymond Collishaw DSO DSC DFC in the cockpit of a Sopwith Camel while serving as Commanding Officer of 203 Squadron RAF at Izel le Hameau on 10 July 1918. Credited with sixty victories during the First World War, Collishaw, a native of British Columbia, destroyed one more aircraft in Russia in 1919. Collishaw served with distinction in the Second World War, commanding 202 and 204 Groups of the Royal Air Force in the Western Desert in 1940-1941. He died in 1976.

The first air Victoria Cross was awarded posthumously to 2nd Lieutenant William Bernard Rhodes-Moorhouse, pilot of a B.E.2 of 2 Squadron RFC for gallantry in a low-level bombing attack on Courtrai railway station on 26 April 1915.

Rittmeister Manfred Freiherr von Richthofen, the top-scoring fighter pilot of WWI with 80 victories. Flying a Fokker DrI triplane 425/17, he was killed near Vaux-sur-Somme on 21 April 1918. The RAF credited his death to Captain A. R. Brown DSC, a Canadian pilot serving on 209 Squadron, although there is considerable evidence to suggest that von Richthofen was killed by ground fire from Australian troops in the area.

A Fokker DR.VII comes to grief.

Captain (later Major) James T. B. McCudden VC DSO MC MM in the cockpit of his S.E.5a (B.4891) of 56 Squadron at Baizieux in February 1918. He began his career in the RFC as an air mechanic in 1913. Most of his 57 victories were scored while he was serving as a flight commander on 56 Squadron in 1917-1918. His engineering knowledge combined with his analytical approach to air fighting helped him to become one of the most influential and successful fighter pilots and patrol leaders of the war. He was killed in a flying accident on 9 July 1918 while on his way to assume command of 60 Squadron.

S.E.5a B603 at Sedgeford.

Camels on 73 Squadron at a landing ground near Humieres on 6 April 1918.

A Sopwith Pup in 1918-19 is inspected for damage to its right landing wheel after a crash.

The Fokker Dr.I triplane 114/17 flown by Leutnant Stapenhorst of Jasta 11 which was brought down almost intact by 'Archie' (Anti Aircraft fire) on 13 January 1918.

RAF officers examining the fuselage of a captured Pfalz D IIIA fighter at No.2 Depot at Candas, France on 26 April 1918. (IWM)

Albatros D.Va Scout (D2359/17) which was forced down virtually intact near Arras on 3 March 1918 by the crew of an R.E.8 on 13 Squadron RFC. The pilot, Leutnant Homuth of Jasta 23, was taken prisoner.

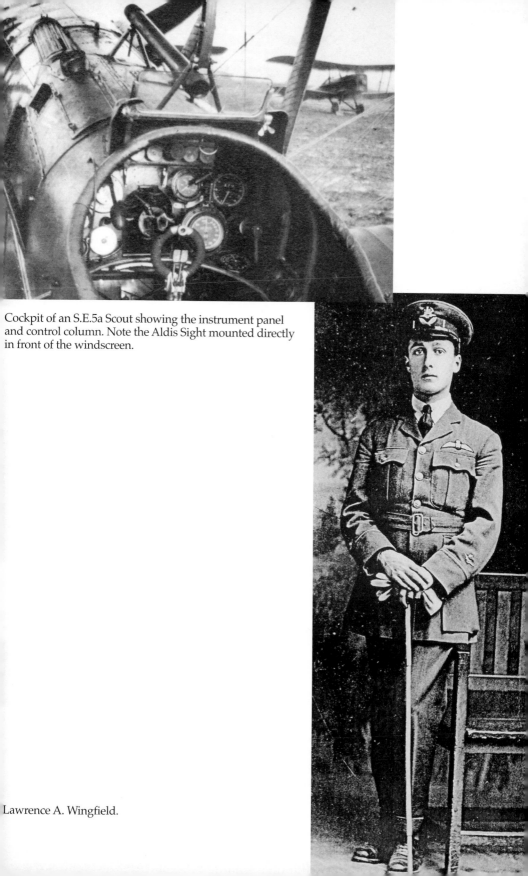

Cockpit of an S.E.5a Scout showing the instrument panel and control column. Note the Aldis Sight mounted directly in front of the windscreen.

Lawrence A. Wingfield.

The 'Blimp' was the smallest of the lighter than air craft employed under the aegis of the RNAS. After a day of coastal and sea reconnaissance this ship is being towed to its moorings.

zigzagging as there was heavy rifle and machine-gun fire from the ground. Suddenly a small flame appeared at the right side of Mannock's S.E. His petrol tank was hit by a random shot from the German trenches, fired by some nameless infantryman.

Mannock went into a slow dive and crashed in flames - not far from his last victim. Inglis described what happened:

'Falling in behind Mick again we made a couple of circles around the burning wreck and then made for home. I saw Mick start to kick his rudder and then I saw a flame come out of his machine; it grew bigger and bigger. Mick was no longer kicking his rudder. His nose dropped slightly and he went into a slow right-hand turn and hit the ground in a burst of flame. I circled at about twenty feet but could not see him and as things were getting hot, made for home and managed to reach our outposts with a punctured fuel tank. Poor Mick...the bloody bastards had shot my Major down in flames'.

Inglis landed safely behind the lines, with a punctured petrol tank. Mannock's body is believed to have been found 250 yards from the wreck of his machine though this is unproven. He did not fire his revolver but it is believed he might have jumped from his blazing plane just before it crashed. Mannock's body was not subsequently recovered by the Commonwealth War Graves Commission (CWGC) so officially he has no known grave. [20]

When the news of Mannock's death reached 85 Squadron, the pilots stared at each other in dazed silence for a moment, then went to their huts and wept. The mechanics and others were similarly affected. And Mannock had only been with the Squadron just over three weeks. The shock of his death was the greater because all who knew him looked upon him as infallible, knowing that he was unmatched in air combat. So died Mick Mannock -acknowledged by many as the greatest air fighter the world has known. In July 1919 many of his former comrades sent a petition to the Air Minister - then Mr. Winston Churchill - urging that no man ever deserved a VC more richly than Mannock.

Mr. Churchill directed that an investigation be made, with the result that Mannock was posthumously awarded the Victoria Cross and officially credited with 61 victories: 1 balloon destroyed, 3 (and 2 shared) captured, 30 (and 5 shared) destroyed, 17 (and 3 shared) 'out of control'.[21] He frequently did not claim a share in kills to which he had contributed - official policy treated a shared victory as a kill for each pilot involved. Mannock himself did not appear particularly motivated to accumulate a score, though he is known to have said, 'If I have any luck, I think I may beat old Mac's (James McCudden) 57 victories. Then I shall try and oust old Richthofen...'

Mannock's Victoria Cross was presented to his father at Buckingham Palace in July 1919. Edward Mannock was also given his son's other medals, even though Mick had stipulated in his will that his father should receive nothing from his estate. Soon afterwards Mannock's medals were sold for £5. They have since been recovered and can be seen at the Royal

Air Force Museum at Hendon. Mick Mannock's career attracted no great public attention until long after his death.

The citation awarding his Victoria Cross ends with these words: 'This distinguished officer, during the whole of his career in the Royal Air Force, was an outstanding example of fearless courage, remarkable skill, devotion to duty and self-sacrifice, which has never been surpassed.'

Footnotes Chapter 8

20   His name is commemorated on the Royal Flying Corps Memorial to the Missing at the Faubourg d'Amiens CWGC Cemetery in Arras. There is also a memorial plaque in honour of Mannock in Canterbury Cathedral.
21   There was a posthumous attempt by former 74 Squadron comrade and fellow ace Ira Jones to credit his old friend with 73 victories and therefore the top scoring British/Commonwealth ace. However research suggests that assertion was not backed by fact.

Chapter 9

McKeever - Two-Seater Ace

'Easy meat,' the pilot of the German Albatros scout must have thought as he
spotted the lone Bristol F.2B fighter droning its way back towards the British lines.
It was 20 June 1917 and in those days, air fighting followed pretty conventional
lines. The German knew just what should happen. He would dive on the Bristol
from dead ahead. The British pilot would see him coming and immediately turn his
aircraft so that the rear gunner could bring his gun to bear. The result of this
manoeuvre was, invariably, a nice juicy broadside target for the Albatros's Spandau
guns. Few qualms troubled the German pilot as he eased his scout into the attacking
dive. But, as it happened, convention on this day was to be flouted. Flying the
Bristol was Second Lieutenant Andrew Edward McKeever, an aggressive Canadian.
McKeever was meeting his first enemy aircraft, but he was not without ideas on
tactics. Among these was the notion that, because the Bristol was fitted with a fixed
forward-firing Vickers gun in addition to the observer's guns, the observer did not
have to do all the fighting. And anyway, McKeever had always wanted to be a
single-seater pilot.
McKeever held steadily to his course and refused to turn for the Albatros. Then,
to the German's astonishment and dismay, McKeever suddenly lifted the Bristol's
nose and pumped a continual stream of red tracer into the Albatros. Unnerved by
this fierce and unconventional onslaught, the German threw his aircraft into a near
vertical dive. McKeever, with a deft movement, brought the heavy Bristol round and
was soon screaming earthwards right on the enemy's tail. One more burst from the
forward Vickers and McKeever had achieved his first victory during his first fight.
Not only was this victory the first of thirty official victories and almost as many
again unofficial victories accorded to McKeever, but it was an event which helped to
change the Bristol Fighter from an aircraft in danger of having its death warrant
signed to one of the most successful aircraft of the First World War.
McKeever-Two-Seater Ace by Frank Levitt, writing in RAF Flying
Review, March 1958. The Bristol Fighter was designed by Captain Frank
Barnwell of the RFC and L. G. Frise and flew for the first time in
September 1916.

It was on 16 May 1917 that Edward McKeever arrived at 11 Squadron after a
period of five months spent in Home Defence in England. He found that the
'Biff or 'Brisfit' as the Bristol Fighter was affectionately known, was regarded
by all pilots as an armed-reconnaissance machine. The F2A's fuselage mounted

high between the wings gave its pilot an excellent view above and below the top wing but the observer was left to do all the air fighting while the pilot merely manoeuvred to give his observer a good field of fire. Even men like Captain William Leefe-Robinson VC commanding 48 Squadron were using these basically wrong tactics. On 8 March 1917 48 Squadron had flown the first production F.2As to France. Used operationally for the first time on 5 April during the spring offensive on the Western Front, 48 Squadron suffered early heavy losses as German fighter pilots exploited the type's poor defensive tactics, attacking from below and directly astern and with such unsuccessful results that the future of the 'Brisfit' hung precariously in the balance. Manfred Freiherr von Richthofen had met the F.2B in combat and reported that it was inferior to the Albatros in 'both speed and ability to climb.' How wrong he was, McKeever was soon to prove.

His successes followed quickly, one after the other. On the day after his first victory another German fell to his guns. On 26 and 27 June 1917 two more followed. Throughout July his score mounted steadily and following McKeever's example, more and more pilots were using the 'Brisfit' as a fighter, the pilot attacking with his Vickers while the observer guarded the rear with his Lewis guns. But McKeever was to remain in the forefront of the select band of pilots who were proving that the 'Brisfit' was not just another two-seater, but a highly dangerous opponent. The RFC soon learned to use the F.2B in an offensive role, for despite its weight and size; the Bristol Fighter was as fast and manoeuvrable as the German single-seat machines and could dive faster than any other type on the Western Front. In a dog-fight the pilot learned to fly it like a single-seater, using his forward firing Vickers gun in the manner of a fighting scout while the observer guarded his rear with single or twin Lewis guns mounted on a Scarff ring. In this role the Brisfit proved a powerful and effective weapon and it developed into the finest two-seat fighter of World War One.

Within two months of arriving at the front McKeever had received the Military Cross and promotion to Captain and Flight Leader. The citation for his award stated that on 10 July, whilst on offensive patrol, he met a flight of nine German aircraft. Single-handed, he attacked them and destroyed three, his observer, Lieutenant Powell, destroyed another. He celebrated the award by bagging another German the following day. This young Canadian had more than his fair share of the ruthless determination and tenacious offensive spirit that was common to all the great aces. He was a non-drinker and gave up smoking so that nothing could affect his skill as a pilot and marksman. He would take on any odds, regardless and attack any target that presented itself on the ground. He was first and foremost an individualist, which accounts for the fact that many of his victories were never confirmed, owing to his fondness for patrolling alone and well behind the German lines. His individuality was also reflected in the little touch of vanity which prompted him to have his aircraft painted white, in defiance of the official orders forbidding the use of personal colours on operational aircraft. In August McKeever's flight was detailed for a raid on a German airfield near Ypres. He led the attack with conspicuous success and gallantry. Three large hangars and many aircraft on the ground were destroyed. On the way home he shot down two Pfalz Dills. For this action he was awarded the Bar to his MC.

Born in the little town of Listowel, Ontario in 1895 to Bella Henderson and William McKeever, a grocer and butcher, Andy McKeever spent much of his spare time hunting in the woods and forests around his home and was a first-class marksman, with the keen eye of the youngster who spent most of his time outdoors. After attending Toronto's Central Technical School, McKeever worked as a teller. He joined the Army soon after the outbreak of war and arrived in France in 1915 as a private in the Queen's Own Rifles of Canada, a militia unit infantry regiment. He remained with them until November 1916 when he applied for a transfer to the Royal Flying Corps and was accepted. He sailed for England for training on 25 November and was commissioned a probationary lieutenant on 5 December. McKeever wanted to fly single-seaters, but his instructors considered him too heavy-handed on the controls and following training he was assigned on 28 May 1917 to 11 Squadron, which was flying obsolete F.E.2s. They re-equipped shortly thereafter with Bristol F.2A fighters, sometimes referred to as the 'Brisfit'. Among McKeever's tasks were photographic reconnaissance, with his observer wielding a hand-held camera and taking the photos. Although the 'Brisfit' could do this job well, it was as fast as the Fokkers that opposed it, as well as maneuverable enough to be flown like a single-seater. Heavy-handed he may have been, but McKeever was a first-rate pilot, able to throw the heavily loaded Bristol Fighter about the sky on equal terms with the highly aerobatic Pfalz and Albatros scouts. Soon the Germans' respect for the Bristol was such that only the very bravest or the most foolhardy Jerry would attack one single-handed. Generally, the favourable odds were considered to be at least three single-seaters to one 'Brisfit."

McKeever began his career as an ace by destroying a D.V on 26 June 1917 and sending down another out of control. On 7 July, he and Powell knocked down three more, with one destroyed and two falling uncontrollably out of the battle. McKeever would repeat this feat of triple victories on three more occasions, on 5 August, 23 September and 31 October 1917. On 3 October, when his score reached 20, Lieutenant McKeever was awarded a Bar to the Military Cross he had gained a month prior. In part, the citation for his Military Cross said: '2nd Lieutenant Andrew Edward McKeever RFC, Spec. Res. For conspicuous gallantry and devotion to duty, particularly when on offensive patrol. He attacked eight enemy aircraft single-handed at close range and by his splendid dash and determination destroyed one and drove five down completely out of control. He had previously shown exceptional fearlessness in attacking the enemy when in superior numbers and in the space of three weeks he destroyed eight hostile machines, setting a very fine example to his squadron.' The citation which accompanied his bar to the MC said: 'Lieutenant Andrew Edward McKeever MC RFC, Spec. Res. For conspicuous gallantry and devotion to duty in aerial combats. He has recently destroyed five enemy aeroplanes and driven down six out of control. On one occasion he encountered five enemy scouts and drove down two out of control. Later, while leading a patrol, he engaged nine enemy scouts. He destroyed two, drove down one out of control and dispersed the remainder. His dash and determination have been a fine example to his squadron.'

The battle of Passchendaele, in which the Canadians suffered enormous casualties, was drawing to a close, when on the morning of 30 November an urgent call for a photographic reconnaissance came through to 11 Squadron from Divisional HQ. Captain McKeever and his observer, Lieutenant Leslie Powell, volunteered, although the chances of success seemed remote. The weather was terrible, with a cloud ceiling of 200-300 feet. Driving rain and mist obscured vision still further. They took off successfully however and the Bristol [A7288], climbed steadily until it was above the clouds, then, by compass and reckoning, he made for his objective, sixty miles behind the enemy lines. When he eventually dropped through the clouds, he found the weather had cleared and the ceiling had improved to about 1,500 feet. Moreover, his navigation had been accurate and he was practically over the recce area in a clear sky. McKeever and Powell made a leisurely reconnaissance and finally turned for home. Suddenly there was a colossal explosion and the earth about five miles to the south spewed up a gigantic fountain of smoke and flame. Immediately, McKeever headed the Bristol towards the scene of the holocaust. A German ammo dump had received a direct hit from a British artillery battery and as they flew above the conflagration they could see hundreds of German soldiers frantically fighting the fires and trying to salvage stores. The temptation was too much for McKeever; he put down the nose of the Bristol and prepared to make things even warmer for the busy Germans.

Both Powell and McKeever were deeply engrossed in the activity below, but luckily McKeever; with the automatic reaction of the skilled fighter pilot, glanced up to look for possible trouble before going into his dive. To his surprise, not more than a hundred yards ahead and to his right, four enemy scouts - sleek Pfalz DIIIs, painted black - were closing in. He turned to yell a warning to Powell and as he did so, saw five more Germans closing in on his tail -three black Pfalz and two blood-red Albatros. He and Powell had been so engrossed in the happenings below that the Germans had had time to manoeuvre them into a virtually inescapable trap. The Germans were obviously expecting the Bristol to pull to the left and had grouped accordingly. Instead, McKeever jerked on full throttle, pulled the 'stick over and ruddered for all he was worth. The Bristol tore straight into the tight-packed flight of Pfalz on his right, taking the Germans completely by surprise. He almost collided with the leader, but, before climbing to avoid him, put in a short ten-round burst. Then, as he flew over, he saw the Pfalz turn on its back and burst into flames. A moment later he got another Pfalz in his sights. He thumbed his Vickers and saw the tracers pour in at point-blank range. The Pfalz seemed to stagger in the air and thick black smoke poured from the engine as the plane side-slipped into a violent dive. At the same time, Powell accounted for another German.

The whole action had taken so little time that no less than three enemy aircraft were falling in flames at the same time. The remaining Pfalz, evidently feeling that there was safety in numbers, had steered clear of the Bristol and joined the enemy planes in the rear. McKeever turned to meet them and as he did so, caught the bright red fabric of an Albatros in his sights Instinctively, he gave it a long burst that raked it from stem to stern as it flew across his line of fire - almost cutting the fuselage in two. As they cut through the enemy formation. Powell was firing like a man possessed at any and every target that presented itself, the fuselage rocking with the recoil of his twin Lewis guns. He destroyed yet another Pfalz.

For a few moments there was a lull as the Germans pulled out of the fight to regain height and renew formation. Then they dived to the attack with renewed fury. McKeever waited for the sound of Powell's guns as they came in too high for him to sight the fixed forward-firing gun, but the observer's guns were silent: he turned to see what was wrong and saw the observer pointing hopelessly at his useless guns, which had caught a burst of fire and were out of action. McKeever immediately pointed his plane's nose at the leading aircraft and climbed to meet him. The German's silver nose and black fuselage came into his sights and he fired at point-blank range. Nothing happened. His own gun had also been hit. The Bristol was defenceless against four German scouts thirsting for blood. Bullets poured into the white-painted Bristol from all angles as McKeever jockeyed it madly, trying to evade the enemy fire. The fuselage and wings had been peppered and tattered ribbons of fabric fluttered in the slipstream. One bullet pierced his flying-boot and grazed his leg. This was the nearest he ever got to being wounded in action.

The position was now hopeless and the young Canadian resolved on the only course of action under the circumstances. He decided to play dead and threw his plane over on one wing in a crazy side-slip. Engine screaming like a berserk banshee, the Bristol tore down to meet the earth. One of the Pfalz followed it down for a few hundred feet, but so swiftly did it fall that the German gave up his pursuit, convinced that the Bristol would never pull out from its dive. In fact, McKeever nearly left it too late, pulling out less than twenty feet from the ground. His performance had been witnessed from the ground and so realistic had it been that British observers had reported him down out of control. The Bristol hedge-hopped back to the Allied lines full-out hidden from enemy planes by a shield of fog and had to run the gauntlet of every German gunner who had witnessed its descent. Tensed in his cockpit, McKeever used every ounce of his great skill as he steered round one tree only to find himself faced with yet another. And when he wasn't evading trees and bushes, McKeever found himself up against the guns. But skill, however fantastic, was not sufficient. McKeever had to have luck and miraculously his luck held. He returned safely to base, to make a perfect landing.

In addition to successfully completing an important mission, under impossible weather conditions - a feat in itself, which would have merited recognition McKeever and Powell had destroyed five enemy aircraft between them. For' their gallantry and devotion to duty they were both decorated. McKeever was awarded the DSO and Powell the MC. McKeever's citation said: '2nd Lieutenant (Temporary Captain) Andrew Edward McKeever MC RFC, Spec. Res. For conspicuous gallantry and devotion to duty. While on patrol by himself over the enemy's lines in very bad weather he encountered two enemy two-seater machines and seven scouts. By skilful maneuvering he engaged one and destroyed it. As he turned to get back to the lines five of the enemy dived on his tail and his observer engaged and destroyed two of them. After an indecisive combat with two others he attacked and destroyed one of the enemy which had overshot him. He continued the fight with the remainder until he was within twenty feet of the ground, when the enemy machines climbed and left him. He has recently destroyed ten enemy machines and has shown great courage and initiative.'

The Canadian was to add only one more victory to his score, on 26 January 1918, before being returned to England with the rank of Major, to take up an administrative post. In seven months at the front, McKeever had piled up a score of thirty-one confirmed victories (his observers accounted for an additional eleven) and his unconfirmed victories are believed to have totalled at least as many again.[22] All but two of those triumphs were over Albatros D.V fighters. Seven different gunners/observers shared his victories. One of these, Lieutenant Leslie Powell, became an ace in his own right, with 19 successes, 18 of which were in tandem with McKeever. His career was unequalled by any other two-seater pilot on either side during World War I. He was never wounded and never had a crack-up. [23]

In England he joined fellow aces William Bishop and Raymond Collishaw in establishing the Canadian Air Force. McKeever organized 1 Squadron of the new air force but the war ended before the new squadron could take its Sopwith Dolphins to battle. Canada's government then dissolved the fledgling air force.

The McKeever story had a tragic sequel. With war's end, he accepted a job managing an airfield at Mineola, New York. Before he could start work, he was involved in a road accident in his home town of Listowel. He broke his leg, complications set in and he died of cerebral thrombosis on Christmas Day 1919. He was aged 24.

Footnotes Chapter 9

22 McKeever and his gunners' 31-claim tally consisted of 18 destroyed and 13 'out of control.

23 By the end of the war Bristol Fighters equipped fourteen squadrons and 3,100 had been built. The type saw widespread post-war service as the RAF's standard army-co-operation aircraft in Ireland and Germany until 1922 and on the Northwest Frontier of India and in Iraq until 1932 when they were finally superseded by Fairey Gordons. Bristol Fighters also equipped eight foreign air forces. When production finally ceased in December 1926, a further 1,369 models had been built.

Chapter 10

Hazards Of Escape

Lawrence A. Wingfield MC DFC

The flying corps perhaps tasted something of a feeling of adventure when the stunts on which they were engaged were not too perilous. For they too, in their own specialised war of single combats must have experienced this sense of personal endeavour and personal achievement, of self reliance and of the sporting chance. And that no doubt is why a better relationship existed between enemy air forces than among other arms. They were not required to live like rats in the ground and did not therefore think of each other as such. On the contrary there seems to have been a curious chivalry among them. They were dealing with individuals whose personal abilities and courage they were able to recognise and acknowledge and the result was, as Captain Wingfield makes clear, that when they took their air-antagonists prisoner they generally showed them an almost ceremonial respect and courtesy, practically unknown among the other arms of the war.
Captain J. R. Ackerley.

Captain Lawrence Arthur Wingfield, known as 'Lawrie', was born in Richmond, Surrey on 17 April 1898. His father started Shoreham Aerodrome in Sussex and imbued in young Lawrie a passion for aviation. Wingfield was commissioned in 1915, aged seventeen, after attending Aldenham School and serving in the Inns of Court Officer Training Corps and the Royal Fusiliers. Training on Maurice Farman Longhorns, he was posted to 12 Squadron in France in September 1915 at St. Omer, where he flew BE2cs on general reconnaissance duties.

'My father started an aerodrome at Shoreham in 1911 when I was a schoolboy and I became interested in flying. As soon as I could, having the intention of getting into the Air Force, I joined the Inns of Court Officer Training Corps. In July 1915, I was commissioned Temporary Acting 2nd Lieutenant in the Royal Fusiliers and after a short time at the Duke of York's School in Dover, I was transferred to the Royal Flying Corps and went up to Castle Bromwich to learn to fly. I learned on a Farman Longhorn, which I found a delightful machine. I was allowed to go solo after about four hours; after eight hours, I got my Aero Club Certificate. I then went to

Netheravon for more training and was awarded my wings in December 1915. I met Billy Bishop at Netheravon. At that time, he was no further advanced than I was, but when I met him many years later in Canada, he was an Air Vice Marshal with strips of medals. [24]

I joined 12 Squadron in January 1916, flying an assortment of aircraft, but mostly B.E.2cs, which were used for gun-ranging and short reconnaissance. They weren't fighter aircraft. We had a couple of Bristol Scouts in our squadron, which were reserved for Flying Commanders, but I was allowed to take them up from time to time. Stationed at an aerodrome a few miles to the north, at Savy Aubigny with 11 Squadron was Albert Ball. I took a Bristol Scout over to that aerodrome to find Ball and get some idea of modern fighter tactics, of which Ball and Bishop were really the pioneers. They had realized that a plane was little more than a gun platform and that what was required was a fixed gun and a movable aircraft. I never got the chance to meet Ball, though, as he wasn't on the aerodrome that day.

My initial posting was to St Omer. Later we moved to Vert Galant and then in February 1916, 12 Squadron went to Avesnes-le-Comte (west of Arras), where we were engaged on every branch of aircraft work. That's where I was stationed at the beginning of the Battle of the Somme. Our reconnaissances were made, in formations of five, about ten miles over enemy lines. One exercise which was set for us was to send one machine every hour to the railhead at St Quentin, a large town then about thirty-five miles on the German side of the lines, there to 'lay' a couple of 'eggs' on the railway station to prevent reserves coming up. I was by far the youngest in the squadron at the time, but this mission struck me as being tantamount to suicide. I went to see the CO and asked him for permission to go first; permission was granted. I didn't do this from any heroism, though; I had the idea that maybe only the first plane to do this would have a chance of getting there and back safely. That didn't happen, though.

On 1 July 1916 I started off at the appointed time and arrived at St. Quentin and dropped my bombs at the railway station. I observed a column of smoke rise to a great height. On the way home I met a Fokker monoplane and that was the end of the story. It took the Fokker about fifteen minutes to shoot me down. I had this Fokker on my tail and the only way of getting back against the prevailing south-westerly wind, was to sideslip. I did this, but the Fokker overtook me and got back on my tail again. I began to see masses of bullet holes appearing in my wings. A bullet smashed into my instrument panel and a bit sheared off and hit the tip of my nose. My engine began to falter and I looked about for a suitable place to land. On my arrival on terra firma, which I achieved without personal injury, I found myself on a parade ground full of German troops. My machine and I were immediately surrounded by souvenir-hunting German soldiers and I found myself amongst men who knew Brighton and London well and who were all questioning me as to the condition of these places. Did I know them? Had they suffered very much through the war? And so on. I was able to reassure them on these points. I entirely forgot that I ought to have done something about my plane, such as set it on fire. I was eventually rescued by three German officers, one of them in mufti, the other two in uniform in a small Mercedes-Benz. The car and the contents belonged to the German Air Force and the gentleman in mufti turned out to be the Commandant of a squadron stationed hard by. This officer apologised to me most profusely for being in mufti, but remarked with mild sarcasm that I had not sent notice of my intention to call. He went on to say, 'We've been running along the road firing at you like anything.' I then noticed that the car had a machine gun mounted in the centre. Now I expect you know that a machine gun fired from the ground is quite ineffective against aircraft flying at any height over 2,000 feet. I had been flying at about 5,000 feet, so with due courtesy I expressed my regret that my attention had been so centred on the Fokker, who shot me down, that I hadn't noticed him. He looked his disappointment and I think the score was mine that time.

A guard was placed in charge of my aeroplane and I was invited to get into the car and was then driven by them to their Squadron Headquarters, which was a magnificent chateau eight miles north west of St. Quentin. I was very impressed by its condition. The gardens were beautiful; all the flower beds in bloom, the lawn mown and everything tidiness itself. I was ushered into a large dining-room, oak-panelled, where I was invited to scat myself next the Commandant and take afternoon tea. I asked what they proposed to do with my aeroplane and was informed that the '2.C.' was considered so ancient and at the same time a survival of such historic interest that it would be handed over to the proper authorities for exhibition in a museum in Berlin. The man who shot me down, Wilhelm Frankl, was introduced to me. He told me that I was his seventh victory.

I was particularly impressed, not to say overwhelmed, by the punctilio with which I was treated by my captors. Each officer, as he came in, clicked his heels in the doorway and saluted in the German manner. Possibly this was all intended for the Commandant. With characteristic British conceit, however, I imagined that the salutes were intended for me. I asked the Commandant if a note might be dropped upon the English side of the lines, so that my relatives and my squadron might have news of my whereabouts. I didn't need to tell the Commandant the number of my squadron or its situation. He already knew it, for he said, 'I will have a note dropped on to 4 Squadron Aerodrome at Albert on our next reconnaissance which showed a fairly good knowledge of the position of the squadrons. At a later date a German aeroplane did drop a note and the note eventually reached my squadron.

When tea was finished the Commandant said, 'I am sorry that you must now go. You have to go into St. Quentin and after that into Germany, but you will be well treated there, have no fear.' I can't say that the subsequent treatment was always good and on some occasions it was far from it, but I firmly believe the Commandant was under the impression that it would be. As I left the squadron chateau the car which was to take me to St. Quentin was drawn up to the steps of the chateau. The whole squadron had been paraded on the terrace and as I got into the car, somebody called them to attention. So they stood, two deep the whole breadth of the chateau. I felt more like a General inspecting his troops than a prisoner of war in the hands of the enemy.

On the way to St. Quentin we passed their aerodrome and as I had never inspected a Fokker aeroplane close to, I asked if I might be allowed to do so. Immediately they stopped the car and we strolled across the aerodrome to where a Fokker was standing on trestles in the machine-gun butts. It was a damn good machine. It was very fast and shot through the propeller [sic]. It was altogether a superb fighting aircraft.

We only restarted when I was quite satisfied. I received the greatest kindness at the hands of that squadron. They were kindness itself.

When we arrived at St. Quentin, I was handed over to one of the Staff Intelligence officers, but he didn't, as I expected, press me for information. He didn't ask me the name of my squadron, who were my squadron commander, or my aerodrome. He told me these things; I felt he would have told me the names and ages of my parents if I but asked. Dazed by his prescience, I was shortly led out and taken to the local gaol. This is the only time I have been in gaol as yet and while some may be good I don't recommend St. Quentin town gaol to anybody. I spent three days in solitary confinement. Another member of my squadron, Van Nostrand, was there. He had been shot down the same day as I had about forty officers and men from the gaol were taken off to St. Quentin Station to go back into Germany. A German officer told me that my plane would be taken to Berlin to be exhibited. I was rather dispirited; after all, I'd lost a serviceable aircraft and a new Lewis gun. I felt that I had failed. Later, though, I learned that the station at St. Quentin was in a terrible state. Apparently I'd been successful. My bombs had hit an ammunition train and the consequent explosion had done the station no good; it was so staggering that I could scarcely believe it. It was obvious that a considerable expenditure upon glass panes would be required to restore its former beauty.

Although three days had elapsed, the Railway Transport Officer in Charge, as I suppose he would be called, was still stamping about and displaying every symptom of emotion at the damage done. I was standing in the company of the only other member of the Royal Flying Corps in our party, a man rather older than myself. Evidently the RTO desired vengeance upon the author of the outrage which had been committed on his station, but didn't know which of us was the guilty party. I didn't enlighten him. At any rate, he clearly suspected my companion rather than myself. He was shouting, stamping his feet and raving at us without being able to make us understand much more than that he loved us dearly. Then he turned and tried to snatch the bayoneted rifle from one of our guards with obvious lethal intent. Happily, the stolid sentry was not used to having his rifle seized in this way by his officers and I am pleased to say, he wouldn't let go. The ensuing tug-of-war recalled the RTO to some sense of dignity and the officer in charge of us managed to pacify him. In the end the RTO contented himself by confiscating all the food we had with us and entraining us in a fourth-class carriage with Senegalese troops. Late the next day we arrived at Mayence and were conducted to the prisoner-of-war camp, an old fortress on the top of a hill overlooking the town. I passed from one camp to another as time went on and about June I went with many others to Ströhen camp which was situated on a sandy moor. The village of Ströhen is about ninety miles from the Dutch frontier and thirty or forty miles from Bremen. We had been housed in a cavalry barracks at my previous camp, but we had only huts at Ströhen.

The camp was surrounded by steel wire trellis work about nine feet high, topped with barbed wire and within was a wire fence creating a neutral zone. The whole of the camp was illuminated by incandescent lamps fixed on high poles at intervals of fifty yards or so and nobody was allowed inside the neutral zone under penalty of being fired on forthwith. Curiosity is so great amongst human beings that if an officer were to be seen lying on his stomach wriggling towards the trellis work, with an eye on the sentries, a pair of wire cutters in his hand and one or two bundles and haversacks festooned about him, ten or more people would be certain to come and stand and gaze at him as if he were doing it for their amusement. So if you had any idea of attempting to get away from the camp, you had to take great care to keep your idea to yourself. Many were the ingenious ways of escaping employed. One man concealed himself in a laundry basket and got out of the camp that way; another man made himself a complete German soldier's uniform, even to the belt and bayonet. He gilded the bayonet with the gold foil collected from cigarette butts. Others went out concealed in the camp refuse.

The plan of escape which had been evolved between a brother officer, Lieutenant B. Robinson and myself, was this. There was an old disused gulley running across the camp. Time and rain had shallowed it, but at night it still provided cover to a man lying full length in it. The drain crossed the neutral zone, passed through the wire and ended in a moat which surrounded the camp. Upon the outer side of the moat was an embankment. The sentries patrolled along the top of this and had a good view down into the camp.

First of all, an escaping kit had to be prepared. I had no civilian clothes, but I took all the stuffing out my cap, removed my rank badges and blackened my buttons. Then I collected goods of small bulk, such as Oxo cubes, milk tablets and so on, matches, chocolate, squares of congealed methylated spirit for cooking and spare socks and shoes for the march, I had made large pockets on the inside of my tunic so as not to resemble a Christmas tree when bearing this assortment. I concealed in these pockets everything required for a week's march, plus maps and compass and found I didn't present an unduly bulky appearance. Such things as maps, of course, were contraband and not easily procured. Malted milk tablets and Oxo cubes were usually obtained from England by parcel post without difficulty. The maps which I had and which are at present in the Imperial War Museum, were tracings of those belonging to a brother officer in the camp and how he'd go them I don't know. Many curious articles arrived from England, in spite of the strict censorship of prisoners' parcel and the constant barrack searches made by our captors never succeeded in unearthing all the battery of wire cutters, files compasses and maps which undoubtedly existed in the camp. The wire cutters used by us arrived in a cake and it may interest you to hear more fully how this smuggling of forbidden things was contrived. The first thing was to make one's needs know to one's friends at home by means of cipher messages ordinary letters. Numerous methods were used and they were all difficult to work. One way was to conceal the message in a sentence which wouldn't puzzle the German censor enough to make him suspicious and yet would puzzle one's friends at home so much that they would scent the trick.

Here's an example from one escaper. He wrote: 'I know young Ambrose (which is not his name) better than you do and if you want to please him send him some of the pictures of the edge of the good old Cheese country.' By the next post he was sent motoring maps of the Dutch frontier.

Then there was invisible writing. Several ordinary liquids such as lemon juice, spittle, or on a certain kind of paper, even plain water, make quite good invisible inks which can be developed by heat. You would, of course, have to explain to your friend at home by some means that the letter he had received was to be cooked to make it yield up its true message. Pricked messages were no good. The Germans knew about them.

In this kind of way secret contacts with home were established and requests for forbidden articles made. The next move lay with one's friends and relatives. They had to procure the required articles, devise ways and means of packing them in food parcels so that the German censors wouldn't find them and finally return word to the prisoner concerned - also by code - so that he would know in what parcel and article the thing was concealed. Major Evans, who has also contributed to this series, describes in his book, 'The Escaping Club,' how he decoded a postcard from home and got the message 'maps in Oswego.' But what was 'Oswego?' He had no idea and he naturally felt a bit nervous when the Germans opened that particular parcel. One of the first things they picked up was a yellow paper packet. They felt it carefully, but passed it to Evans without opening it and he saw 'Oswego' marked on it. It was a packet of flour and contained a large bundle of maps in the middle of it. He also tells another amusing story how one prisoner borrowed another prisoner's dried fruit to make a stew for the mess and when he was cooking it, found messages from home floating about on top. Apparently they'd been substituted for the stones in the dried prunes'.

Many and various were the ways and places in which these messages and contraband articles were concealed and the final move lay with the prisoner again, to get them out of the parcel room undiscovered. Sometimes, of course, the Germans just handed them over as in the case of 'Oswego' but it was often advisable to try to prevent the guilty article receiving too close a scrutiny and many devices were successfully tried. One way was to tempt the censor by offering him a tin of food and then, while his attention was thus agreeably distracted, pocket the particular article in the parcel one didn't want examined. At one camp the censor used to cut cakes of soap in half to see if there was anything inside, as there often was. This went on until a prisoner showed him how he could see right through the soap if he held it up to the light. This interesting experiment was carried out with a cake of Pears transparent soap and thereafter the intelligent censor held up all kinds of soap to the light and never cut another cake. Well, now to get back to my own escape.

The outstanding difficulty of the 'getaway' was that it would take us three or four minutes at least to cut through the wire. We had to wait until the two sentries who ordinarily patrolled the embankment were both standing still at the opposite ends of their beats. The attempt was to be made after dark on a wet night. My friend and I waited for a fortnight without obtaining favourable conditions and during this period we took a third officer into our scheme. We arranged with him that he should be the first to enter the drain and cut the wire and we would watch how the two sentries were behaving and signal to him by a prearranged series of taps upon a china plate. This method of signalling was adopted because we proposed to use the kitchen window as our vantage point and because in the general noise of the camp it was less likely to attract attention, than whistling or using lights.

At length our patient waiting night after night was rewarded It was a very dark night, raining hard and the sentries were still. At about 9 pm Somerville, our third confederate, entered the gully and crawled along it to the wire. He cut through the wire and crawled through the hole he had made without making a sound. In some miraculous way he managed to pass, running, through the zone of light into the darkness surrounding the camp, without being seen by either of the sentries.

We gave him four minutes start and then Robinson and I entered the gully at a point about seventy-five yards from the wire. We began to wriggle on our bellies keeping one eye on the sentries. When they moved we waited. Unknown to us we had been observed by brother officers in the camp and two of them, seeing what was happening, had joined the escape procession and entered the gully behind us. I don't know whether you've ever done it, but it's quite exhausting to wriggle seventy-five yards on your face, in mud and water, clad in a raincoat and encumbered as we were, I was fairly tired when I reached the wire. So when my coat caught in the loose strands of wire, I stuck, but the chap behind me, with herculean strength, seized hold of my legs and shot me through the hole like a cork from a bottle. The noise attracted the attention of the two sentries, who came up at the double. I have an impression of scrambling over the embankment and of the fleeting figures of my comrades receding into the darkness. There was a lot of noise and shouting as the whole of the camp guard, numbering about twenty, turned out. Luckily there were so many that those who had rifles could hardly fire for fear of hitting the others. My friends' speed was so much greater than mine that I sought safety by cover rather than flight and dived into a ditch nearby. I stayed as nearly as possible below the surface of the water, with only my head out. The guards continued to fire in all directions in the pitch dark, which chiefly endangered themselves. The bugle sounded throughout the camp and the roll-call was taken, all while I was lying in this ditch close by. My most vivid impression of that time was the wish for some means of taking a photograph of myself, because I am sure that a more unhappy looking object would be impossible to find.

I was about three-quarters of an hour under water in the ditch and when the commotion had died away I got out made off across the moor. When I had put some distance between myself and the camp, I stopped and took stock of my stores. I had left my light raincoat in the ditch, because was so wet; I found that my matches and cigarettes we spoilt, also my compass wouldn't work. It was a home-ma one, consisting of a card swinging upon a gramophone need which had been magnetised by rubbing it on a magnetic steel razor. The whole thing was encased in a cardboard pill box and although it was still intact the bath hadn't improved it. Everything else was soaked.

For the first two days I tried to avoid roads and go across country. In a dry country this might have been all right, but the country in this neighbourhood was very low-lying with a lot of water about and when I left the roads I got into trouble. So I wasted a great deal of time stumbling into back gardens a arousing dogs by the hundred or getting soaked by falling into streams. At this rate I didn't make much headway to beg with. I only travelled by night and very soon discovered good plan for keeping warm during the day. Hay in German is invariably kept under cover in open barns, so I would find good stack and bury myself about four feet down in it. This would keep me very warm, without in any way interfering with breathing. Towards the end of the second night, after I'd been soaked by the rain, I took cover in the straw of one of the barns. I hadn't been there long when I heard voices and found to my horror that someone was removing the straw. The voices turned out to belong to French soldiers, prisoners of war I should explain here that on-commissioned prisoners were usually employed on some work not connected with the war such as farming and were only under lock and key at nigh' When I realized who they were, I took them into my confidence and they were most anxious to help me. That night they brought me a black cloak, took me back with them to their quarters and found me a hiding place up in a loft. So there I was, back again in a prison camp, although not as a prisoner. I stayed with them two nights to recuperate. They were naturally rather anxious to get rid of me, as my presence was a danger to them and at the end of the two days they gave me a clay pipe, three pounds of the strongest tobacco I have ever come across and quantities of provisions and saw me off down the road. I had only two whiffs of that pipe before I hurled it and the tobacco over the hedge and as the rain continued I went back to the same place again unknown to them. I thought I might just as well stay in such a good place during the rain and was actually there three days and nights. In this way I got through the Sunday, the day when all Germany takes to the country, which was dangerous for me as it increased the possibility of an encounter with someone.

It took me four days more to get to the Dutch frontier, travelling always at night, in stages of about twenty miles. It rained every single day and the rest of the journey was without serious incident. The French prisoners had given me an old great coat, to replace the raincoat which I had lost. I must have looked like an animated scarecrow. I had long since lost collar and tie but I had five socks in my possession; I wore two on my feet, two on my hands as gloves and one round my neck and I used to change them over occasionally to dry them when they got wet. I followed railway tracks, rather than roads, whenever possible, as naturally they were deserted. One had, of course, to avoid being run down by passing trains.

On the eighth day after leaving Ströhen I came to the river Ems, near the Dutch frontier. It was about ten o'clock at night and I went down into the marsh and reeds which fringed the east bank and was looking for a narrow place where I might swim across when a man came up behind me and said something. I don't speak German, so I didn't understand what he said, but as he waved his arms and his revolver, I thought I'd better stop.

He was in uniform; a frontier patrol. As I appeared so dense he said: 'Do you speak French,' and I explained in that language that I was an English officer, a prisoner of war. He said 'I can help you. I am an Alsatian and will show you where to cross.' He told me to follow him at about fifty paces and if I saw anybody coming to slip into the wood and hide, until they were gone. In my excitement I didn't ask his name and unless this book should get into his hands there is no hope of my being able to find him and express my gratitude. He led me about a quarter of a mile and then said: 'There you are.' The river at this point was only about one hundred yards wide. I went down to the water's edge, found a plank of wood and tied my clothes on to it with my puttees. Then I asked him if there were any patrols on the opposite bank and he said 'No.' It was certainly lucky for me I met him. I swam over pushing the plank in front of me, dressed on the far bank and started off west again. I got lost once or twice during that night and at about two o'clock I arrived at a new canal in course of construction and presumed that I had arrived in Holland. I had.

After incarceration in various camps, he escaped in October 1917 and reached Holland safely after walking over ninety miles in ten days. Later he was awarded the MC and DFC. He noted, 'I was decorated once for being shot down and once for running away.'

After the war Lawrence Wingfield served as solicitor to the Royal Aeronautical Society starting in 1920. He joined the Institute of Aeronautical Engineers and founded the Guild of Air Pilots and Air Navigators. He retired from GAPAN in 1955 but continued as its legal advisor. Wingfield wrote a book, *The Law in Relation to Aircraft*. He died on 23 October 1989, aged ninety-one. [25]

Footnotes Chapter 10

24   In England as a cavalry subaltern in the Canadian Mounted Rifles in 1915, William Avery Bishop decided he would see more action as a pilot and transferred to the RFC in July of that year. He flew in France as an observer on 21 Squadron for several months and was hospitalised as the result of a crash-landing and frostbite. He trained as a pilot and in March 1917 joined 60 Squadron, flying Nieuport 17 scouts. On 25 March he scored his first victory over an Albatros and repeated the feat on 31 March. During the following week he shot down three more enemy aircraft and on 7 April destroyed one aircraft and one observation balloon. His MC was awarded for this exploit. His score continued to mount at a phenomenal rate; he frequently flew for seven hours a day and by early May he had destroyed 20 enemy machines. His DSO was awarded for his actions on 2 May, during the course of which day he attacked a total of 19 enemy aircraft in nine separate engagements, shooting down two. He was awarded the Victoria Cross after an engagement on 2 June when flying alone over an enemy airfield at dawn; he shot down three of the aircraft which took off to intercept him, damaged others on the ground and returned safely to his home base for a late breakfast. When his score reached 45 Bishop was promoted Major and awarded a Bar to his DSO. Late in 1917 and early in 1918 he carried out a number of non-combat duties, including recruiting drives in Canada and instructing at an aerial gunnery school. Subsequently given command of 85 Squadron, flying S.E.5As he led them back to France on 22 May 1918. Despite orders to avoid risking his life in combat he returned to the fray, shooting down 25 enemy aircraft in a period of 12 days, 12 of them in the last three days and all within a total of 36½ hours flying time. He was then recalled to England and never flew operationally again; his DFC was gazetted on 2 July. Bishop rose to the rank of Honorary Air Marshal in the Royal Canadian Air Force. He died in Florida in September 1956.

25   *Voices In Flight: Conversations with Air Veterans of the Great War* by Anna Malinovska & Mauriel Joslyn (Pen & Sword Aviation 2006).

Chapter 11

Duel In The Dark

Like a dome filled with light, the entire heavens were transformed into a vast, brilliantly-lit area. With thousands of others, I stared up to the east, where a small, intensely brilliant pencil of light rode high in the sky. For a brief spell it seemed motionless, then pointed downwards and like an arrow of fire, plunged from view. As it fell the night's silence was broken. From everywhere there arose a great crescendo of sound, a raucous, wild discord. It was a far-reaching, echoing cacophony of thousands of cheering, shouting, screaming voices. There had been 37 airship raids on Britain up to that September night in 1916. The 'gas-bags' would come, cruise serenely in our skies, drop their bombs and drone homewards unmolested and unscathed. The British people were left with feelings of doubt, resentment and alarm. But now there could be no doubt what that strange spectacle we had witnessed signified. It was the end of a duel in the dark - the first one to end in success for Britain. It was also the moment when a new name was added to the immortals of the air. We did not then know what the name was, but by the end of the week it was spoken by millions of lips.
Duel In The Dark by Grenville Manton, writing in RAF Flying Review April 1957. [26]

All this happened on the night of 2/3 September 1917. Sixteen German airships struck en masse at the City of London. On 24 August, four airships had raided East Suffolk, Essex and Kent. One of these ships, L 31, a Zeppelin, succeeded in penetrating the defences of London. It entered by the Thames estuary and on reaching Barking turned to the south, crossed the river at Millwall, circled round Woolwich and returned home via Shoeburyness. Bombs were dropped at Millwall, Blackheath, Deptford, Eltham, Greenwich and Plumstead, killing nine persons, injuring 40 and doing considerable damage to property in these thickly populated areas. Several of the raiders were sighted by airmen; but only one, L 32, was attacked and this managed to get away.

The raid on 2 September was the greatest yet planned. Every available naval airship was sent out and in addition several military vessels cooperated. Altogether 16 airships started, 14 of which crossed the English coast. The object of the raid was to lay London in ruins and attack the great manufacturing centres of the Midlands, but it ended in almost grotesque failure. In the eastern and south-eastern counties the airships wandered about, lost in the upper air, evidently quite uncertain of their position and dropped a large number of bombs at random, with so little result that only 16 casualties were reported. Two of the airships were hit by the British artillery, but were not set on fire. One of them threw overboard many objects, including an observation car and portions of the machinery and armament. Badly damaged, it limped home by way of the Dutch coast. The squadron of military airships was less fortunate. Two were driven off London by the fire of the anti-aircraft guns. Another attempted to attack by the east.

At 10.40 pm observers both ashore and afloat reported that an airship was flying inland above Foulness Point, Essex. Messages were passed to headquarters and elsewhere and swiftly a solitary biplane sped across the grass of a field at Sutton's Farm near Hornchurch, Essex. No sooner was it airborne than it was lost to view in the dark. It was one of a mere half-dozen 90 hp converted B.E.2c night fighters of a Flight of 39 Squadron RFC charged with the task that night of intercepting the raiders. Its pilot had been instructed to patrol a stretch between Sutton's Farm and Joyce Green across the Thames. Seated in his open and draughty cockpit, he set course and began to climb. It took 53 minutes to reach 10,000 feet. Up there the night at first was clear and there were few clouds below him. But he could see little except the stars above, the red glow of the engine's twin exhaust stacks, jutting up above the centre-section and the glint of the lighted instrument panel. Below him he could see here and there pinpoints of light - the curves of the Thames and the momentary appearance of searchlight beams. And that was all.

To and fro he flew along his sector keeping a constant lookout. For more than an hour his vigil seemed fruitless. Then suddenly in the apex of two searchlight beams he saw clearly and unmistakably an enemy airship. By this time our pilot had climbed to 12,900 feet and was feeling intensely the bitter cold. He eased over the stick, applied a shade of rudder and his aircraft wheeled round.

Very slowly he began to gain on the raider. For ten minutes the chase was held and then, at a most critical moment, clouds collected and the airship disappeared. In vain did the pilot continue his search, descending, climbing and turning, ever watchful. But the 'gasbag' evaded him and after 15 minutes had elapsed he returned to his patrol. After a while in the North-East area of London he saw the red glow of a fire. Yes, the bombing had started now with a vengeance. At the time he was flying at close on 13,000 feet and he turned and headed towards the scene. Somewhere down below, the searchlight crews seemed to be making feverish efforts to locate an enemy aircraft. Their long shafts of light swung swiftly and wildly through the darkness and then suddenly one fixed firmly on its prey. A second beam joined it. No time to lose now. The B.E. was put instantly into a dive! With screaming bracing-wires, wing tips quivering and the Royal Aircraft Factory engine roaring, the machine sped towards the airship. As he drew close, the pilot saw sinister streams of ack-ack and tracer shells from our batteries, bursting all around him and he could hear their crack and crump. Pulling out of the dive and climbing he began to close in on his adversary. With intense deliberation he sighted his Lewis gun on the great bulk he saw above him and then he opened fire. Brock and Pomeroy bullets poured into the airship from bow to stern. But - Hells bells! To his chagrin this opening attack seemed to have had no effect. Away he turned, lowered his gun on its mounting and reloaded feverishly with another drum. He launched a second attack from the side but again there was no effect! Then came the third assault. Closing in to less than 500 feet, the B.E. approached the airship's stern and once again its machine-gun barked. It was the lethal blow. For inside the great envelope the ominous glow showed up and the next moment the whole stern of the craft was enveloped in flames. When this final blow was struck the guns below were silent, the searchlights out. As the blazing wreck plummeted earthwards it threatened to encompass the victor in its fall, so that he had to dive flat-out and turned away in the nick of time.

Tremendously elated by the triumphant end of his mission, the pilot proceeded to fire red Very lights and dropped a parachute flare to mark his exultation. He had been in the air for more than two hours and his fuel supply was getting perilously low. For a while he had difficulty in locating his landing ground, but ultimately he recognised once again the tiny lines of paraffin landing flares at Sutton's Farm. He began his descent and when he touched down without a bump - a perfect three-point landing - it was a quarter to three in the morning. [27] At the same time, not so many miles away a hideous mass of metal, wood and fabric was sprawled in a field at Cuffley, Hertfordshire; crackling, crumbling and writhing in an immense shroud of hellish flames. The enemy airship was plainly seen in the very clear starlit night by spectators over a vast area near London at about 2.20 am. Suddenly a taint glow of red showed towards the stern of the airship; it spread with great speed and the whole huge structure began to fall, slowly at first, but gathering momentum and blazing more fiercely as it approached the earth, when it lighted up the whole sky with a blaze that was seen for over 50 miles. The grim carcase of the Schutte-Lanz (the S.L.11 - so often wrongly described as a 'Zeppelin L 21') was still smouldering when dawn broke that day. The bodies of the crew lay about. Some had evidently leapt out, or had been flung out, as the airship fell. The flames of the blazing airship must have been seen by several other airships appropriating the metropolis and it produced on these a very marked morale effect. The commanders of the remaining airships lost heart and dropping their bombs hurriedly, made for home as speedily as possible. The ships which attacked the country north of London met with little or no success. L.22, concentrating on the Humber area, dropped most of its bombs in open fields, while L.13, probably the most successful of the fleet, bombed East Retford and destroyed three gasometers. The casualties, however, were small in view of the magnitude of the effort; only four persons were killed and 12 injured.

From then on the story began to unfold and before the week was out a name - Lieutenant William Leefe Robinson of the Royal Flying Corps - was known to everyone in Britain'. [29] In a memo to his Commanding Officer, Leefe Robinson wrote:

'September 1916 From: Lieutenant Leefe Robinson, Sutton's Farm. To: The Officer Commanding No. 39 H. D. Squadron.

Sir: I have the honour to make the following report on night patrol made by me on the night of the 2-3 instant. I went up at about 11.08 p.m. on the night of the second with instructions to patrol between Sutton's Farm and Joyce Green. I climbed to 10,000 feet in fifty-three minutes. I counted what I thought were ten sets of flares - there were a few clouds below me, but on the whole it was a beautifully clear night. I saw nothing until 1.10 am, when two searchlights picked up a Zeppelin S.E. of Woolwich. The clouds had collected in this quarter and the searchlights had some difficulty in keeping on the airship. By this time I had managed to climb to 12,000 feet and I made in the direction of the Zeppelin - which was being fired on by a few anti-aircraft guns - hoping to cut it off on its way eastward. I very slowly gained on it for about ten minutes. I judged it to be about 800 feet below me and I sacrificed some speed in order to keep the height. It went behind some clouds, avoiding the searchlight and I lost sight of it. After fifteen minutes of fruitless search I returned to my patrol. I managed to pick up and distinguish my flares again. At about 1.50 am I noticed a red glow in the N.E. of London. Taking it to be an outbreak of fire, I went in that direction. At 2.05 a Zeppelin was picked up by the searchlights over NNE London (as far as I could judge). Remembering my last failure, I sacrificed height (I was at about 12,900 feet) for speed and nosed down in the direction of the Zeppelin. I saw shells bursting and night tracers flying around it. When I drew closer I noticed that the anti-aircraft aim was too high or too low; also a good many shells burst about 800 feet behind - a few tracers went right over. I could hear the bursts when about 3,000 feet from the Zeppelin. I flew about 800 feet below it from bow to stem and distributed one drum among it (alternate New Brock and Pomeroy). It seemed to have no effect; I therefore moved to one side and gave them another drum along the side - also without effect. I then got behind it and by this time I was very close - 500 feet or less below and concentrated one drum on one part (underneath rear). I was then at a height of 11,500 feet when attacking the Zeppelin. I had hardly finished the drum before I saw the part fired at, glow. In a few seconds the whole rear part was blazing. When the third drum was fired, there were no searchlights on the Zeppelin and no anti-aircraft was firing. I quickly got out of the way of the falling, blazing Zeppelin and being very excited, fired off a few red Very lights and dropped a parachute flare. Having little oil or petrol left, I returned to Sutton's Farm, landing at 2.45 am. On landing, I found the Zeppelin gunners had shot away the machine-gun wire guard, the rear part of my centre section and had pierced the main spar several times. I have the honour to be, sir, Your obedient servant, (Signed) W. Leefe Robinson, Lieutenant No. 39 Squadron, RFC.

It was Robinson who so tirelessly searched the dark sky for the marauder and having found him, had struck and sent him to his doom. A wave of enthusiasm swept the country and this 21-year-old pilot became a national hero. On 5 September an announcement appeared in the London Gazette announcing the award of the Victoria Cross to Lieutenant Leefe Robinson 'for most conspicuous bravery. He attacked an enemy airship under circumstances of great difficulty and danger and sent it to the ground as a flaming wreck.'

For weeks Robinson was news. One read of how his car broke down when he was on his way to Windsor Castle for the investiture, of how the mayor sent him a message of welcome, of incidents when he was overwhelmed by joyous crowds. Songs were sung about him and his exploit. The debonair, good-looking Robinson was photographed, welcomed, mobbed, everywhere he went. In spells of leave he was the guest of honour at lunches, dinners. [30]

He was promoted to Captain and in April 1917 he was posted to France as a Flight Commander on 48 Squadron, flying the then new Bristol F.2 Fighter. (He had served in France before, in 1915 as an observer and had been wounded). On 5 April he set off to lead an offensive patrol over the lines. It was the last flight he ever made. While high above Douai Robinson's formation of six aircraft encountered the formidable Albatros D.III fighters of Jasta 11, led by Manfred von Richthofen. Robinson was shot down and wounded by Vizefeldwebel Sebastian Festner. Bullets riddled Robinson's machine, the engine was wrecked and he dropped from the sky to fall into enemy hands. Three other Brisfits met their end, too.

On 7 April Richthofen followed his success over the new Bristol Fighters by another exploit. Flying in the Arras area with four other Albatros scouts, he met a flight of six British machines of 60 Squadron. The latter were of the French Nieuport type; though quickly manoeuvrable, their rotary engines had not the power of those of the Albatros and their single Lewis gun put their pilots at a disadvantage. Consequently, when Richthofen met them over the German lines, they were soon in difficulties and only one pilot succeeded in returning to his aerodrome; all the others were shot down.

The day on which Richthofen won his greatest success was also memorable as the date of the last British raid into German territory made for some months. Under Lieutenant-Colonel C. E. H. Rathborne, naval airmen combined with a French flying force, in a bombardment of Freiburg. Two daylight attacks were made and large buildings were shattered.

Owing to a lack of machines which could equal those of the German fighting squadrons, it was decided by RFC headquarters that the only possible means of checking enemy predominance in the air was by attacking their aerodromes and a campaign of night bombing was introduced for this purpose. This work was allotted to squadrons 10, 27, 55 and 100 and during April a number of raids were carried out. Douai, where Richthofen's squadron was stationed, was subjected to much bombing and hangars containing aircraft were demolished; other enemy aerodromes at Mouveaux, Provin and Wervicq were also attacked.

But while these raids doubtless disorganized the preparations of the German squadrons and harassed their personnel for a time, the results were not decisive. Moreover, the British bombing planes did not carry out their work without great difficulty and a considerable number of machines were shot down. In May the tide began to turn, however. The men of the RFC, who had been fighting under tremendous strain with daily losses, were gradually regaining the power that they had lost; the new scout machines of the S.E.5 type, which had been so badly needed, were at last dispatched in quantities and with their arrival in France the British pilots were able to meet the Germans on much more equal terms.

Leefe Robinson was not well treated by the Germans. He made several attempts to escape but all failed; his health was badly affected during his time as a prisoner. He was imprisoned at Zorndorf and Holzminden, being kept in solitary confinement at the latter camp for his escape attempts. When he returned home on 14 December 1918 he was a grievously sick man. He did not live to see the New Year in, dying on the night of 31 December at the Stanmore home of his sister, the Baroness Heyking, from the effects of the Spanish flu pandemic to which his imprisonment had left him particularly susceptible. He was buried at a little cemetery at All Saints' Churchyard Extension in Harrow Weald. [31] Barely ten miles away sixteen bodies are buried. They were once the crew of the S.L.11 whose fiery end is now a dim memory. Victor and vanquished have joined the ranks of half-forgotten men.

Footnotes Chapter 11

26 Robinson was born in Coorg, India on 14 July 1895, the youngest son of Horace Robinson and Elizabeth Leefe. Raised on his parents' coffee estate, Kaima Betta Estate, at Pollibetta, in Coorg, he attended Bishop Cotton Boys' School, Bangalore and the Dragon School, Oxford, before following his elder brother Harold to St. Bees School, Cumberland in September 1909. While there he succeeded his brother as Head of Eaglesfield House in 1913, played in the Rugby 1st XV and became a sergeant in the school Officer Training Corps. In August 1914 he entered the Royal Military College, Sandhurst and was gazetted into the Worcestershire Regiment in December. In March 1915 he went to France as an observer with the RFC, to which he had transferred. After having been wounded over Lille he underwent pilot training in Britain, before being attached to 39 (Home Defence) Squadron.

27 The propeller from the B.E.2C Leefe Robinson was flying when he shot down the airship is on public display in the Armoury of Culzean Castle in Ayrshire. It was given to the Marquess of Ailsa in thanks for letting his land at Turnberry be used for an RFC flying school.

28 Undeterred by the loss of the SL 11, the Germans launched another raid on the night of 23 September. On this occasion 11 ships took part, three of which, L 31, L 32 and L 33, were the best and most powerful of the German naval airships. They were ordered to attack London, whilst the older ships were to concentrate on the area between the Wash and the Humber. L31 and L32, in order to avoid, if possible, the increasingly efficient defences, approached the capital from the south, whilst L33, the very newest ship, came in from the north-east. Of these three super-Zeppelins only one, L31, under Captain Mathy, Germany's most brilliant commander, was destined to return home. (Mathy and the crew of L.31 were killed on 1 October when they were shot down near Potters Bar by Lieutenant W. J. Tempest). But the other two ships were less fortunate. L32, after reaching London about 1 am, was heavily engaged by the Dartford defences. The commander hurriedly dropped his bombs and made for home, but was spotted by Lieutenant F. Sowrey, who was out on patrol. L.32 caught fire and plunged to the ground, painting the sky for miles with a crimson glare. It dropped near Billericay and burned for nearly an hour. All the crew perished. The L33, which came in from the north-east, dropped bombs on Bow and Bromley-by-Bow, damaging many houses, factories and business establishments and killing 11 and injuring 25 persons. But L33, coming under a very heavy fire from defences, made off quickly to the north-east. Apparently it had been badly hit, for L.33 jettisoned much of its gear in order to gain height. Approaching Chelmsford L.33 was picked out by Lieutenant Brandon of the RFC who engaged the airship hotly without result. By the time L.33 reached the coast however, it was losing gas and rapidly descending. L.33 proceeded to sea for about two miles, but its condition was so bad that it was forced to turn back. The airship came gliding in at a low speed, almost touching the water and took the land safely not far from the coast. After setting fire to their ship the crew marched off on the road to Colchester, which one of them knew well and presently, meeting a special constable they surrendered to him. The loss of these two airships and the serious damage done to a third caused dismay in Germany. The official report spoke of the "extraordinarily heavy fire with incendiary shells' which had destroyed the two airships.

29 The S.L.11 was one of 16 which had left bases in Germany for a mass raid over England. The airship was the Robinson made an attack at an altitude of 11,500 feet approaching from below and closing to within 500 feet raking the airship with machine-gun fire. As he was preparing for another attack, the airship burst into flames and crashed in a field behind the Plough Inn at Cuffley, killing Commander Wilhelm Schramm and his 15-man crew. This action was witnessed by thousands of Londoners who, as they saw the airship descend in flames, cheered and sang the national anthem, one even played the bagpipes.

30 The propaganda value of his success was enormous to the British Government, as it indicated that the German airship threat could be countered. When Robinson was awarded the VC by the King at Windsor Castle, huge crowds of admirers and onlookers were in attendance. Robinson was also awarded £3,500 in prize money and a silver cup donated by the people of Hornchurch.

31 A memorial to him was later erected near the spot where the airship crashed.

Chapter 12

Black Leader Ace

Hit 'em hard, hit 'em often and then hit 'em again. But never let them know where you're going to hit 'em next.' That was the motto of Raymond Collishaw and as he wheeled around high over the French city of Lille in Northern France at the controls of his all-black Sopwith Triplane, he was resolved to put his motto into good effect. 'Collie' was not by nature a killer, but there was death in his eyes and heart on 25 June 1917 - death which was directed towards the pilot of the green-striped Albatros which was circling with Collishaw, warring for an opening.

Leslie Hunt, writing in *RAF Flying Review,* September 1962. Raymond Collishaw was the most successful RNAS fighter pilot of the War and with 60 confirmed victories, third in the over-all British and Empire aces' list. A member of No 3 Wing RNAS he gained his first air victory on 12 October 1916. In February 1917 he joined a scout unit, No 3 (Naval) Squadron and in April was posted to No 10 (Naval) Squadron as commander of 'B' Flight. Equipped with Sopwith Triplanes, the 'Black Flight' of 'Naval Ten' earned a reputation as one of the most formidable Allied units of the war. The Flight was composed entirely of Canadians; their aircraft were decorated with black paint and named *Black Maria* (Collishaw), *Black Prince, Black Sheep, Black Roger* and *Black Death.* Between May and July 1917 the Flight destroyed 87 enemy aircraft and during June Collishaw shot down 16 in 27 days. After the Armistice, Collishaw commanded 47 Squadron in the Russian campaign of 1919-20, where he destroyed two more aircraft. He remained in the RAF, serving in the Second World War and reaching the rank of Air Vice-Marshal with CB DSO and Bar DSC DFC and Croix de Guerre, as well as both military and civil grades of the OBE.

Twenty-four years old, Collishaw was the proud Flight Commander of 10 (Royal Naval Air Service) Squadron which flew the famous all-black Triplanes - the first Squadron to fly the 'Tripe' on the Western Front. Under the young Canadian's leadership victories had been many, but then there had come a tragedy. Lieutenant J. E. 'Jerry' Nash, one of the five Canadians comprising this special flight, had been shot down by a distinctive green-striped Albatros of the Richthofen Circus flown by Leutnant Karl Allmenröder, a top-scoring member of the famous 'Circus' and a close personal friend of Richthofen himself. Collishaw had sworn revenge on this pilot and now he had met him, high over Lille. It was the Albatros which moved first. Seizing what seemed an opportunity, Allmenröder swooped in to the kill. But Collishaw had been in too many battles to be caught that easily. A brief change of bank was sufficient to make the German miss. The Albatros swooped past, climbing and turning on a wing tip. This was Collishaw's chance. He threw the Triplane into an almost flat turn and opened fire as he did so. His burst of bullets caught Allmenröder's aircraft amidships. The Albatros seemed to hang motionless for a few seconds and then it spiralled down, streaming black smoke. Collishaw followed. He saw the smoke become tinged with brief stabs of flame. Then the German aircraft exploded. Of Allmenröder there was no sign. Among the witnesses of Collishaw's spectacular victory was von Richthofen himself. Too high and too far away to have been of any help to his friend Allmenröder, von Richthofen turned disconsolately back to the German lines as Collishaw was speeding back to his base to recount his victory.

Adventure was no new thing to this tough Canadian, who was born in Nanaimo, British Columbia on 22 November 1893. His father was John Edward Collishaw an itinerant miner from Wrexham who was raised in Pantygog, Garw Valley and his mother Sarah 'Sadie' Jones from Newport. John Collishaw had stopped his wanderings in Nanaimo to earn some money coal mining so he could continue to prospect in California. Ray dropped out of grade 8 at age 15 and his father got him a job as a cabin boy on the Alcedo a Canadian Fisheries Protection Service ship, when it sailed into the Arctic Circle in search of the Stefansson expedition. It had been crushed by ice and some of the crew were dead. Collishaw applied for and received the British Polar Ribbon. It was not, as some reports have it, for sailing to Antarctica with Robert Scott's ill-fated South Pole Expedition while only eighteen years of age. The furthest south he got was China. Later, he found out that he was not really eligible for the medal and he had to remove it from his military tunics. It was a hard, but exciting life and one that taught you obedience to superior officers. He worked for seven years on the west coast, eventually rising to the post of First Officer on board the Fispa, later going to sea on a Pacific steamer. By 1915, he had worked his way up to first officer.

When war started in 1914, Collishaw was 21. His first idea was to join the Royal Canadian Navy, but he did not hear from them for some time. Having attended a flying meet at Lulu Island near Vancouver and hearing that the Royal Naval Air Service was recruiting, he decided to apply for them instead. He applied in Esquimalt, BC and then was sent to Ottawa, Ontario for a final interview. He was enrolled as a Probationary Flight Sub-Lieutenant and would become a full one upon completing a flying course. At his own expense! He then travelled to Toronto to attend the Curtis Flying School, the only flight training school in Canada at the time. The candidates waited a long time to get into the school, throughput was slow and the weather was getting cold and would soon curtail flying. Due to the destitute condition of many of the RNAS 'students' the Royal Navy decided to give them basic naval training in Halifax and then ship them to England and have them do their flight training there. He did his basic training on the cruiser HMS *Niobe* until January 1916.

It was then that he boarded the White Star liner Adriatic for England with a bunch of other Canadians, including Lloyd Breadner, who was to become the RCAF's Air Chief-Marshal in WWII. In England he was posted to the naval air station at Redcar for what passed as flight training. It was the start of a distinguished flying career which was to last through two world wars. Flying in 1916 was very hazardous. He usually flew in a French-made Caudron G.3. It was a crude aircraft that was tricky to fly because of its use of wing-warping instead of ailerons for banking. Ailerons were not in wide use at the time, but would be within two years. They provided much more control over the banking movements of an aircraft, providing more control and enabling more severe lateral movements. They also trained on the Avro 504c and a wide variety of other aircraft. The RNAS believed that a broad base of knowledge of aircraft would stand them in better stead than learning a single type. Despite problems with landings Collishaw soloed with only 8½ hours of flying time.

At the time the German Zeppelins were raiding southern England with impunity and the RNAS pilots were in more danger from irate towns folk than they were from Germans. Collishaw was more fortunate than many pilots as John Alcock, who made the first non-stop flight across the Atlantic with Arthur Brown in a converted Vickers Vimy bomber, gave him extra tuition, making him a better pilot than most of his contemporaries. Even so Collishaw made some serious mistakes. Once while attempting to deliver a note from a friend to a local girl he crashed into a row of outhouses and destroyed the aircraft. The girl was not impressed.

Collishaw received his wings and first went to France flying a Sopwith Pup on escort duties. On 2 August 1916 he was posted to 3 Naval Wing, a bomber wing at Luxeuil-les-Bains, flying Sopwith 1½ Strutters. Some of the Sopwiths were equipped as single-seater bombers, while others were configured as two-seat fighter fighter scouts. They had been outfitted with special fuel tanks so they had an endurance of 7.5 hours. They were to conduct long-distance bombing raids over Germany. On 12 October he participated in the first strike on the Mauser Arms Works at Oberndorff, Germany. His duty was as a pilot in a two-seater fighter-scout as cover for bombers. Over 80 aircraft, including 40 1½ Strutters and French Breguet V bombers and Nieuport 11 scouts from the 'Lafayette Escadrille' participated in the raid. It was a large one by 1916 standards. Unfortunately, the Nieuports did not have the range of the other aircraft and had to turn back before they reached the target, thus exposing the rest of the flight to attacks by German fighters. Past the Rhine River the armada was intercepted by Albatros DIIs of the 'Grasshopper' Jasta that included future ace, Ernst Udet. He claimed his first victory that day, a Breguet V bomber. Collishaw and his gunner shot down the future ace, Ludwig Hanstein. His gunner put bullets into Hanstein's engine and Collishaw followed him down firing at him with his forward Vickers. This was his first victory, but his engine acted up and he barely made it the 200 miles home. According to the German authorities, they lost no aircraft during the engagement, but it was not unheard of for combatants to attribute their losses to accident rather than enemy action.

The raid was a failure with the loss of nine aircraft and little damage done to the rifle works. But 3 Naval Wing learned its lessons. The next week they destroyed the furnaces at a steel works with a much smaller force that got in and out of Germany without being spotted. But in the raid after that one he was shot down, fortunately the aircraft of the time were good gliders. He coasted into Allied France near Nancy and crash landed.

Collishaw's next two victories a fortnight later, near Luneville, were properly witnessed by thousands of French troops. He was ferrying a new aircraft from Wing Headquarters when six German Albatroses dived out of the clouds and attacked him. It was six to one and the Germans had the advantage of height. Collishaw, like William Barker and Edward McKeever, was happiest when close to the ground in such a spot. He went down. At tree-top level the advantage of numbers meant much less. In two quick bursts, he sent two Albatroses crashing into the trees, after which the others flew off. The flight so impressed the French that a grateful French government made him an immediate award of the Croix de Guerre. On 27 December, while returning from a raid on the steel works at Dillingen, Collishaw's machine was damaged in flight; he only just succeeded in gliding back over French lines near Nancy where he crashed and his plane was a total wreck. It was the first of a number of crashes and Collishaw on that occasion set the pattern which he followed throughout. He stepped out of the wreckage grinning and ready to fly again.

Early winter halted operations until January 1917. On one supposedly easy flight he was ferrying a Sopwith 1½ Strutter to their new base at Ochey without a rear gunner. He accidently strayed over the front and was jumped by six Albatros DIIs. The first hint he had of their presence was tracer bullets slamming into his instrument panel, one hitting his goggles and partially blinding him with glass. In desperation he dived for the trees hoping to lose them. One Albatros followed and crashed, another cut in front of him and presented a point-blank target. Collishaw did not miss and sent him into the ground with an accurate burst. Now he had to get home without instruments and nearly blinded. He guided his way home by the sun and landed, gratefully, on a field. Men came running to his aircraft, he thought to help him. That is until he saw a line of Fokkers on the field. He had landed at a German aerodrome. Quickly he gunned the motor and took off with Fokkers behind him and clipped two trees at the end of the field. They caught his slower plane and riddled it with bullets, but he managed to lose them in clouds. He was several miles past the front before he realized it and managed to land at a French airfield near Verdun. He stayed several days to have his eyes patched up by a local doctor. The French were so impressed with his feat that they awarded him the Croix de Guerre on 21 April 1917 and the British posted him to No. 3 Naval Squadron, which was operating with the army near Cambrai. During his two months there, Collishaw was employed as escort to the Corps Squadron bombers, downing one German aircraft in the process.

In February 1917 the Allied squadrons on the Western Front were being pulverized during the Arras offensive. Several Naval squadrons were sent to lend a hand. The RFC did not view them as a real benefit, however, as the RNAS had a fairly easy time of flying compared to them. Many RNAS pilots were shocked to find the fighting over the front was continuous, with three and four flights a day and every one guaranteeing a battle with the Huns. Several times Collishaw found himself alone just as the Albatroses showed up, the rest of the RNAS pilots skipping out with 'engine trouble'. He flew the Sopwith Pup, a single-gun, underpowered aircraft that was easy to fly and very manoeuvrable. He brought down an Albatros just after arriving at the front, but then had trouble with his gun freezing up in the frigid air. It wasn't until March that he brought down another aircraft while escorting F.E.2bs on a spy mission over Cambrai. He shot down the leader of a flight of Halberstadt fighters that were trying to intercept the 'Fees'. In another mission his goggles were again shot off and his gun jammed so that he had to lean into the slipstream without eye protection to unjam the gun. He froze his face quite badly and was hospitalized for a month.

Soon the Royal Flying Corps was badly in need of reinforcements, much due to the after-effects of 'Bloody April'. As a result, upon returning to the front on 26 April Collishaw was posted to 10 Naval Squadron as a flight commander, engaging in mainly coastal patrols. Naval 10 was equipped with the new Sopwith Triplane, which was even more agile than the Pup. It had an incredible rate of climb, better visibility above and a small turning radius. It was slower than the Albatros DIII but in WWI aircraft agility counted for a lot. Its major drawback was the single machine gun, as the Albatroses had two forward firing guns. Even so, the Germans had a nasty surprise with the appearance of the Triplane. 'Collie' brought down a Roland Scout near Ostend on his first day flying the Triplane in combat. In the next few weeks he shot down four more aircraft. Then Naval 10 was moved to Droglandt, near Belgium. Preparations for the Messines offensive were underway and the RFC needed assistance in providing protection for reconnaissance and bombing flights. Collishaw and Naval 10 were facing the cream of the German Army Air Service and would be in the thickest air combat facing Baron von Richthofen's Flying Circus.

Thanks to the marked promise he showed as a leader and as a fighter pilot, Collishaw's 'B' Flight would be composed entirely of five Canadians. The fighters in Naval 10 had painted the cowlings of their Triplanes to identify the various flights in the air. Collishaw had always been impressed with the German idea of distinctive markings for fighter aircraft. Although British commanders strongly discouraged pilots painting their aircraft, Collishaw ordered his flight's Sopwith Triplanes be painted black (though appearing dark brown) and called themselves the 'All-Black Flight', later known more simply as the 'Black Flight'. The aircraft of the 'All-Black Flight' were christened with suitable names. Ellis Reid of Toronto flew *Black Roger*; John E. Sharman of Winnipeg flew *Black Death*; Jerry Nash of Hamilton called his machine *Black Sheep* and Marcus 'Mel' Alexander of Toronto christened his plane the *Black Prince*. Collishaw's machine gloried in the name *Black Maria*. Within weeks they were the terror of the German Army Air Service.

In April 1917 and added three more enemy aircraft to his mounting score during the first two weeks of May. During their first two months they claimed a record 87 German aircraft destroyed or driven down - which, strangely enough, brought Collishaw and the unit no wide publicity, though it produced a great deal of renown among their German opponents in the area. Collishaw later claimed that this was because officials in the regular Royal Flying Corps were loath to give credit to naval pilots. Then the unit was moved from attachment to the Home Fleet and transferred to the Royal Flying Corps' 11th Wing near Ypres. During what remained of May 1917, each member of the 'Black Flight' shot down at least one German aircraft and Collishaw himself destroyed four recce machines in five days' patrolling. On 5 June 'Collie' brought down a two-seater and on the following day added another three to his score, which by then stood at 16 confirmed. The 'Black Flight' were flying offensive patrols with ten Triplanes. Collishaw was leading a patrol when they came across an Albatros two-seater escorted by 15 Albatros and Halberstadt fighters. In the maelstrom that ensued Collishaw shot down three Albatroses, Gerry Nash destroyed an Aviatik two-seater and an Albatros, Ellis Reid destroyed a Halberstadt scout and Sharman and Alexander each destroyed an Albatros. In total the RNAS shot down ten German aircraft without loss.

Two days later Collishaw was shot down. He had been in a tight circling fight with an Albatros and was about to fire on it when German bullets from an aircraft behind him smashed into his cockpit. His aircraft fell out of control in a dizzying series of spins, cartwheels, swoops and dives from 16,000 feet. Just before he hit the ground the Triplane pulled nose up and slammed belly down into the ground. British Tommies pulled him from the wreck, dazed but unhurt.

The 'Black Flight's first loss came when they had achieved an aggregate of fifty victories. On 26 June Collishaw's Flight became embroiled with Richthofen's Jagdstaffel 11. Gerry Nash found that he was fighting two German pilots single-handed. One of them was Leutnant Karl Allmenröder, victor in 30 air battles and second only to Richthofen among the German pilots then in action. Nash's other opponent was Richthofen himself. Yet, faced by the two deadliest German pilots, Nash fought a tremendous battle. He twisted and turned, looking for openings, but at last Allmenröder got in a telling burst and Nash's controls were damaged. He fell out of the fight and managed to land safely - but behind the enemy lines, where he destroyed his Sopwith before he was captured. The four survivors were bitterly grieved by the loss and they vowed immediately to avenge him by engaging and destroying the Albatroses of Richthofen's Jagdstaffel which had brought down Nash. At the same time they thought that Nash was dead.

On the morning of 27 June Collishaw's Flight met the Richthofen Staffel near Courtrai and this time Collishaw found himself engaged with the bright-green and red Albatros of Allmenröder - though he was not aware at the moment that he was fighting the conqueror of Nash. It was one of the classic dogfights of the war, like William Barker against Linke, like Hawker against Richthofen - two skilled and experienced fighters, who knew every trick, had met. They met head-on and then they went into the 'waltz' (dog-fighting). Collishaw fired at Allmenröder mostly as a matter of course, not really expecting to hit him, but Allmenröder went down out of control, to crash to his death near Lille. Nash, lying in a cell, heard a church bell tolling that afternoon and learned from his guard that it was the funeral of Allmenröder, who had shot him down. Allmenröder, the guard said, he been shot down by the leader of the 'Black Triplanes'. While there have been claims that Collishaw shot down German ace Karl Allmenröder, this has been disputed and remains difficult to verify.

The revenge was carried out with interest because Collishaw added another eleven to his score during the early part of July, as well as the unfortunate Allmenröder. For his combats in June 1917 he was awarded the Distinguished Service Cross. In part, the citation said that 'On July 2nd, Collishaw was involved in the air battle that nearly killed Baron von Richthofen. Six FE2bs had been set upon by 30 Albatroses, some from Richthofen's Jasta 11. One FE2b gunner grazed Richthofen's skull with a bullet. The German 'Ace of Aces' was lucky to come to before he crashed and managed to land his aircraft. The wound put him out of action for a month. In fine style Collishaw shot down six Albatros scouts, Alexander got two and Reid one.'

In July Collishaw was again shot down. This time, a powerful burst of bullets from a German aircraft broke the wires keeping the two sides of the metal cowling on the aircraft. One side piece flipped off and jammed into his wing struts causing an immediate and rapid, spin. His Triplane began tumbling end-over-end; with the added stress his seat belt snapped and he flew out into space. Frantically, Collishaw grabbed a centre-section strut and hung on for dear life. His arms were being slowly pulled out of their sockets and his hands were losing their grip as he was flung about by the wildly gyrating aircraft. In one of its swoops he was thrown part ways into the cockpit. With strength borne of desperation he hooked a boot around the control column and pushed it forward enough that he could get further into the cockpit. By now he could pick out individual trees. With an immense effort he levered himself into the cockpit with his foot and pulled back on the stick. The aircraft levelled out before slamming into the ground and was destroyed, but he walked away unhurt.

By the end of July 1917 'Collie's' score stood at 37 destroyed; the British Empire's second-highest-scoring living ace. He had destroyed 27 German aircraft during his command of the Black Flight of Naval 10. Altogether the Black Flight was responsible for the destruction of 87 German aircraft for only two losses (Nash and Sharman). Collishaw was granted a three-month leave in Canada. He was virtually unknown, in stark contrast to the grand reception given to the top-scoring living ace, Billy Bishop, when he returned on leave at about the same time. In August Collishaw was awarded the Distinguished Service Order 'For conspicuous bravery and skill in consistently leading attacks against hostile aircraft'. The citation said that 'Since the 10th June Flight Lieutenant Collishaw has himself brought down four machines completely out of control and driven down two others with their planes shot away. Whilst on an offensive patrol on the morning of the 15th June he forced down a hostile scout in a nose dive. Later, on the same day, he drove down one hostile two-seater machine completely out of control. On 24th June he engaged four enemy scouts, driving one down in a spin and another with two of its planes shot away; the latter machine was seen to crash'.

Returning to the war late in November, Collishaw was given command of

128

No. 3 Naval Squadron, which was flying Sopwith Camel F.1s in what was known as the Seaplane Defence Flight from Dunkirk, performing escort duty with the Channel Patrol. The new fighter was tricky to fly without considerable experience but once mastered it was a dangerous aircraft to the enemy. And it came with two synchronized Vickers machine guns. Posted to St. Pol in northern France, there was little action, even so 'Collie' shot down an Albatros while escorting D.H.4 bombers. The squadron commander was killed shortly after and Ray Collishaw took over. The action for the RNAS in the north typically consisted of escorting bombers over the German ports of Zeebrugge and Ostende. He celebrated his appointment with a string of three victories on 1 December - two enemy seaplanes and an L.V.G. two-seater. His most amazing experience on this tour of duty was an air battle between his squadron and a formation of German Scouts in which no shot was fired. The squadron was providing protection for an observation machine, which was ranging guns for a fleet firing on Zeebrugge. The German formation approached and Collishaw led his pilots to the attack but found that his guns had jammed, owing to the congealing of the oil in the low temperature. Several times he turned to attack the Germans and each time they withdrew, until the navy's shoot was finished. Then Collishaw learned that all the squadron's guns were jammed - possibly all the guns of the German Scouts as well.'

Mel Alexander survived the war and remembered Ray Collishaw as a charismatic leader and an inspiration to others. He would fly with new pilots letting them spray lead at enemy two-seaters and then with little effort slipping in and downing the plane. He would slap the newcomer on the back and congratulate them on their first victory. Fortunately, for them, the action on the coast was not like the RFC had on the front lines. Collishaw developed a taste for attacking enemies head-on, firing until the other aircraft fell or swerved away and then using the Camel's right-hand manoeuvrability to pounce on their tail. He destroyed two Pfalz's and two of the new Fokker DVIIs with this technique in two days.

In October 1917 Collishaw received a Mention in Despatches for particularly fine work in the air. The flying and fighting kept up throughout the winter of 1917-1918 with brief respites due to poor weather. Much of the combat in the summer of 1918 was strafing German troops. Flying low over the trenches and firing on the troops was exceedingly hazardous, as many rifles and machine guns would bear on the aircraft. Many pilots died in this activity. Collishaw shot down four aircraft and a balloon in August and five more in September. He led a low level bombing attack with a mixed flight of planes, including Camels, SE5s and Brisfits on an airfield at Lieu St. Amand. They set three hangers on fire and shot down a handful of Fokker pilots, with Collishaw getting two. On the way home they strafed ground troops. As Collishaw put it, 'All in all it was a most successful affair'. He was awarded the bar to the DFC. His citation noted that he had 'carried out numerous solo patrols and led many offensive patrols, on all occasions engaging the enemy with great bravery and fearlessness. Up to date he has accounted for forty-seven enemy machines, twenty-two in the last twelve months'.

On 23 January 1918 Collishaw returned to the embattled area of the Western

Front to command No. 3 Naval Squadron, which was equipped with the more deadly Sopwith Camel fighters. On 1 April the RNAS and the RFC merged and No. 3 Naval became 203 Squadron Royal Air Force. Collishaw remained in command with the new rank of major, finding that serving as a Commanding Officer took up a great deal of his time with 'paper work'. But he was able to make time for flying and by the end of the summer he was one of the first to receive the newly conceived Distinguished Flying Cross as well as being awarded a bar to his Distinguished Service Order in August 1918.

Collie's finest day was very much like Billy Bishop's raid on an airfield that earned him the Victoria Cross. Collishaw and Leonard Rochford raided an airfield 15 miles behind enemy lines in Camels each carrying four 25lb bombs and extra bullets. Rochford swept in low strafing and bombing as Collishaw provided top cover. Once Rochford had shot up the hangers, barracks and mess and lit a large tent on fire, Collishaw swept in and shot up the flight line of Albatroses. Circling up he spotted a large two-seater coming in for a landing, both pilot and observer being very non-observant of the proceedings. He shot the plane down in flames. They returned to home base and Collishaw re-armed with bullets and went back to view the damage. Upon arriving he shot down an Albatros circling above the field, took a look at the damage and headed home. Collishaw received a Bar to Distinguished Service Order and Rochford received the DFC for his part. 'Collie's' citation, in part, said that he was 'A brilliant squadron leader of exceptional daring who has destroyed 51 enemy machines. Early one morning he, with another pilot, attacked an enemy aerodrome. Seeing three machines brought out of a burning hangar, he dived five times, firing bursts at these from a very low altitude and dropping bombs on the living quarters. He then saw an enemy aeroplane descending over the aerodrome; he attacked it and drove it down in flames. Later, when returning from a reconnaissance of the damaged hangars, he was attacked by three Albatros scouts who pursued him to our lines, when he turned and attacked one, which fell out of control and crashed'.

Collishaw had quite a few close escapes during the war. His plane was hit often by bullets, but Collishaw escaped unscathed in the air. His aircraft was shot down out of control and crashed several times. Once, lost in a fog, he landed on a German aerodrome and was actually taxiing to the tarmac when he saw German insignia on the grounded planes and German troops rushing out to arrest him. He opened his throttle wide, took off and escaped. On another occasion, his goggles were shattered by an enemy bullet. He once had his controls disabled by German machine gun fire from the ground and had to ride out the flight until the aircraft crash-landed - luckily near the British front trenches.

While in command 'Collie' destroyed twenty more German aircraft in four months, many of them the much-vaunted Fokker. An airman who flew with him claimed that he would often 'give' a victory to a new, green pilot, just to bolster his confidence. The new pilot would be taken out by the renowned Collishaw to 'bag one'. Anxiously following the leader, he would find himself diving on the tail of a German reconnaissance plane. Trying to control the machine, so that the nose would stay still, he would find his gun-sight wobbling all over the sky. He would press the firing button, spraying bullets like a lawn sprinkler. Then suddenly Collishaw would appear alongside; there would be a short, deadly burst and the new pilot would turn sick as he saw the enemy plane catch fire and plunge to earth. He would fly back to the aerodrome, where the flight commander would clap him heartily on the shoulder and insist 'You got one! Grand show old boy!' The new pilot, unable to speak, would nod timidly and thereafter he would fly into battle with Collishaw anywhere. That was - according to the story - part of Collishaw's great quality of leadership.'

Collishaw was officially credited with 60 kills (28 enemy aircraft destroyed (including one shared victory), 30 enemy aircraft driven down 'out of control' (including two shared wins) and one enemy aircraft 'driven down').

But this does not take into account the eight balloons he shot down. Balloons were frequently more hazardous to attack than enemy aircraft were, but they were not credited as an aircraft kill. Collishaw claimed that he destroyed 81 aircraft and balloons. Had be flown for the RFC this total would have been closer to his credited kills than 60, as the RFC was more lenient in awarding kills to pilots. In the RFC Raymond Collishaw would have been the highest ranked ace of the war and would undoubtedly have been awarded the Victoria Cross. [32]

The war was nearly over, but Collishaw persisted in attacking enemy aircraft, almost getting shot down in October 1918. Collishaw was given another Mention in Despatches for exceptionally fine work in the air. He was ordered to report to the Air Ministry in London and three weeks later the Armistice was signed. Collishaw was to be sent back to Canada to help form the Royal Canadian Air Force, but the end of the war delayed this and he stayed on in the RAF with a permanent commission. Collishaw was in England working on the formation of the Royal Canadian Air Force when the Armistice was signed. He was promoted to Lieutenant Colonel during this time. He took some leave in Canada in December before returning to England. He was planning on attempting to fly across the Atlantic using a long range bomber but his plans were interrupted by events for in November 1918 the decision was taken to send a squadron to help General Denikin's White Russian forces in the Russian Civil War against the Bolsheviks, who had skilled German pilots manning some of their aircraft.

Collishaw was chosen to be in command. As CO of 47 Squadron he left for the Middle East and from there joined the RAF Training Mission in South Russia, leading ten pilots south to Nororossiiski flying Camels and D.H.9 two-seater bombers to fly and fight for the Czarists under General Denikin. At first death from typhus was the greatest hazard as there were no medical supplies and there was little they could do for typhus in any event. In late August Collishaw went into battle dropping bombs from his Camel on Bolshevik troops crossing the River Volga on rafts. He sank a gunboat and became one of the few aces to sink an enemy vessel. It was a nasty civil war, with no thought given to the safety of civilians and waged by any means possible. Cavalry charges with Cossacks and Muslims were still held, with Sopwith Camels flying top cover. In one sortie four Camels caught a large troop of

Bolshevik cavalry in the open. Their eight machine guns cut them down without respite, inflicting 1,600 casualties. It stopped only when the aircraft ran out of bullets. In October Collishaw shot down his first aircraft in Russia, an Albatros D5 that crashed into the Volga. He destroyed another a few days later, but then was put out of commission with typhus. Collishaw, as usual, was fortunate in being tended by a homeless Russian countess who likely pulled him through the disease.

Collishaw's Squadron were credited with 19 successes but the campaign eventually turned into a retreat and then a rout. They had to abandon their aircraft and flee with the aristocrats and anti-soviet peasants on an old train. It was nearly their undoing. The Bolsheviks chased them for 500 miles in an armoured train mounting a 9 inch cannon. Civilians along the way tore up track in front of them or fired on the cars as they passed. Typhus ran through the train, dead bodies were simply hurled from the cars. They had to collect snow and firewood for the engine and themselves. At one point a local body of Bolsheviks ran a railroad engine into the train, but failed to derail it. Finally, in January 1920 they made it to Crimea and relative safety. He admitted in his autobiography that Russia was far more frightening than the Western Front. Once they were in the Crimea they reassembled their planes and were back in action. Collishaw blew an enemy train off the tracks and damaged a second one with bombs. On the second foray his motor was damaged and he was forced down behind enemy lines. Fortunately, the ground was frozen so he taxied back to his lines. By the time the Allies pulled out of Russia, with the collapse of the White Army in the spring of 1920, Ray Collishaw had destroyed two aircraft, two trains, a gunboat (with a bomb dropped from his Sopwith Camel) and a bridge. Collishaw admitted in his autobiography [33] that his experiences Russia (particularly the escape from) was far more frightening than the Western Front. For his work in Russia the Air Ministry gave him his third mention in dispatches. The Czarists, before he left, invested him with the Orders of St. Anne (White Russian) and St. Stanislas (White Russian) and the Order of St. Vladimir.

After 47 Squadron was withdrawn from Russia, Collishaw was sent to Egypt to command 84 Squadron. The squadron was moved to Persia, which was made a British protectorate after the war, to defend against the Bolsheviks. After arriving back in England he took three months leave and returned to Canada. Following this leave he returned to England in August 1920 and spent time at an RAF depot and was then posted to Mesopotamia (now Iraq). He took command of 30 Squadron equipped with D.H.9a's. Iraqi tribes were revolting against central authority under King Faisal and the 'British Mandate'. The RAF was sent to crush the rebels. As there was no air opposition the entire activity was bombing and strafing rebel positions, troops, villages and stock. Many of the pilots had no compunction about bombing civilian villages, but refused to bomb their livestock. Collishaw thought bombing non-combatants to be dishonourable. The only real danger to the pilots was being forced down in rebel territory due to engine problems. The rebels had little respect for their aerial tormentors and would kill them if they captured them. They all carried papers written in Arabic, Syrian and Turkish called 'blood chits'. They promised that a substantial reward would be paid to those who helped a downed airman. He spent three years in freezing cold weather with deep snowdrifts in Kurdistan, to temperatures of 130 with no shade, dusty, dysentery, thirst and other equally unpleasant discomforts. Part of their operations were against more Bolsheviks in North Persia at Kazvin in support of units under General Ironside. As winter set in most of the action consisted on desultory bombing and reconnaissance and the maintenance of communications between the Kazvin base and Baghdad. The planes would take off from airfields made of deep, packed snow (done by camels) and landed in temperatures over 120.

No. 30 Squadron was then involved, along with 47 and 70 Squadrons, in setting up the Baghdad to Cairo air route to enable easy military access to Mesopotamia and Britain. Also, it was to make Baghdad part of a projected Australia, India, Cairo, Baghdad, London air route that would, of course, be controlled by the British. They worked with two truck crews in identifying landing areas 20 miles apart, preferably near water on flat ground. At one oasis water was required for the aircraft. The water was nearly 80 feet down in the well and no one was stepping forward to descend for it. Collishaw had a rope tied onto himself and with bucket in hand descended to get the water. By the time he reached the bottom his eyes had adjusted to the dark and he was horrified to see the walls crawling with large, black scorpions. Quickly he scooped up a bucket of water and rose out of the well. One bucket was all they got. The provision of water was a continual problem. Collishaw thought that they could use the inner tubes from the tires of Handley-Page 0/400 bombers. The concept was to fill an inner tube in a tyre with water and drop it from an aircraft to resupply distant airstrips. They experimented with one such tyre weighing 750lbs. The pilot came in low over the Baghdad airfield in a Handley-Page bomber and released the tyre. Travelling at 100 mph the tyre hit and rebounded off of the field changing course for the hangers. Everyone dropped or ran like mad away from the tyre travelling towards them. It hit a hanger in the side and went through the offices of several flight commanders, out through the other side of the hanger and demolished an aircraft. Needless to say, they went back to delivering water by truck.

By the spring of 1921 the British had had enough and were not prepared to fight any major battles against the Bolsheviks over Kurdistan. His work 'in recognition of distinguished services in Iraq in 1921' was noticed with another Mention in Despatches dated October 1922. In the 1921 New Year's Honours List, Collishaw was made an Officer of the Order of the British Empire. By 1923, the RAF was back in Kurdistan and Turkey fighting a breakaway rebellion by Sheik Mamoud, the self proclaimed King of Kurdistan with Turkish backing. A column of 5,000 mounted British troops was sent into Kurdistan and Collishaw went along as RAF Liaison Officer. After six weeks on horseback and the burning of a number of rebel towns the British withdrew, not really accomplishing anything.

Following the Mesopotamian excursion Collishaw commanded 41 Squadron at Northolt equipped with Armstrong-Whitworth Siskins. From there he attended the RAF Staff College at Andover. He found the College to be run along very unimaginative lines, with little thought given to actual field problems and how commanders in the field overcame them. The Naval Staff saw no need for aircraft that could sink an enemy battleship, that was what they had battleships for. They prepared plans to refight WWI, not a coming war. From the Staff College he went to command 23 Squadron flying the new Gloster Gamecock. They often flew at night in cooperation with the London anti-aircraft batteries. One night his Gamecock flipped onto its back while he was landing. He was in fine shape, nothing broken or bent, but he was stuck in the plane soaked with fuel. A few feet away there was an airstrip marking flare burning merrily away. He expected to be burned to a crisp at any moment, but help came eventually.

In 1927 Collishaw was posted to a new organization that had developed in response to continuing poor relations with France and the lack of aircraft squadrons in England. He became the Head of the Department for Operations and Intelligence working under Air Marshal Sir John Salmond of the Air Defence of Great Britain. They all assumed that if war came, it would be with France. During this period there was a strong anti-military lobby in the League of Nations. Part of this was a movement to outlaw aerial bombing. Collishaw blamed this activity for limiting England's bombing abilities at the beginning of WWII. By the end of WWI the Handley-Page 0/400 bombers were dropping 1,650lb bombs and the Handley-Page V/1500 bomber was capable of dropping a 3,360 pounder by the time the war ended. At the beginning of WWII the maximum bomb size carried by English aircraft was a 500lb bomb. In July 1929 Collishaw was sent as Senior RAF Officer aboard HMS *Courageous,* England's newest and largest aircraft carrier located in Malta. He spent three years aboard the ship. From there he spent three years commanding RAF Station Bircham Newton where Nos. 35 and 207 Squadrons were stationed flying Fairey Gordon light bombers. The only respite he had from boredom was the rare visit from the King and Queen. In 1935 he was finally promoted to Group Captain and was sent to command RAF Station Upper Heyford. After a few months the Italians invaded Ethiopia and the government wanted an experienced commander in the region. He was sent to Sudan to take over 5 Wing of the RAF's Middle East Command. The Wing was composed of 35 and 207 Squadrons still flying Gordon bombers and 3 Squadron flying Bristol Bulldogs. Nothing much came of the British response to the Italian campaign and the Wing was disbanded in 1936. Collishaw however, took over command of the RAF Station at Heliopolis, Egypt. Here there was a lot to do, especially considering the Nazi and Fascist menace that was growing in Europe. On leave one time, he and his wife took a motor trip from Cairo through Cyrenaica (north eastern Libya). He took careful note of military installations along the way (there was only one road) for future reference that was to stand him in good stead.

Collishaw was appointed AOC Middle East Bomber Group in April 1939. Just before the start of the Second World War, Collishaw was fortunate in being the guest of the Italian Air Marshal Balbo, a great air leader and the man responsible for building up the Italian Air Force. It proved a most valuable visit for Collishaw. Long discussions with Balbo gave him an insight into the

Italian's way of thinking and from what he saw in Italy he was almost able to jot down the Italian Order of Battle from memory. So, although British forces were extremely thin on the ground when 'Collie' took over control of 204 Group in the Western Desert as the Italians entered the war, he had a very shrewd idea of enemy plans. The old motto of 'Hit 'em hard, hit 'em often and then hit 'em again,' still held good.

When the Second World War began in September 1939, Collishaw was promoted to Air Commodore and took over as Air Officer Commanding, 204 Group ('Egypt Group') in North Africa. He concentrated on strategy and tactics to neutralize the Italian air force and to gain aerial superiority in North Africa. This was a tough challenge considering that his men were flying outdated Gloster Gladiator biplane fighters and Vickers Wellesley bombers. Within two days of the commencement of hostilities Collishaw's pilots attacked an Italian airbase destroying 18 aircraft with only three aircraft losses. He then turned their efforts to bombing harbours, ships and troops to hold up the reinforcement of North Africa. They sunk the Italian cruiser San Giorgio and blew up an ammunition dump. His pilots were badly outnumbered and outgunned. But he countered these deficiencies with expert advice on aerial tactics, aggressive attacks and trickery. He had only a single modern Hawker Hurricane fighter to use at the front (three others were relegated to training) dubbed 'Collie's Battleship'. He made the best of it by constantly moving it from base to base and letting the Italians see it. He came up with the idea of making many, single plane attacks on Italian formations to fool the Italians into thinking he had many Hurricanes. The result was that the Italians spread their superior fighters thinly across North Africa and seriously diluted their strength... Collishaw implemented a continual harassment procedure that forced the Italian's into having standing patrols over their forts. This was incredibly wasteful of men, fuel and machines. They should have been on the offensive and yet were not.'

Collishaw had no time for the obvious targets but specialised in non-conventional raids. His aircraft were, at first, just Bombays, Blenheims and a handful of Gladiators. Then in August 1940 the first Hurricane arrived. Collishaw gathered together as many Hurricane pilots as he could and flew the single aircraft continuously each day, several sorties a day, always from different landing strips. The result was an undermining of Italian morale because the enemy thought that the Hurricanes had arrived in strength.

With his uncanny insight into Italian thinking, he would often challenge Intelligence reports sent to him from Middle East HQ and would play his own hunches very boldly - almost always with incredibly successful results. With uncanny accuracy he would bomb airfields just before Italian aircraft took off for a raid against the British, or strafe roads just as the enemy were making 'top secret' moves. More than one Italian prisoner of war swore that the British had a secret agent at their headquarters who was able to transmit top secret plans almost as they were formulated. Collishaw aimed at cutting the Italian lines of communication and depriving them of spare parts. He also laid traps to draw fighter protection off the bombers and strafed soldiers until morale cracked. Just how effectively his plans worked was discovered when British forces at last took Cyrenaica and found some 1,100 enemy aircraft destroyed on the ground - many of them had just been unserviceable and were waiting for the spares which Collishaw had denied them.

In September 1940 the Italians under General Grazziani finally started a ponderous offensive from Libya into western Egypt. The British pulled back to Marsa Matruh, allowing the Italians to capture an airbase at Sidi Barrani. The Italians stopped there until December to regroup and restock supplies. Collishaw implemented a continual harassment procedure that forced the Italian's into having standing patrols over their forts. This was incredibly wasteful of men, fuel and machines. They should have been on the offensive and yet were not. While the Italians were in Sidi Barrani someone in the rear area of Cairo found a large stock of old English anti-personnel mines in a storehouse. Bristol Bombay transport/bombers were used to 'bomb' the Italian forts with these 20lb anti-personnel mines. Each Bombay could carry 200. As the plane circled a fort, one man would arm the AP mine, hand it to another who would then toss it out the fuselage door. They kept this up all night alternating planes and forts. It was reported to have lowered the Italian's morale even further. Reinforcements arrived in the shape of Vickers Wellington medium bombers and two squadrons of Hurricanes. Collishaw used them to good effect during Operation 'Compass'. It was originally designed by Generals Wavell and O'Connor as a reconnaissance in force around Sidi Barrani. The RAF was tasked with harassing the Italians and making sure that their reconnaissance and bomber planes did not find out what was going on in the British sector. They were very successful as the Italians were taken completely by surprise by the opening attack of 'Compass'. He even had a Bombay fly back and forth over the tanks moving to the front the day before the attack to cover their noise. The Bombays were very noisy aircraft. With the overwhelming success of the initial days of 'Compass', General Wavell pushed further into western Egypt and entered Libya. Collishaw's men were extremely busy keeping the 'Regia Aeronautica' at bay and strafing rear areas and lines of communication and retreat. Eventually the British captured Benghazi. However, the Germans realized they could not afford to lose North Africa so easily and despatched General Erwin Rommel to retake it. A fact of warfare in North Africa worked alternately in the attackers favour and then in his disfavour. The more successful the attack, the further the enemy was pushed back, the longer became the supply lines for the offense and the shorter became the supply lines for the defence. This is a main reason for Rommel's success in the Libyan Desert and then for the British and American success over him.

Finally, the time came for Collishaw to be given a well-earned rest, after which he became AOC 14 Group at Inverness. He still had the happy knack of getting the best out of his men and one young aircrew sergeant, who had just escaped from Germany and was visiting 'Collie's' Group to give a lecture on his experiences, recalls how the much-decorated Collishaw made him - a lowly sergeant with only the DCM - feel the most important person at the HQ. This was one of 'Collie's' greatest gifts.

In July 1942 Collishaw was recalled from the desert and was replaced by Air Vice-Marshal Coningham. He was given a posting in Fighter Command in Scapa Flow and remained there until he retired, involuntarily, from the RAF in July 1943. Collishaw attained the rank of Air Vice Marshal; he was awarded a Companion of the Order of the Bath during his service. He spent the rest of the war as a Civil Defence Regional Air Liaison Officer. Following the war he returned to British Columbia as part owner of a mine near Barkerville. He finally settled down to a good and finally, peaceful life. Air Vice Marshal Raymond Collishaw died in West Vancouver in 1975 at the age of 82.

He was the highest scoring RNAS flying ace and the second highest scoring Canadian pilot of the First World War.

Footnotes Chapter 12

32 As early as the 1950s, there has been debate over whether his kills had been understated, due to the Royal Naval Air Service receiving less credit than the Royal Flying Corps. Some historians credit him with 81 (unofficial) kills, which would place him at the top of First World War flying aces, ahead of the 'Red Baron' and top British Empire ace Billy Bishop.
33 His memoirs were titled *Air Command, A Fighting Pilot's Story* and were published in 1973.

Chapter 13

The Flying Hussar

The roar of tortured engines and the staccato chatter of machine guns reverberated across the crater-pocked fields of Northern France. Battle-weary troops peered over the edges of their sandbagged trenches, straining to glimpse the melee raging over their heads in that [23rd] September evening sky of 1917. Twisting and turning, each straining to gain an advantage, were a handful of fighting scouts - six S.E.5As of 'B' Flight, 56 Squadron RFC, a silver-blue Fokker Dr.I and a red-nosed Albatros D.V. Each pilot strove to bring his gun sights to bear on one of his antagonists, but neither the British nor the German pilots were new to the art of 'dog-fighting' and the little biplanes and the sole triplane cavorted about the sky for a full ten minutes before any pilot succeeded in placing a decisive shot. The two German pilots fought in a masterly and courageous fashion and every S.E.5A was hit, but the result of such a one-sided contest was a foregone conclusion - the British fighters were led by the redoubtable Captain (later Major) James B. McCudden and his skill, together with that of Lieutenants Rhys Davids and Hoidge, added to their numerical advantage, gradually began to wear down the German pilots and first the Fokker and then the Albatros spiralled down out of control.
Douglass Whetton, writing in *RAF Flying Review*, February 1957.

Major James Thomas Byford McCudden VC DSO* MC MM is officially placed fourth in the roll of British and Empire aces with 57 confirmed victories which included 19 captured, 27 and 1 shared destroyed, 8 and 2 shared 'down out of control'. One of the first truly 'professional' airmen, who applied a scientific approach to air combat, McCudden took great pains over his guns, aircraft and tactics, dismissing choices of last resort such as deliberately crashing a plane into the enemy. Using his knowledge as a mechanic, he tuned his aircraft to give it an additional 4,000 feet altitude ceiling. This resulted in him specialising in carefully stalking high altitude reconnaissance aircraft, leading to an unsurpassed total of captured enemy aircraft (21 fell within Allied lines).

He was born in Gillingham, Kent on 28 March 1895 to ex-Sergeant-Major William H. McCudden and his wife Amelia. Two of his brothers Willie (killed in 1915) and John McCudden (killed in 1918) were also military pilots. He joined the Royal Engineers as a bugler in 1910, but after a flight with his brother Willie across Salisbury Plain requested transfer to the RFC, Military Wing, which was granted in 1913. He arrived in France on 13 August 1914 as a First Class Air Mechanic on 3 Squadron and was allowed to fly as an observer over the next few months. By the summer of 1915 he had reached the rank of Sergeant, had made a few flights as an observer and was gaining some piloting experience by strictly unofficial flights in a Morane Parasol. His first combat, as an observer, took place on 19 December 1915 and he was awarded the Croix de Guerre the following month. Late in January 1916 he was promoted Flight Sergeant and posted home for flying training at Gosport where he obtained his pilot's licence that April. He joined 20 Squadron as an NCO in June 1916 flying reconnaissance and escort flights in the F.E.2d from Clairmarais, near St. Omer. After just a month he soon switched to 29 Squadron flying DH-2 scouts. He made his first claim for an aircraft - a two-seater - on 6 September 1916. His DH.2 could just keep pace 400 yards behind an enemy two-seater in a slight dive, so he fired three drums of Lewis ammunition while in pursuit. Three days later, an Allied intelligence agent behind the German lines confirmed the victory. He was awarded the Military Medal on 1 October.

Sergeant McCudden and several of 29 Squadron encountered Jasta 2 and Leutnant Manfred von Richthofen in a prolonged dogfight on 27 December 1916. The Baron claimed a 'pusher' shot down during this fight and research seems to indicate it was McCudden's D.H.2 he claimed, although none of the 300 bullets fired by the Baron had even hit McCudden's machine and he returned safely to base. He was commissioned on 1 January 1917. He shot down an Albatros C-type on 6 February and a Roland C II on the 15th. His Military Cross was awarded the following day. He returned to England having claimed five air victories. During this spell, McCudden was twice involved with attempted intercepts of formations of bombers in a phase of Gotha Raids. In the second raid on 17 July 1917 on London, out of a defending force of 95 aircraft, McCudden alone was able to achieve sufficient altitude in his Pup to engage the enemy. Having insufficient ammunition, he was unable to make any significant impact. After a spell with 66 Squadron on Sopwith Pups, he was appointed as a flight commander with 56 Squadron, flying SE5as in mid 1917.

During the first half of 1917 he served with various training establishments and did a short 'refresher course' on 66 Squadron. At the end of July McCudden found himself at Estree Blanche, 56 Squadron's new home in France, researching current methods of flying with another of the Squadrons. He hit it off with Major Blomfield immediately and managed to make a patrol flying the S.E.5 for the first time, deciding that he should like to join his unit. By the middle of August the necessary moves had been made and McCudden joined 56 as 'B' Flight Commander. He had seven victories to his name and in the six months which he spent with 56, he raised that total to at least 57. Many of his victims fell after a long 'stalk'; he was an instinctive lone hunter and would wait patiently for the right moment to attack. He was also a sound patrol leader and his technical background led him to make a thorough study of his engine and guns and of the potentialities of enemy machines. [34]

On 23 September McCudden and his six S.E.5As of 'B' Flight were just on the point of engaging six Albatros Scouts away to the right, when they saw ahead of them, just above Poelcappelle, an S.E. half spinning down closely pursued by a silvery blue German triplane at very close range. It was an evening patrol and several members of 56 Squadron, including Arthur Rhys Davids and Cecil Lewis were patrolling. [35]

'The S.E. certainly looked very unhappy' wrote McCudden later, 'so we changed our minds about attacking the six V-strutters and went to the rescue of the unfortunate S.E. The Hun triplane was practically underneath our formation now and so down we dived at a colossal speed. I went to the right, Rhys Davids to the left and we got behind the triplane together. The German pilot saw us and turned in a most disconcertingly quick manner, not a climbing nor Immelmann turn, but a sort of flat half spin. By now the German triplane was in the middle of our formation and its handling was wonderful to behold. The pilot seemed to be firing at all of us simultaneously and although I got behind him a second time, I could hardly stay there for a second. His movements were so quick and uncertain that none of us could hold him in sight at all for any decisive time.

'I now got a good opportunity as he was coming towards me nose on and slightly underneath and had apparently not seen me. I dropped my nose, got him well in my sight and pressed both triggers. As soon as I fired up came his nose at me and I heard clack-clack-clack-clack, as his bullets passed close to me and through my wings. I distinctly noticed the red-yellow flashes from his parallel Spandau guns. As he flashed by me I caught a glimpse of a black head in the triplane with no hat on at all.

'By this time a red-nosed Albatros Scout [piloted by the ace Carl Menckhoff] had arrived and was apparently doing its best to guard the triplane's tail and it was well handled too. The formation of six Albatros Scouts which we were going to attack at first stayed above us and were prevented from diving on us by the arrival of a formation of SPADs, whose leader apparently appreciated our position and kept the six Albatroses otherwise engaged.

'The triplane was still circling round in the midst of six S.E.s, who were all firing at it as opportunity offered and at one time I noted the triplane in the apex of a cone of tracer bullets from at least five machines simultaneously and each machine had two guns.

'By now the fighting was very low and the red-nosed Albatros had gone down and out [36] but the triplane still remained. I had temporarily lost sight of the triplane whilst changing a drum of my Lewis gun and when I next saw him he was very low, still being engaged by an S.E. marked I, the pilot being Rhys Davids. I noticed that the triplane's movements were very erratic and then I saw him go into a fairly steep dive and so I continued to watch and then saw the triplane hit the ground and disappear into a thousand fragments, for it seemed to me that it literally went to powder. Strange to say, I was the only pilot who witnessed the triplane crash, for even Rhys Davids, who finally shot it down, did not see its end.

'It was now quite late, so we flew home to the aerodrome.'

McCudden was only one of a handful of people who had cause to lecture Rhys Davids about unnecessary risks and their consequences. During one of the first patrols Arthur was involved in an accident when he was supposed to be familiarizing himself with the local landscape. In an incident he blamed on the quality of his goggles he misjudged his landing and in the process of writing off his machine he also badly sprained his back. Without a plane to fly he found himself out of action for almost a month. Arthur would confess to his mother that once in the air he became a different man and that people could not understand the nature of aerial combat. His reckless bravery did not go unrewarded. Arthur continued to be successful and later received a bar to his MC.

After McCudden and his pilots had landed from the prolonged dogfight, the sole topic of conversation in the officers' mess was concerned with the possible identity of the German pilots and particularly that of the pilot of the Fokker Triplane, who had fought with particular brilliance and verve. Speculation had reached a height when a telegram arrived from Wing Headquarters. The wrecked Fokker Dr.I 103/17 had been found. Its dead pilot had worn the Boelke collar and the 'Ordre pour le Mérite' or the 'Blue Max' as it was widely known - it was the almost legendary Werner Voss. Scarcely twenty years of age, Werner Voss's rise to fame was little short of meteoric - his fighting career lasted barely ten months, but in that time he was to build up a score of forty-eight victories that placed him fourth in the roll of German aces and gain a place among the ranks of the finest fighter pilots of all time. Born in 1897, he first saw service in a cavalry regiment, a fact which resulted in his becoming known as the 'Hussar of Krefeld' but late in 1915, when still only eighteen years of age, he succeeded in transferring to the Imperial German Air Force, serving initially as an observer.

But the relatively passive occupation of flying up and down to observe the enemy's movements did not appeal to Voss's temperament and he soon applied for permission to train as a fighting pilot. He became a pilot in May 1916 and served his apprenticeship in Jagdstaffel 2 - the famous Boelke Staffel - in the late autumn of 1916. He had found his true metier for, a few weeks later on 27 November he made his first two 'kills' - a Nieuport Scout and a B.E.2c. A month passed before he could claim a further victim, but between 1 February and 24 March 1917 he accounted for no less than nineteen Allied aircraft - victories 102 to 120 in the official ' Game Book ' of Jagdstaffel 2 and in those four weeks he had risen from the large ranks of capable pilots to the small group of aces.. During the spring of 1917 he is believed to have served briefly with both Jasta 5 and Jasta 14. In July 1917, at the request of his friend Richthofen, Voss was posted to command Jasta 10 in Jagdgeschwader Nr. 1. During their lifetimes, Voss was second-ranking ace to Richthofen. A born flyer and fighter, he nevertheless lacked the leadership qualities of Richthofen and Hauptmann Rudolf Berthold the commanding officer of Jagdgeschwader Nr. 2. Voss was not only a courageous and highly skilled fighter pilot, he was a brilliant tactician and he foresaw the next move to be made by his antagonist before the enemy pilot had conceived it. During his spectacular career he flew several fighter types, but he will always be most closely associated with that supreme 'dogfighter,' Fokker's Dr.I Dreidecker. Anthony Fokker, in his book *The Flying Dutchman*, claimed subsequently that Voss gained his last twenty-two victories while flying aircraft of the Dr.I type, but this is extremely improbable, as it would suggest that Voss was flying a Dreidecker in April 1917 and although no official date is available, the famed Richthofen

Geschwader appears to have been the first unit to be re-equipped with Dr.I fighters in August 1917; von Richthofen gaining his first victory with this type on 2 September by destroying an R.E.8 and incidentally, bringing his personal score to sixty. It is possible however, that Voss was flying a Dr.I on 10 August 1917 when he gained his thirty-fifth victory.

In common with many other German pilots of this period, Werner Voss adopted distinctive markings for his mounts. These varied from aircraft to aircraft, but included a checker-board design on the fuselage accompanied by red wings and tail, an overall black finish with a white 'skull and crossbones' design either side of the fuselage, or, alternatively, a white heart surrounded by a wreath of leaves. One of his Albatros D.V scouts was pale green overall, while one of the Dr.Is, in which he scored his last dozen victories, had a face painted on the engine cowling. The Dr.I in which he was killed was not his usual machine, which was undergoing repair at the time.

Werner Voss certainly employed the Dr.I with devastating effect during the last weeks of his life, destroying a further fourteen aircraft. On 5 September 1917 during an engagement with a formation of Sopwith Pups, he sent one down for his fortieth victory and later the same day accounted for a Caudron bomber. Five days later, on 10 September, flying unaccompanied, he ran into a formation of three Sopwith Camels. Taking them completely by surprise, he sent one Camel down in flames with his first firing pass, made short work of a second Camel and then chased the remaining member of the unfortunate trio back over his own lines. Twenty minutes later he dived on an F.E.2d, which immediately broke up.

On the next day Voss destroyed two more Allied aircraft to bring his score to forty-seven, but his next victory on 23 September was to be his last. On that fateful day, after destroying a D.H.4, he rearmed and took off again, despite poor visibility, shortly after 18.00 hours and over the British lines he attacked a lone S.E.5A. The British fighter was soon in trouble, with Voss driving it eastwards towards the German lines. But above the Fokker Dr.I was Captain McCudden, leading the six S.E.5As of 'B' Flight, who was flying north to intercept a formation of six Albatros scouts. Seeing the S.E.5 in trouble, McCudden led his formation down on the silver-blue Fokker. McCudden banked to starboard and Lieutenant Rhys-Davids banked to port, but Werner Voss was too old a hand to be caught in this manner and allow himself to be boxed in. Leaving his victim, he whipped his triplane around sharply, turning to face his attackers and firing as he came, the first bursts from his Spandaus rippled through the wings of McCudden's S.E.5A. Simultaneously, a red-nosed Albatros D.V joined the one sided combat, its pilot, flying with skill second only to that of Voss himself, doing his best to guard the tail of the Fokker triplane.

The end of the combat is told by Lieutenant Rhys-Davids in his report:

'The red-nosed Albatros and the triplane fought magnificently. I got in several bursts at the triplane without apparent effect and twice placed a new drum on my Lewis gun. Eventually I got east of and slightly above the triplane and made for it, getting in a whole Lewis drum and a corresponding number of rounds from my Vickers. He made an attempt to turn in and we were so close that I was certain that we would collide. He passed my starboard wing by inches and went down. I zoomed and saw him next with his engine apparently out, gliding east. I dived again and got one shot out of my Vickers. I reloaded, keeping in the dive and got in another good burst, the triplane effecting a slight starboard turn, still going down. I had now overshot him, zoomed, but never saw him again.'

McCudden was the only pilot to see Werner Voss crash and wrote afterwards:

'As long as I live I shall never forget my admiration for that German pilot, who single-handed fought seven of us for ten minutes and also put some bullets through all of our machines. His flying was wonderful, his courage magnificent and in my opinion he was the bravest German airman whom it has been my privilege to see fight.

'We arrived back at the mess and at dinner the main topic was the wonderful fight. We all conjectured that the enemy pilot must be one of the enemy's best and we debated as to whether it was Richthofen or Wolff or Voss. The triplane fell in our lines and the next morning we had a wire from the Wing saying that the dead pilot was found wearing the Boelcke collar and his name was Werner Voss. He had the 'Ordre Pour le Mérite.'

'Rhys-Davids came in for a shower of congratulations and no one deserved them better, but as the boy himself said to me, 'Oh, if I could only have brought him down alive' and his remark was in agreement with my own thoughts.'

The remarkable career of Werner Voss was finished, but no finer and more fitting epitaph could have been written than those words of his enemy.

McCudden wrote that 'Nothing happened of interest that I am able to recall until the 27th, when I brought down my first German machine in our lines. I left the ground soon after lunch and very soon saw a Hun two-seater flying round over Houthoulst Forest, apparently ranging. Whilst waiting for a favourable opportunity I saw a SPAD attack this Hun and I saw the Hun twisting and swerving about with the French SPAD in pursuit and then suddenly the SPAD appeared to be hit and went down out of control. The Hun went off east a little and then came back, apparently very pleased at having shot the SPAD down.

'He now came to within reasonable distance of where I was waiting and after him I went. When I got to my two-seater position, the Hun was going due east and I fired a good burst from both guns until I had to turn sharply to the right to avoid colliding with the Hun. As I turned I saw the Hun gunner at a range of twenty yards with his gun central to the rear waiting to see which way I would turn, for he had seen me overtaking him too fast and knew that I should have to turn and as I did turn I saw him turn his gun and fire just four shots, each 'Cack, cack, cack, cack,' two bullets of which I distinctly felt hit my machine. I half rolled and got clear of him glanced round to see where he was.

'When I did see him he was in flames going down in a vertical dive, after which he went past the vertical and then onto his back, so that he was now falling towards our lines, into which he fell near St. Julien, although when I had shot him he was flying east.

'When the machine went beyond the vertical and onto its back, the enemy gunner either jumped or fell out and I saw him following the machine down, twirling round and round, all arms and legs, truly a ghastly sight. A queer thing happened; the enemy gunner fell into his own lines and the machine and the pilot in our lines.

'I flew back to my aerodrome very pleased, for it is the wish of most pilots to bring Germans down in our lines, so as to get souvenirs from the machine.

'The next morning, September 28th, I led my patrol over the lines at 11,000 feet over Boessinghe and before crossing the lines I saw a patrol of Albatroses going south over the Houthoulst Forest. I signalled to my patrol, who understood what I wanted and down went our noses and although I thought I was going down fairly slowly, my comrades afterwards said they were recording 180 mph to keep up with me. I picked out the Albatros who was on the east of this formation and opening fire at 200 yards, released my triggers about 50 yards short of the Albatros, whose left wings at once fell off and then the whole machine fell to pieces at about 9,000 feet. The enemy pilot also fell out and went down much quicker than the machine.

'I then flew onto the leader, who was still in front of me and having apparently seen me shoot his comrade he was very wide awake. Before I got to close range he had turned round and we now started to do the usual circling, each trying to get behind the other. Meanwhile, all my comrades were also busily engaged with their partners.

'My opponent and I continued to circle round from 8,000 feet down to 4.000 feet, when, as the German passed directly below me in the opposite direction, I did a steep Immelmann turn to get on his tail, but in doing so I lost a good deal of height and now I found the German above me. I continued to circle, but at last the German got behind me and commenced to shoot.

'We were now 2,000 feet over the Forest of Houthoulst and things for me did not look very cheerful, for I had been out manoeuvred by the German pilot and was now over a mile behind his lines. I continued to manoeuvre to prevent the Hun from shooting at an easy target and when we were down to about 1,000 feet I dived with engine on almost to the ground, intending to contour chase back at a few feet when the silly old Hun turned off east and flew away just at a time when things were looking rather black for me.

I heaved a sigh of relief as I recrossed the lines and then I went up to my rendezvous, to reform my patrol, but could not find them. So, after climbing up to 10,000 feet I flew towards Menin and found Barlow leading them miles east of the lines, with dozens of Huns west of them. I flew towards them and fired two recall signals and then they rejoined me, but there was nothing more that happened of interest to relate.

'This is peculiar. While the Hun who had outmanoeuvred me was engaging me, at about 2,000 feet, I happened to see one wing of the Hun whom I had shot to pieces floating down like a leaf quite near me, three minutes later.

'Our patrol time being over we flew back to our aerodrome and had breakfast and [Richard] Mayberry, who was also having breakfast when we trooped in, remarked that I was becoming expert at turning Huns out of their aeroplanes. We chatted over breakfast and found that Rhys-Davids and Barlow had each got a Hun out of the first formation whom we attacked, so out of the five we attacked only two went home.

The Hun who outmanoeuvred me was very good indeed, but I never have understood why he left me at a time when he could have most likely shot me down.'

Arthur Rhys Davids DSO MC and Bar had a hand in 25 victories before he disappeared flying East of Roulers on 27 October 1917. In the absence of McCudden he had been leading a patrol and in following him the rest of his flight had been distracted by an attack from the side. When they turned around he had gone. Arthur Rhys Davids was one month past his 20th birthday. His family hoped he had simply been caught and imprisoned and continued to write to him despite a message claiming he was dead that was dropped over British lines by the Germans. Arthur carried a book of poetry by William Blake with him into combat every day in case he was shot down and captured. The British Army declared Arthur Rhys Davids as having been killed in action on the date that he disappeared, on 18 March 1918. On the same day he was gazetted again, this time for the Voss victory, obtaining the Distinguished Service Order: 'For conspicuous gallantry and devotion to duty in bringing down nine enemy aircraft in nine weeks. He is a magnificent fighter, never failing to locate enemy aircraft and invariably attacking regardless of the numbers against him.' When Richard Mayberry died in 1918 their commanding officer wrote: 'He and Captain Ball and Lieutenant Rhys Davids did more harm to the morale of the German Flying Corps than any other fifteen pilots between them. They all, always, took on any odds. They were too brave and reckless.'

By 23 November 1917 McCudden had earned a Bar to his MC and his score stood at 20. Between that date and 31 December he destroyed at least a further 17 aircraft, four of them falling on 23 December. He repeated this quadruple victory on 16 February 1918, bringing his score to 51. On 25 February he destroyed his last victim, a Hannover CL III. He returned to England for an instructional tour. Shying away from this publicity, McCudden did not even tell his family of his attendance at Buckingham Palace on 6 April to receive his Victoria Cross from King George V. McCudden was also awarded his DSO and bar and a bar to his Military Cross at the same time. The citation for his Victoria Cross published in the London Gazette read:

'For most conspicuous bravery, exceptional perseverance and a very high devotion to duty, Captain McCudden has at the present time accounted for 54 enemy aeroplanes. Of these, 42 have been destroyed, 19 of them on our side of the lines. Only 12 out of the 54 have been driven down out of control. On two occasions, he had totally destroyed four two-seater enemy aeroplanes on the same day and on the last occasion all four machines were destroyed in the space of one hour and thirty minutes. While in his present squadron, he has participated in 78 offensive patrols and in nearly every case has been the leader. On at least 30 occasions, whilst with the same squadron, he has crossed the lines alone, either in pursuit or in quest of enemy aeroplanes. The following incidents are examples of the work he has done recently: on 23 December 1917, when leading his patrol, 8 enemy aeroplanes were attacked between 1430/1550 and of these 2 were shot down by Captain McCudden in our lines; on the morning of the same day, he left the ground at 1050 and encountered 4 enemy aeroplanes and of these he shot 2 down; on 30 January 1918, he, single-handed, attacked 5 enemy scouts, as a result of which 2 were destroyed. On this occasion, he only returned home when the enemy scouts had been driven far east; his Lewis gun ammunition was all finished and the belt of his Vickers gun had broken. As a patrol leader he has at all times shown the utmost gallantry and skill, not only in the manner in which he has attacked and destroyed the enemy, but in the way he has, during several aerial fights, protected the newer members of his flight, thus keeping down their casualties to a minimum. This officer is considered, by the record he has made, by his fearlessness and by the great service which he has rendered to his country, deserving of the very highest honour.'

Promoted to the rank of Major, while on leave in London he socialised a great deal with Edward 'Mick' Mannock. The friends ended up competing for the love of West End theatre dancer Teddie O'Neill, whom McCudden took on a joy ride. McCudden wished to return to the front, but because he was now a high-profile celebrity the Air Ministry was not keen. McCudden eventually won this discussion, but was reportedly turned down for command of 85 Squadron because of his lack of a 'public school education'; in other words, because of his relatively humble origins. A pilot on 85 Squadron at the time, Lieutenant John M. Grider, wrote in his diary: 'The General came over and had tea with us and asked who we wanted as CO. He wanted to send us McCudden but we don't want him. He gets the Huns by himself but he doesn't give anybody else a chance at them...We asked for Mickey Mannock who is a flight commander in 74 Squadron.'

On 8 July, now a Major and commanding officer designate of 60 Squadron RAF, McCudden collected his new Royal Aircraft Factory S.E.5a outside London and flew to Kent to spend the night with his family before flying to France. Next morning, before flying over the English Channel towards Boffles, over breakfast he handed his sister an envelope, which was subsequently found to contain all of his medals. With his six British medals and one French one, McCudden received more medals for gallantry than any other airman of British nationality serving in the First World War.[37] He landed at Auxi-le-Château to get directions from the RAF personnel stationed there. Shortly after take-off, the S.E.5a's engine failed, possibly due to a wrongly installed carburetor. McCudden committed the basic error of trying to turn back to land rather than proceeding straight on and the aircraft stalled on the turn and spun into the ground. The accident happened within sight of RAF personnel, who quickly drove over to render assistance. McCudden was found at the crash site with severe multiple injuries. He was taken to hospital where he died two hours later, without regaining consciousness. McCudden's remains were subsequently buried at the nearby Wavans war cemetery in the Pas de Calais. He was 23. His death occurred only two months after the death of German ace Manfred von Richthofen, whom some commented had been honoured with a longer and more elaborate funeral by the British.

Footnotes Chapter 13

34 *Air Facts and Feats: A Guinness Record of Aerospace Achievement,* compiled by Francis K. Mason and Martin C. Windrow (Guinness Superlatives Ltd 1970). Some of these stalking techniques are described in McCudden's autobiography, entitled Flying Fury - Five Years In the RFC.

35 Cecil Arthur Lewis MC (29 March 1898-27 January 1997) joined the RFC in 1915 after lying about his age. In 1916 he flew the Morane Parasol in combat with 3 Squadron and was awarded the Military Cross for his actions during the Battle of the Somme. Flying the S.E.5a with 56 Squadron, he was credited with eight victories during May and June 1917. Back in England, Lewis served with 44 and 61 Squadrons on Home Defence before returning to France in late 1918 with 152 night-fighter Squadron, flying the Sopwith Camel. He went on to co-found the BBC and enjoy a long career as a writer, notably of the aviation classic Sagittarius Rising (inspiration for the movie *Aces High*).

36 Menckhoff survived the engagement, as did all the British pilots.

37 Today all of McCudden's medals including his Victoria Cross are displayed at the Royal Engineers Museum in Chatham, alongside those of two of his brothers and his father. The original brass engraved grave plaque used, along with a wooden propeller are also displayed. The shattered windscreen from McCudden's crashed SE5a is preserved in the collection of the Imperial War Museum. The museum's collections also include McCudden's uniform 'maternity jacket' and a half-length portrait of McCudden by William Orpen. McCudden and two of his brothers are also memorialised on a panel on the Carlow Great War Memorial, Leighlinbridge Memorial Garden, Leighlinbridge, Co. Carlow, Ireland which notes also that their father was born in Carlow.

Chapter 14

The Circus

F. Suckling

F. Suckling joined the Army in April 1917, at eighteen years of age. He served in infantry training battalion for three months before becoming an officer cadet in Royal Flying Corps. He received his Commission in October 1917 and 'wings' as flying officer in March 1918. He went to France in April 1918 and served with 65 Squadron until October of the same year. From April to August 1918 he was engaged on the Somme front, chiefly against hostile fighting machines. He did his first 'show' before nineteen years of age. During August to October 1918 he was on the northern section of the front; his chief duty escorting bombers to Bruges and other Belgian towns. He returned to England for brief period of Home service, during which time the Armistice was signed. [38]

By the side of a cottage in an insignificant French village one morning in the spring of 1918, a group of khaki-clad figures stood gazing intently at a sheet of foolscap bearing a few typewritten names. By the cap and cut of the jacket, these lads, none of them more than nineteen years and all just from England, could be seen to belong to the Flying Corps and they were eagerly scanning the newest list of postings. One of them, by hurrying out from his billet immediately after breakfast, had been the first there and although he had been at the Pilots' Pool only two days, it was with intense satisfaction that he read: To 65 Squadron: Lieutenant Suckling. Lieutenant K. 'X seems to be having a thin time; that's ten new pilots in a week,' a voice remarked. 'Heaven help those two poor devils. They've got the 'Circus' on their front.' For a moment Lieutenant S. felt a tinge of dread; he had heard much of the 'Circus' of forty picked fighters, led by the redoubtable Richthofen and here was he - a mere child in matters of aerial warfare - to be pitted against the best pilots of the German Flying Corps.

About eleven o'clock that evening a tender came for the two 'unfortunates' and after a chilling ride which brought them ever nearer to the sound of big guns and a sky perpetually bright with their flashes, Suckling arrived at his squadron in the blackness of night that preceded dawn. War seemed far away when a few hours later, looking out from the tent flap, he found himself in a little wood where a bright sun made the dew on the green leaf-buds glisten and revealed patches of violets among the moss. The sight of these flowers brought to his mind a vivid picture of

Sussex woods and an English girl. It was her favourite flower!

At the end of a fortnight he was told to be ready to be one of three for a two hours' 'show' over the lines. As he gazed up at the blue sky, broken from time to time by drifting clouds, which the enemy well knew how to use as a hiding place, the young officer pondered over his first outing. There was his 'bus,' a scout which needed delicate handling and instruments which required occasional watching. He must keep a wary eye all round and at the same time look out for landmarks; he must also keep his place in formation and an eye on the leader's plane for the 'waggle' which should tell of hostile aircraft.

Once up aloft, all apprehension left him and the clear spring air acted as a tonic. The sense of adventure became uppermost. In a close triangle the machines climbed to gain height before crossing into enemy territory and after an hour's flying the planes of the front machine rocked.

Enemy! Another waggle, more violent! He looked in front... behind... above... and then over the side he saw them. A few hundred feet below cloud vapours were drifting across the sky and as the machines circled above a gap in the golden mist he could see an old R.E.8 lumbering along with three 'Tripes' buzzing round like hornets. Only the 'Circus' flew triplanes and here were three of them, their variegated colours turned into gold by the brilliance of the sun, playing about with one of the slowest machines then on the Front. Why didn't his leader dive into them and give him a chance of using his guns on a live target, instead of letting the unequal battle go on?

Suddenly across the sun shot some black specks and a flight of Camels streamed down on to the scene below. There was a mix-up of red and blue circles and black crosses and one machine went down in flames, but the three machines above flew straight on and finished their patrol. When they came down S. asked the leader why he had not taken them into it, for they had been in a good position and the numbers were even.'

Say, youngster, do you realize who they were? If we had mixed it, you would have been dead meat before now. They are not new hands! And I had seen our chaps - even if you hadn't!'

A few weeks afterwards he met the 'Circus' again, not three of them, but the whole bunch. For several days things had been quiet on the Front and the absence of hostile planes, which was attributed to a threatened offensive against the French south of Moreuil, had engendered a greater boldness in our young flying lads. Miles beyond the trenches they would fly, a few feet from the ground, bombing dumps and 'shooting up' anything moving. There was no opposition whatever until a certain Sunday in mid-June when, at a height of 15,000 feet, three of them had ventured about eight miles into the enemy's territory. The clear sky, the absence of noise beyond the hum of the engine, the apparent peace all round, made it seem really a day of rest. Once during the patrol I had noticed about a mile away and 1,000 feet below a large flight of machines. Since his arrival at the squadron he had learned how to identify all types of machines in the air and now, with the momentary thought 'Bristol Fighters,' he dismissed them from his mind. For a few minutes only!

Suddenly, without any preliminary waggle, the leader climbed sharply to the right. Suckling, flying on the right corner of the triangle, climbed at an even steeper angle to keep formation and what happened then was recorded as a series of blurred impressions. As he turned, the air was filled with tracer bullets and before he was on an even keel his partner on the left burst into flames, fell and went out. He had heard such happenings reported by others, but the quickness of it appalled him. There was by now no sign of his leader and coming straight at him was the 'Circus!' His mind, in a flash, remarked the bizarre appearance of these triplanes with the sun behind them; they resembled so many sets of empty bookshelves as they flew at him, the first a blood-red one. Only Richthofen flew a blood-red machine!

The air seemed alive with white-hot bullets passing over his head, beneath his wheels and even between his planes. Instinctively he pressed his gun controls; there was no time to use telescopic sights. He blazed away in a vain effort to stop these flaming specks which were streaming past like fiery hail and forgot that he had been told to fire always in short bursts. His guns stopped - jammed; the 'Circus' all round and he helpless at a height where the thin air made his controls slow to act. There was one thing he could do, dive - and the 'Tripes' could not dive steeply for long without a plane lifting off!

Pulling the joy-stick over to the right, he kicked the rudder bar hard with his right foot. Up and over came the nose of the little Camel, then down, down, engine full on. The pointer on his air-speed moved rapidly round 150, 170 and 200 and still he kept his nose down. Even as he had begun his dive he had seen four enemy machines dive out of the crowd and give chase. Could he go more steeply? He had heard of his own type of bus sometimes not coming out of a vertical dive. By this time the rush of cold air would have cooled his guns and he could scrap again, but one against four of Germany's best! A backward glance revealed the enemy beginning to flatten out and lose distance, so he himself flattened out. By the time he was out of the dive and had turned his machine back, only two of his attackers were at all near. He climbed after them, but instead of turning to fight they simply flew eastward. His own bus, built more for rapid manoeuvring than for great speed, was gradually outdistanced and all he could do was to fire a burst in farewell.

On his return home he found his flight leader awaiting him, unhurt.

'Gee, that was a warm two minutes,' the captain said.

'There were well over thirty of the blighters.'

Two minutes! To Suckling it had seemed a lifetime!

July came in and was very hot and in that part of the Front, both on the ground and in the blue, there was great activity. No longer did our young pilots seek adventure in threes or sixes; a 'squadron show' was now the rule. Every evening at 7 the whole of the eighteen machines went up together and as soon as they were high enough and formation was made, the three triangles, each of six machines, flew east in quest of trouble with the red sun behind them. Nor did it take much looking for. Invariably about the hour of 8, the 'Circus' was there, always waiting at the same spot and a perfect formation dive soon developed into a 'dog-fight.' It was then a case of every man for himself, singling out an enemy 'bus' and sticking to it until one or the other went down or ammunition gave out.

In the twilight of the evening our machines returned singly or in pairs; names were checked and the pilots gathered together by a hangar, looking out for those not yet in. Soon all but one were back and as long as light permitted them to discern anything moving in the sky, so long they stood there, cap, goggles and gloves in hand, just as they had climbed out of the cockpit. But something strange was happening and as the days wore on a gloom settled upon the squadron. Every night with unfailing regularity one of the lads did not return and this went on for the greater part of a fortnight. On no occasion had a Camel been seen to go down in flames or out of control. In the excitement of a 'dog-fight' this was to be expected, but there seemed something uncanny in the monotonous regularity with which just one failed to return. A less buoyant air was to be noticed among the pilots on the 'drome and in the mess and unconsciously everyone knew the unspoken question uppermost in every mind, 'Whose turn to-night?' Something had to be done and quickly.

One evening during the middle of that month, the men in the trenches must have looked up when they heard the roar of more than fifty English scouts crossing over like three great arrowheads. The boys in those machines that evening were feeling 'bucked,' for that self-same morning another squadron had met a section of the 'Circus' and satisfactorily disposed of ten of them. With this knowledge and no time to think of the nightly missing pilot, they sailed across to their evening tryst. Of the scrap that followed, one of the largest ever seen over the lines, one vivid picture remains to Suckling. He is on the tail of a small, fast German scout, barely 100 feet away and even while keeping an eye on it until he cannot fail to hit it, he is able to glimpse in the sky all round him countless specks of different sizes, wheeling, 'split hairing,' half-rolling, diving, at times spitting flame. To his right and just above him there are five balls of fire falling earthwards, a moment ago swiftly moving machines guided by living minds. As he watches, flames lick out of the side of a bus not far away; in a fraction of time it is consumed with fire and hurtles down, leaving streaks of flame behind. No shrieks are heard, the comfortable hum of the engine removes any sign that a boy has gone to his death.

His own quarry is doing its level best to escape, but, although actually faster, it is inferior at stunting and the crowd of eighty odd specks makes straight flying impossible. Suddenly; during a short dive, the German pilot's neck fills the ring in his sight. Suckling presses his gun controls. There is a short burst, a wisp of grey smoke, but before he can see the result the nose of his machine rises quickly and turns to the right. Why he never knew; he hears the rattle of machine guns and looking to his left, sees within a few feet a black bus with tiny white crosses on the upper plane streak past in a headlong dive. The pilot's head is turned towards him, so near that he would recognize him again. In a flash he pushes the joy-stick forward to the left, rudders in the same direction and dives after this new adversary. Comes another burst of bullets, more prolonged and an S.E.5, in a vertical dive, shoots between them and separates them. How he went into the fight, what else happened in it and the flight home, have gone from memory.

Back at the hangars, pilots related individual experiences and there was great satisfaction when it was clear that the Camels alone, apart from the other two squadrons, had accounted for eleven of the 'Circus.' But no one had destroyed a red machine. That honour fell to Brown on 209 on the following Sunday morning. [39] On the evening of the same day Suckling saw the dead body of the famous German pilot. As a doctor cut open the leather flying suit, Richthofen's underclothing was revealed - of the same blood-red colour as his triplane.

Footnotes Chapter 14

38   First published in 1930 under the imprint of Messrs J. M. Dent / Quoted in *On The Front Line: True World War I Stories* (Constable & Robinson Publishing Ltd 1997).

39   Richthofen's death on 21 April 1918 has been the subject of controversy ever since. He was flying a Fokker Dr I when he became engaged in a low-level combat with two Sopwith Camels of 209 Squadron RAF over Sailly-le-Sec. At one point the aircraft of 2nd Lieutenant W. R. May was flying at low altitude with Richthofen in pursuit and the aircraft of Captain A. Roy Brown DFC, behind the German; Brown opened fire in an attempt to save the inexperienced May from the enemy ace and Richthofen's triplane was then seen to break away and crash-land. Richthofen was found dead in his cockpit with a bullet wound in the chest. Brown was officially credited with his death, but prolonged research has failed to settle with any certainty whether the fatal shot was fired by Brown or by a member of an Australian Field Artillery battery which was putting up a considerable volume of small-arms fire at the time. Richthofen's 80th and last victim was 2nd Lieutenant D. G. Lewis, a Camel pilot on 3 Squadron RAF who was shot down, wounded and taken prisoner near Villers-Bretonneux the day before Richthofen's death.

The RAF credited Brown with shooting down the Red Baron, but it is now generally agreed that the bullet that hit Richthofen was fired from the ground. Richthofen died following an extremely serious and inevitably fatal chest wound from a single bullet, penetrating from the right armpit and resurfacing next to the left nipple. Brown's attack was from behind and above, and from Richthofen's left. Even more conclusively, Richthofen could not have continued his pursuit of May for as long as he did (up to two minutes) had this wound come from Brown's guns. Brown himself never spoke much about what happened that day, claiming, "There is no point in me commenting, as the evidence is already out there".

Many sources, including a 1998 article by Geoffrey Miller, a physician and historian of military medicine, and a 2003 U.S. Public Broadcasting Service documentary, have suggested that Sergeant Cedric Popkin was the person most likely to have killed Richthofen. Popkin was an anti-aircraft (AA) machine gunner with the Australian 24th Machine Gun Company, and was using a Vickers gun. He fired at Richthofen's aircraft on two occasions: first as the Baron was heading straight at his position, and then at long range from the right. Given the nature of Richthofen's wounds, Popkin was in a position to fire the fatal shot, when the pilot passed him for a second time, on the right. Some confusion has been caused by a letter that Popkin wrote, in 1935, to an Australian official historian. It stated Popkin's belief that he had fired the fatal shot as Richthofen flew straight at his position. However, in the latter respect, Popkin was incorrect: the bullet that caused the Baron's death came from the side.

A 2002 Discovery Channel documentary suggested that Gunner W. J. 'Snowy' Evans, a Lewis machine gunner with the 53rd Battery, 14th Field Artillery Brigade, Royal Australian Artillery is likely to have killed von Richthofen. However, Miller and the PBS documentary dismiss this theory, because of the angle from which Evans fired at Richthofen.

Other sources have suggested that Gunner Robert Buie (also of the 53rd Battery) may have fired the fatal shot. There is little support for this theory. Nevertheless, in 2007, a municipality in Sydney recognised Buie as the man who shot down Richthofen, placing a plaque near Buie's former home. Buie, who died in 1964, has never been officially recognised in any other way.

The commanding officer of No. 3 Squadron AFC, Major David Blake, initially suggested that Richthofen had been killed by the crew of one of his squadron's R.E.8s, which had also fought members of Richthofen's unit that afternoon. This claim was quickly discounted (if only because of the time factor) and withdrawn. Following an autopsy that he witnessed, Blake became a strong proponent of the view that an AA machine gunner had killed Richthofen.

Chapter 15

The Casualty

Reverend John H. W. Haswell[40]

Reverend J. H. Haswell enlisted as a private in the Royal Welch Fusiliers in 1916, becoming a corporal and in 1917 was commissioned in the Royal Flying Corps as second lieutenant. Promoted lieutenant in May 1918, he proceeded to France, serving there until May 1919 with the Royal Air Force. He became a missionary in West Africa (Primitive Methodist).

It happened over Ypres.

I was a member of a Royal Air Force unit, nineteen years of age. The infantryman was one in a tiny circle of pals, each circle but one wavelet in a huge-sea. His was a hard life - mud and blood and losing chums and ever conscious of being but a cog in a mighty and soulless machine. We, on the other hand, were neither wavelets nor cogs. We were *it*.

Our squadron was, like a battleship, a unit in itself and every individual was important. We were a small family of officers living in decent huts, partaking of decent meals, sleeping in, clean pyjamas and generally living in comfort for eighteen hours of the twenty-four. In the remaining six we might plunge into the welter of war in which the infantryman lived, but we did our particular job in a clean atmosphere in a clean way and when we killed or were killed it was done in that same inevitable and highly respectable manner.

The infantryman looked up from his rat hole and said, with his hair on end, that he wouldn't have our risky job for anything, while we looked down on his muddy wastes and said, 'Poor devils!' (Or words to that effect) and flew home to a hot dinner served on a clean tablecloth while he cut his fingers opening bully-beef tins.

The family were, of course, occasionally bereaved and we talked rather awkwardly at dinner and avoided each other's eyes and were relieved when, at the end of the meal, the OC briefly called us to silent remembrance. But coffee, smokes and piano quickly saved us from overmuch thought. When these bereavements became frequent, we had to receive others into the family and every few days there would arrive a number of strangers looking very self-conscious and humble, as well they might before us hardened warriors of two or three months' experience! Only a few hours after their arrival each one was instructed to report to a senior pilot and the process of initiation began. The observers had revision of the mysteries of maps, machine guns, cameras and many other strange things with which these poor benighted ones deal, while the pilots, to whose skill (or lack of it) the former entrust their lives, were told to memorize the map of the sector until they knew it better than anything else on earth and then were taken to 'have a look at the war.'

I was a senior pilot of about ten weeks' standing and to me there was detailed a new pilot, a youngster of about twenty-one (two years older than I!) and after a serious conversation on what London looked like when he left and what 'shows' were running at the time, we agreed to go and have a peep at the front line. My machine stood waiting; we put a couple of bombs in 'for luck,' and in a few minutes were heading eastward towards that horror of mud and waterlogged trenches.

We soon caught sight of the flooded area which had been the Yser Canal and then of that dark blotch called Ypres and being now about 10,000 feet up, I beckoned my 'pupil' to lean over from his seat behind me and shutting off the engine and falling into a glide, I pointed out to him the various beauty spots of the district, Ypres, Poperinghe, the Menin Road, etc, yelling the names at the top of my voice, lest the fierce wind should snatch them out of hearing. He nodded, glancing at his map and I saw with joy that he was keen.

For some little time we flew up and down the line (but keeping on our own side of it!), waved our hands to some kite-balloon folk who occupied lofty positions in a row behind Ypres, while at the same time I took the opportunity to indicate the cables mooring the balloons, for it is not wise to collide with them. Then came the second stage of the initiation - to go over the line and receive a baptism of fire from 'Archie,' the enemy anti-aircraft batteries. There is an art in this game. On a cloudy day one can hop in and out of the clouds, greatly to the annoyance of some Archie commander who, just when he has got range and direction and is about to let fly, finds that his bird has disappeared into a cloud. He fills that cloud with HE but his quarry emerges from another nearby with a gesture of derision which the gunners below may imagine, though cannot see. On a sunny day, Archie is up early, for he knows that aircraft will be silhouetted against a blue sky. Then the experienced pilot hops in and out of the sun, there being no clouds, while the Archie commander rubs his smarting eyes and uses strong words. Today favoured the latter game, which we played with zest for some little time. Then, having carefully spotted the AA position, we got it carefully on our bomb sights and sent our greetings in the form of the two bombs we had brought.

I was about to swing round and head for home and tea, when I espied a spot on the horizon towards the south-east. It might be an enemy raider coming to pounce on our helpless balloons, or it might be one of our own.

Anyway, we would see and pointing out my intention to my companion, we speeded off in pursuit. We were in luck! From far off the shape of the aircraft showed its alien origin and we began to prepare for chasing him home again. First I pressed the trigger of my forward gun, which loyally answered with a rapid 'Ta-ta-ta-ta,' a noise which, my companion told me afterwards, nearly made him jump overboard with fright. I had forgotten him and he had forgotten my front gun! Then quickly I beckoned him, quietened down the engine and shouted a series of instructions and as the engine roared out again, I heard a few rounds fired from his rear gun and knew that all was well.

The next minute we had come to grips with the enemy, a wicked looking single-seater, much lighter and faster than us and with every advantage except that his one gun fired only forwards, while, in addition to my similar gun, my companion had one on a swivel mounting which revolved easily and allowed him to fire in almost every direction. Our plan of campaign, therefore, was that I should manoeuvre the machine so as to keep the enemy in a position where he would be a good target for the rear gunner, who could give all his attention to firing. We circled round each other looking for an opening. Then I suddenly reversed my direction, bringing the other alongside us and within easy range where he would be simply raked from stem to stern, while his fixed forward gun pointed harmlessly away from us.

I waited to hear my companion's gun as he took advantage of the position, but not a sound came and the next fraction of a second I was swinging round for dear life with the 'Zip-zip!' of bullets round my ears. The second's delay had given the other the chance he wanted, for he was now under our tail out of reach of both of our guns and it was some seconds more before I could shake him off. However, I got him once more in a good position, waited for the sound of gun-fire, but again silence and again I dived desperately out of a stream of bullets. 'Fire, you fool!' I yelled, though not a word could reach him and I dare not turn round, while all the time the darting little wasp who seemed aware of my plight, came buzzing behind and resisted all my efforts to avoid him. There was only one thing left to do. I must try to fight him off with my forward gun and I turned to do so, when, wonder of wonders, I saw him fall into a steep dive and make for home, having seen a triangle of our machines appearing out of the blue. And now for an explanation from this idiot behind! I spun round angrily, but words were impossible. He was sitting there strapped as usual to his seat, but with his face a mass of blood, while his gun hung uselessly from its mounting! After a rapid spin to earth and a landing at the first favourable spot, he told me what had occurred. We had not been hit by Archie's shrapnel. I had seen him quite fit after that. The disaster had befallen him before we engaged in the air duel.

It was that silence after the first gun-test which should have told its tale. He had decided to test the gun-mounting also, but, being accustomed to the poorly kept machines at home, had expected to find it equally difficult to move. He had not thought that here on active service, where the space between life and death is measured in hundredth parts of a second; each mounting is kept thoroughly oiled and will spin round at a touch. Consequently he had seized the mounting, pulled it round quickly and the heavy gun, resenting such rough treatment, had revolved on its easy bearings and had smitten him violently over the head, knocking him out completely. Well might I have waited for the sound of his gun. He had not even been aware of the fight!

Footnotes Chapter 15

40   First published in 1930 under the imprint of Messrs J. M. Dent/Quoted in *On The Front Line: True World War I Stories* (Constable & Robinson Publishing Ltd 1997).

Chapter 16

1st Lieutenant George W. Puryear, USAS 95th Aero Squadron

In April 1917, after many diplomatic exchanges, Woodrow Wilson, then president of the United States declared his country at war with Germany. By October 1917 the first arrivals among the American troops were considered ready to take their place in the front line. The first offensive action by American troops was in the middle of February 1918 when American batteries took part in the artillery preparation for an attack by the French at the Butte du Mesnil. The 27th, 94th, 95th and the 147th Pursuit Squadrons in the 1st Pursuit Group became operational at the beginning of 1918. Although the 95th was the first to arrive in France, at the small village of Villeneuve-les-Vertus on 18 February, none of the pilots had training on the machine-guns, so the honour of being the first into action went to the 94th Squadron, later commanded by Captain Eddie Rickenbacker, which had as its emblem the famous 'Hat-in-the-Ring'.

Lieutenant George W Puryear, it is believed, was the first American officer to escape from captivity in Germany and a narrative of his experiences is one of vigour and youthful audacity. From the time of his capture, partly due to his own eagerness in a moment of success, he made it his aim to escape from the clutches of the Hun and in the face of tremendous obstacles he accomplished his purpose. On 14 July 1918, having completed his training in the United States, then at Issoudon and Cazeaux and having served for two months as a ferry pilot, he was ordered to join the 95th Aero Squadron of the 1st Pursuit Group. At that time the 95th was changing over from the Nieuport Type 28 machines to SPADs and on 18 July from the Saints aerodrome, Puryear made his first flight over the Chateau-Thierry sector. With a week of patrol experience behind him, he went up with four other SPAD Scouts to patrol the lines from Chateau-Thierry to Neuf-le-Chateau. It was a day of mist and rain, so thick that two of the machines turned back. The other three had an engagement with a German biplane machine, but Puryear ventured on alone in spite of the bad weather. The Hun observer was shot and the pilot forced into a landing. Puryear, in the enthusiasm of probable victory, followed the German plane down, shooting continuously and thinking himself in Allied territory he landed not far from the wrecked Hun.

As he taxied around the field in his plane he suddenly realised that he might be behind German lines, so he headed his machine round to face the long way of the field and prepared to take off. As he was running up into the wind the machine struck a ditch and nosed over. In the distance behind him and around him, machine-guns were snapping; overhead he saw the white puffs from the bursts of other aircraft barrage, but still he was undecided as to his location. He jumped from the cockpit of his own machine and hunted around for the other planes. The German pilot, in the meantime, had pulled his dead observer out of his aircraft and taken him away. By a gradual process of assessment Puryear became convinced that he was behind German lines and somewhere near machine-gun emplacements. The first man he saw was an unarmed German who accosted him in a friendly manner. As the man spoke French and wore no helmet, Puryear was suddenly taken with the idea that the man was an Italian. The American asked where he was. The Hun told him civilly the thing that he feared, namely that he was within German lines and asked him if he was an American officer. Puryear replied that he was, whereupon the German saluted him at attention. A crowd of Germans then began to gather about him from various sides (presumably a German observation balloon had telephoned, warning of his descent) and he was taken captive. He was conducted straight away to a house which was being used as an emergency hospital, where he was relieved of his flying suit, belt, goggles and other leather equipment except for his helmet, which was taken later and searched for firearms. During the search he chatted in English with the officer in charge. From this point he was put through a series of quizzes by intelligence officers who sought to enhance their knowledge of Allied aviation by every sort of question. Four different times he was quizzed and on each occasion in a separate office, but of all the questions the only one he considered to have any particular importance was the enquiry as to where his aerodrome was located.

After these inquisitions he was placed with two hundred prisoners (including two French officers) in a temporary concentration camp, where he was given his first German meal. The meal consisted of old German bread, soddy and stiff like a piece of bacon and so unappetising that he was unable to eat it although it was then about noon and he had had nothing but a cup of coffee since the time when he had tumbled out of bed in the morning and started from his aerodrome at five am. Thus he hungered until six o'clock in the evening when a German soldier in the guard house gave him some barley soup and some horse meat, which his fatigue from marching flavoured sufficiently for him to call it good. There was here a private who was a German-American, quite familiar with Broadway and Brooklyn Bridge. The Hun treated him quite well, but food was scarce and unappetising. That night, as he looked outside, he estimated his chances of getting away and though he did nothing at that time, he began to make his plans for escape which culminated in the bold venture of 6 October that opened the way to freedom.

The next morning he was taken along for an all-day march on a meal of so-called coffee, made from brown barley and some unappetising bread. Upon reaching another town he was engaged by a third in the series of German intelligence officers who, after questioning him, told him in English that he would now be conducted to his 'room and bath'. The 'room and bath' were found to be an old barn with an insufficient layer of straw gathered in one corner. Here he seated himself and fed himself jam and bread, a type of potato bread which Puryear characteristically referred to as a 'clod of dirt' and finally went to sleep with a chill creeping up his back.

The following day he joined a large detachment of prisoners which included 400 French and 80 British, mostly Hospital Corps men and 28 Americans who had been captured from the 26th and 42nd Divisions during the Château-Thierry fight. The march to Laon which followed was one fraught with discomfort and suffering for many of the men. Puryear, although still possessing his officer's suit with insignia, was lightly clad and during the night of the 28th would have suffered much but for the generosity of a British Hospital Corps soldier who gave him food and a blanket. To add to his difficulties his shoes wore through during the long tramp and his feet became sore. It was during this trip he first made the acquaintance of Adjutant Andre Conneau, a French pilot, with whom he was to make his first attempt to escape.

The treatment of the prisoners on this long trip was one to aggravate them and beat down the morale. On the way Puryear made friends with 1st Lieutenant Zenos Miller, who had been a pilot in the 27th Aero Squadron of his own group and with the following lieutenants: Willard Bushey, Crawford J. Ferguson, H. W. Shea and Oats. Between them the men continually complained, 'kicked', swore and precipitated arguments with the more conservative members of the group about their philosophy of accepting the hardships of war with equanimity. Around them the men saw German wounded lying without care, as if they were so many dead horses; a country savagely devastated by the wastes of war; British captive soldiers, starved, pale and unshaven, toiling for the Huns behind their lines, brutally discriminated against and a few solemn-looking French civilians. The atmosphere was anything but encouraging.

The next day, which was the third on starvation rations of soup and bread, they took a train into Germany, starting at five am and arriving next day at eleven pm at Rastatt, Baden, where they were quartered in an old fortress overnight and then inducted into the Friedrichsfeste camp. There they first received passable food, which came via the British Red Cross. This food was distributed, after being inspected and checked by the Germans, by an American prisoner designated to issue it according to his own methods. At this point they discovered that they were only 160 kilometres from the Swiss border; already strongly urged by a desire for freedom, Lieutenant Puryear made a mental calculation of the number of days' travel that would be necessary to carry him to the border in case he should escape. He estimated that he could do it in between seven and thirteen days.

On the following day he discovered an easy way to get out of the camp. The method, so far as the writer knows, still remains a secret in the minds of those who employed it. As Puryear gave this story to the interviewer prior to the Armistice, he desired to keep secret the means of escape in order that he might do nothing that would reveal to the Germans how a number of Americans had found their way out of Rastatt prison. Puryear decided to couple his chances with those of Conneau the Frenchman, who, he said, looked mean, hard and game enough to do anything and together they planned escape. Puryear depended upon Conneau, who appeared to have considerable knowledge of the country over which they were about to travel and the only preparations which he personally made were to borrow a substantial pair of shoes from a British captain to replace his own, which were in a very dilapidated condition.

On 5 August at 11.30 pm Puryear succeeded in making his escape unnoticed. He proceeded to a prearranged spot where he waited for an hour and a half, until after the next change of guard, when Conneau appeared. Together they started on their journey. The Frenchman had a map and compass which they used to guide them and a heavy French leather and fur coat which he loaned to Puryear from time to time to warm him. After a few hours they entered the Black Forest. At about two o'clock it started to rain and from that moment it seemed that the heavens never ceased to cast a deluge upon the fugitives. During three nights of travel there were about three hours when it was not raining hard. During the daytime they hid in the forest, resting on the Frenchmen's coat, trying to snatch moments of sleep, but no sooner would they fall asleep than it would start to rain and they would have to take the coat from under them and crouch beneath it, using it as shelter. The Frenchman was a true comrade and gave Puryear a full share of what he had. They finally invented the method of thatching themselves in for the day with branches leaning against a tree, a method which succeeded in turning away the rain. After resting by day they would start at 10.30 pm when darkness had fallen and travel onwards.

Conneau, however, was mistaken in his direction and bore too much to the west with the result that they found themselves on the second day still at the edge of the forest, with peasants working quite near them in the fields. Again, on the next night they erred and at three am on 8 August they came out on the banks of the Rhine. Realising that they were off course they took a small road southwards and just as they were intending to stop for the day at four am walked into a German sentry on duty. They knew the Rhine was well guarded with the more conservative members of the group about their philosophy of accepting the hardships of war with equanimity. Around them the men saw German wounded lying without care, as if they were so many dead horses; a country savagely devastated by the wastes of war; British captive soldiers, starved, pale and unshaven, toiling for the Huns behind their lines, brutally discriminated against and a few solemn-looking French civilians. The atmosphere was anything but encouraging.

The next day, which was the third on starvation rations of soup and bread, they took a train into Germany, starting at five am and arriving next day at eleven pm at Rastatt, Baden, where they were quartered in an old fortress overnight and then inducted into the Friedrichsfeste camp. There they first received passable food, which came via the British Red Cross. This food was distributed, after being inspected and checked by the Germans, by an American prisoner designated to issue it according to his own methods. At this point they discovered that they were only 160 kilometres from the Swiss border; already strongly urged by a desire for freedom, Puryear made a mental calculation of the number of days' travel that would be necessary to carry him to the border in case he should escape. He estimated that he could do it in between seven and thirteen days.

On the following day he discovered an easy way to get out of the camp. The method, so far as the writer knows, still remains a secret in the minds of those who employed it. As Puryear gave this story to the interviewer prior to the Armistice, he desired to keep secret the means of escape in order that he might do nothing that would reveal to the Germans how a number of Americans had found their

A Sopwith Camel of 208 Squadron RAF which crash-landed on a German support trench near Cherisy on 4 September 1918. The pilot was slightly injured. (IWM)

A crashed aircraft in trees above the trenches.

This aircraft made an undignified dive into a hangar.

RAF mechanics removing a Siddeley Puma engine from a damaged fuselage at No.2 Depot, Rang du Fliers-Verton near Etaples on 12 July 1918. (IWM)

F.E.2b two-seater.

D.H.4 day bombers of 'A' and 'B' Flights on 27 Squadron RFC at Serrny on 17 February 1918.
(IWM)

R.E.8s of 15 Squadron RFC lined up by a roadside near Albert on 25 March 1918 during the German offensive in Picardy.

Avro 504 B3189 around 1918-19.

HM Queen Mary accompanied by Major-General Hugh Trenchard (far right) inspecting a Bristol F.2b on a visit to St. Omer on 5 July 1917. Trenchard, (later Marshal of the Royal Air Force Lord Trenchard CB DSO) commanded the RFC in France from August 1915 until January 1918, when he became the first Chief of the Air Staff in the newly-created Air Ministry. He resigned in April 1918 following a disagreement with Lord Rothermere, the Secretary of State for Air and returned to France to command the Independent Bombing Force from June until the end of the war. 'Boom' Trenchard served again as Chief of the Air Staff from 1919 to 1929 and died in 1956.

An F.E.2b night bomber of 100 Squadron – the first British night bomber squadron - ready to leave an airfield in France on a raid.

SPAD SVII which became one of the most famous French fighters used in WWI. Large numbers also saw action with the RFC, US Army Air Service and Belgian and Italian air arms. The Spad took its name from the initials of the *Societé pour Aviation et ses Derives*, the French firm which originally designed and manufactured the type.

F.E.2b built by G & J. Weir Ltd.

RFC Armourers at work loading bombs.

RFC pilots pose for the camera in front of an Avro 504K.

Freddie West VC.

Freddie West (right) as an observer on 3 Squadron RFC in 1917 with his pilot, Lieutenant Edgar Golding.

Leutnant Werner Voss, credited with 48 victories between 27 November 1916 and 23 September 1917. Voss became commander of Jasta 10 in the 'Richthofen Jagdgeschwader' at the end of July 1917. On 23 September 1917, flying a Fokker DrI triplane, Voss fought virtually alone for some ten minutes against six SE5as on 56 Squadron, led by James McCudden, before being shot down by 2nd Lieutenant Arthur Percival Foley Rhys-Davids.

Rittmeister Manfred von Richthofen (left) with pilots of Jagdstaffel 5 in March 1918.

The SPAD XIII was a favourite mount of the American contingent on the Western Front. Second Lieutenant Frank Luke Jr, of the 27th Aero Squadron, flew SPAD XIII fighters to score 21 aerial victories in just seventeen days. He finished as the second top American ace to Captain 'Eddie' Rickenbacker, last CO of 94th Aero Squadron who achieved most of his record 26 confirmed kills in a SPAD SXIII.

Opposite page: German troops watch an observation balloon being tethered on the Western Front. Balloons were a favourite target of 'Balloon Buster' Frank Luke.

S.E.5a-equipped American unit on the Western Front. The American Air Service had no indigenous aircraft of their own and used French and British aircraft.

Louis Arbon Strange DSO MC DFC..

Flight Sub-Lieutenant Reginald
Alexander John Warneford of 1
Squadron RNAS. He was flying a
Morane-Saulnier Parasol from
Dunkirk on the night of 6/7 June
1915 when he destroyed Zeppelin
LZ37, the first airship to be shot
down. Warneford returned safely
to base after making a forced
landing to repair a broken fuel
line. He was informed the
following evening that he had
been awarded the Victoria Cross.

An RAF padre conducts a Sunday morning service from the gunner's cockpit of an F.E.2b night bomber at No.2 Aeroplane Supply Depot in France on 1 September 1918.

way out of Rastatt prison. Puryear decided to couple his chances with those of Conneau the Frenchman, who, he said, looked mean, hard and game enough to do anything and together they planned escape. Puryear depended upon Conneau, who appeared to have considerable knowledge of the country over which they were about to travel and the only preparations which he personally made were to borrow a substantial pair of shoes from a British captain to replace his own, which were in a very dilapidated condition.

On 5 August at 11.30 pm Puryear succeeded in making his escape unnoticed. He proceeded to a prearranged spot where he waited for an hour and a half, until after the next change of guard, when Conneau appeared. Together they started on their journey. The Frenchman had a map and compass which they used to guide them and a heavy French leather and fur coat which he loaned to Puryear from time to time to warm him. After a few hours they entered the Black Forest. At about two o'clock it started to rain and from that moment it seemed that the heavens never ceased to cast a deluge upon the fugitives. During three nights of travel there were about three hours when it was not raining hard. During the daytime they hid in the forest, resting on the Frenchmen's coat, trying to snatch moments of sleep, but no sooner would they fall asleep than it would start to rain and they would have to take the coat from under them and crouch beneath it, using it as shelter. The Frenchman was a true comrade and gave Puryear a full share of what he had. They finally invented the method of thatching themselves in for the day with branches leaning against a tree, a method which succeeded in turning away the rain. After resting by day they would start at 10.30 pm when darkness had fallen and travel onwards.

Conneau however, was mistaken in his direction and bore too much to the west with the result that they found themselves on the second day still at the edge of the forest, with peasants working quite near them in the fields. Again, on the next night they erred and at three am on 8 August they came out on the banks of the Rhine. Realising that they were off course they took a small road southwards and just as they were intending to stop for the day at four am walked into a German sentry on duty. They knew the Rhine was well guarded and the troop concentrations thick and they were so fatigued and discouraged that they made no attempt to run from the guard. The Hun turned them into the guard house, where they were equipped with blankets and passed a good night in rest. They found that they had been captured 50 kilometres from Rastatt and now, after being rudely thrust into cells for a night's rest at Kehl, they were to be sent straight back to Rastatt. Without any quiz or trial they were sent into confinement for five nights before being transferred to Rastatt.

Puryear was searched and relieved of his helmet. This left him without a hat. The commanding officer of the camp questioned him closely as to his escape and Puryear disclosed everything except the means he had used to get out. Within a short time he was sent with fifteen other American officers to Landshut, Bavaria, where he was assigned to the old castle on the hill north-east of the town which had been set aside as a concentration prison for American aviation officers. There were eighteen of them there, ten of whom were Major Harry M. Brown and his pilots and observers of the 96th Aero Squadron, who had been captured on 10 July after an unsuccessful bombing expedition in thick weather. The newly arrived captives were quarantined and inoculated for cholera, typhoid and smallpox.

The food there was good but meagre. They received meat once a day and white flour twice a week, occasionally pancakes and although the Red Cross food was excellent they found it scarce. There were no special facilities for entertainment and the days dragged. Under such conditions the minds of the officers often turned towards the chance of escape, but it was now 240 kilometres to the Swiss border and this, combined with the approach of autumn and its cold nights, was strong persuasion against attempts to escape.

It was a congenial group, however. Among the officers who were there were 1st Lieutenant Carlisle 'Dusty' Rhodes, also of the 95th Aero Squadron, who had been reported dead but had come down in a vrille in Germany, unhurt; Lieutenants H. F. Wardle, Herbert Smith, James E. Lewis and George Ratterman and Captain James Norman Hall, who had previously been reported dead and was the first American officer captured by the Germans. To pass away the time the men played cards and an occasional package from home received through the Red Cross added to the comfort of all. The commanding officer of the prison camp was reported by Puryear as being one of the worst of the Huns, a man of mean disposition who 'bawled them out' in German every day by the clock, had their shoes taken away every night at eight pm and counted them in their beds with the guard. In spite of this some of the officers planned an escape. They succeeded in getting out by cutting through the wooden wall, but they were recaptured.

Puryear's mind was still bent on escape, but he was wiser than to attempt it here. He applied, therefore, for a transfer to the prison at Villengen. There was in the employment of the Germans a civilian by the name of Pasteur, who had been married to an American girl and who owned property in New York. He was apparently the intermediary between the prisoners and the Germans and carefully reminded them: 'I am a German, be careful what you say.' Through this individual Puryear made his application for transfer early in September. Major Brown was also transferred. Another lieutenant who had a hole cut through his wall preferred to remain and take his chances of escape. 1st Lieutenant Carlisle Rhodes, who was in the group that had left Landshut, pretended that he was sick and escaped from the train; when Puryear actually became ill, he got no sympathy and nothing but 'hell' from the guards. Lieutenant Rhodes was later recaptured.

Puryear and the party, after two days in stuffy cars - during which time the German guards exercised the strictest rules, forcing them to keep their shoes off, giving them no food for one and a half days and allowing them to go to the toilet only once every five hours - arrived at Villengen. This was a new American officers' camp, fair according to the general standard, but better than others as it developed. It was 15 September when they arrived. The food supplied by the Red Cross was good and the clothing sufficient.

After four or five days Puryear was informed by an interpreter that he had some good news for him. The news was that he was entitled to fourteen days' solitary confinement for his previous escape and since he had served only five of the days he would be given the pleasure of nine more days in jail. Between 20 and 29 September he languished in a six feet by twelve feet cell with nothing but a bed, table and chair, with a small window above him which let in a few rays of the sun.

He was released on the 29th and by 6 October he had escaped from the camp.

In the interim he did considerable figuring. It was 36 kilometres in a direct line to the Swiss border, but to the point to which he later tramped and crossed into Switzerland it was 65 kilometres and he estimated that he must have tramped a hundred kilometres in order to reach it. But to return to the plans for escape. The Americans had determined upon concerted action and decided that they would select a night and all attempt to escape from the camp at several points at the same time. Two of them were in such a hurry that eleven others altered their plans and agreed to the same night rather than have their own chances spoiled by the special measures of discipline which which would follow any one attempt. They waited for three nights for plans to develop before making the dash for freedom. Puryear had equipped himself with a hand-drawn map, made by a fellow captive and a small compass purchased from a Russian officer at a price of one sack of coffee, one box of Red Cross meat, one package of hard-tack and an OD army shirt, the total of which looked like a million dollars to the Russian.

The men had carefully studied the defences of the camp. The barracks were located in an enclosure of about 800 by 200 metres, which was surrounded by a high board fence peaked with barbed wire. Outside that was a wire fence and still further on, a ditch set with barbed-wire entanglements. The main wire fence was about nine feet tall and on the inside iron hooks were fastened, intended to prevent persons from climbing over it. Both inside and outside the camp powerful electric lights and posts of guards of about one hundred German soldiers, men of some age and limited vigour, were set over the 200 Russians and 77 Americans confined there.

On the night of 6 October thirteen Americans were waiting impatiently, bent on escape. At 11.15 pm the lights flickered and went out (they had been short-circuited by an accomplice who had thrown chains across the wires at a prearranged signal). Apparently there had been some suspicion among the Germans, who were prepared for the trouble; nevertheless, the Americans made their rush from four different points of the camp. Three of the men, including Puryear, had posted themselves in a barracks window on the south side. As the lights went out they pulled from the window its iron grating, which in advance had been carefully cut with a file and Puryear jumped through to the ground. They had already constructed a fourteen-foot ladder from bed slats, the rungs of which had been fastened in place with wire in the absence of screws. Puryear pulled the ladder through the window and placed it against the fence while Lieutenant Ticknor, a fellow captive, braced it at the bottom. By climbing to the top of this ladder it was possible to jump and clear the main fence, the low fence and the barbed-wire ditch in one leap.

It was a starlit night, but dark. As Puryear scrambled up the ladder it squeaked and aroused the suspicion of the guard who was but ten steps away. 'Halt!' the German guard cried. Puryear was at the top of the ladder. 'Halt!' came the warning cry again. The American jumped, got to his feet and dodged behind a tree four paces away, but the guard had seen him. A second guard was approaching about thirty paces away. Puryear figured that he could not keep one tree between himself and two guards for very long, but a desire to play fair and to still leave a chance for his accomplice, who had not yet jumped from the ladder, made him remain a moment in his place of hiding. Suddenly he ran past but eight feet from the guard.

The stolid German followed his instructions and challenged him twice before shooting. The first time the fugitive was three steps away; by the time he could shout again Puryear was ten paces beyond and running a zigzag course. The German fired and missed. Another shot from the other guard. The bullet whizzed by him in the darkness. On he sped until at length, just as both guns fired again, he stumbled into a ditch which in the excitement he had forgotten about.

'Forgetting about that ditch probably saved my life,' said Puryear later. 'The Hun thought he had winged me and immediately turned towards the others who were breaking out on every side. There were all kinds of excitement; guns were firing and men were shouting. I heard two more shots behind me and kept on running until my breath gave out about a quarter of a mile away. I went to a prearranged spot where we were to meet and waited for fifteen minutes, during which time there were about fifty shots exchanged, I should judge. No one came, so I got down on my knees, prayed for luck and started off.'

In his travels towards Switzerland Puryear used the tiny compass which he had received from the Russian. Realising that he would be travelling by night and that it would be difficult to get his directions in the dark he had contrived to make the compass points visible by scraping the phosphorescent material from the face of his wrist watch and applying it to the compass needle. By this means he was able to travel in the dark and still keep himself constantly appraised of his direction. Frequently he heard Germans approaching on the road, whereupon he would step off and into the woods to avoid them, as he was travelling in Russian coat and cap which formed a distinctive silhouette against the sky. One man, who caught him unawares, spoke to him in passing and Puryear replied Gute Nachf in his best German.

The journey to the border was without unusual incident. On the night of Thursday, 10 October, he came out south of Walshut about eleven pm. Believing he was near the Swiss border, he climbed the mountain to assure himself, having seen a picture of the town. The only element between him and freedom was the Rhine. It was only 200 metres across but the current was flowing at a speed of several miles an hour and Puryear had not been in water for two years. He selected a point near a bend where the current would assist in carrying him to the other shore. Then he went into the woods, stripped off all garments but his underclothes and breeches and gradually crept down to the bank, shedding a garment every few feet. At 5.30 in the morning he sprang into the river and swam it. It was about a fifteen-minute job, but the swift current was so great that eddies and whirlpools pushed him about and very nearly exhausted him before he reached the other side. He crept up the bank, stared back into Germany and cursed it. Several peasants approached, took him into their home and gave him food and clothing and he was later assisted by the American Red Cross.

Puryear was the first American officer to escape from Germany according to available records, but was in fact preceded by three days by an American private. In general he regarded his treatment in Germany as fair. Men were paid sixty marks a month by the German government, but had to spend fifty-two of this for mess and with the balance they could buy only two mugs of poor German beer.

'It was an experience,' said he, 'which I am glad I had, but would not go through again voluntarily.'

Chapter 17

1st Lieutenant J. D. Fuller Jr (pilot), USAS. 2nd Lieutenant Virgil Brookhart (observer), USAS. 135th Aero Squadron

On the morning of 12 September, which marked the beginning of the Ste. Mihiel drive, Lieutenants Fuller and Brookhart set out from their aerodrome near Toul on a mission for reglage of artillery fire in the vicinity of Mont Sec. The weather was quite unfavourable owing to low, hanging fog and the south-west wind. At a height of 1,500 feet they encountered thick clouds and after five minutes' progress in a west-to-east direction they became temporarily swallowed up in the clouds. By chasing holes in the clouds they managed to catch glimpses of the various towns over which they were passing. Though this presented some difficulties, since it was their first flight together over the lines, they identified Nancy and then found themselves over Thiaucourt (west).

They were having such difficulties that they decided to abandon their mission and started south-west with the Ourches aerodrome as a goal. Climbing to 10,000 feet, they proceeded for about half an hour in what they believed to be a south-easterly direction. When they came down they found they were over a range of mountains and later discovered they had been near Mulhausen. They could see trenches as they neared the ground and therefore ascended again and proceeded for some time toward the south-west, as they believed and again came down to find themselves over the frontline trenches. It became apparent to them that a fairly strong wind was blowing them off their intended course. The wind at that time was westerly and since they had been heading south-west, they concluded that the wind had been forcing them in a southerly direction and at the same time sweeping them constantly with an eastward inclination towards the Swiss border.

Finally they flew below the clouds again and finding that they had left the trenches behind them they landed. Peasants and soldiers appeared from all directions and as the country looked strange they took off again with the intention of rising, but the motor died and they were forced to stop and land a second time. People crowded about them. They were not sure just what the trouble was with the motor, but as they had started to rise after the first landing, the Swiss soldiers had fired upon them and they believed that a bullet had torn the jacket of the motor thus rendering it useless.

The inquiry showed that they were only 600 metres from the border in one of the projections of Switzerland into French territory and they believed that had they been able to proceed for a few moments longer they would have landed in French territory. The Swiss authorities took charge of the two men and sent them to Berne and thence to Lucerne. There they were informed of their rights: they could either go free on parole or go to prison. It appears from the statements of both men that they were much chagrined over their internment and realising that they could not escape while on parole owing to the responsibility of the United States government to surrender them if they broke leave of honour they preferred to take their chances of escape. Fuller, in particular, stated to the writer that he did not fancy the prospect of being interned in Switzerland for the period of the war and therefore decided to take his chances in prison with the prospect of escape.

It was agreed, therefore, that Brookhart would go to the hotel at Lucerne on parole, while Fuller would enter the military prison at Andermatt near the St. Gotthard Tunnel, where he would reconnoitre the prison, study the chances of escape and communicate his plans by code in letters to his comrade. It was planned that ultimately Brookhart would also come to the prison and they would escape together.

It happened, however, that by the time Fuller was able to make any substantial plans for escape the prospect of the signing of the Armistice was at hand. Having received no word from his comrade, Fuller decided to make his own escape single-handed. He was on the fourth floor of the prison. Near his cell was a toilet, from which opened a window overlooking the ground below. To this toilet he was ordinarily accompanied by a guard. He made it his habit to stay in the toilet room longer and longer each day, so that his delay on the night of the escape would not excite any suspicion. The night he chose, in early November, was dark and foggy. He cut his bed sheet into seven strips, which he tied together. These he tucked about his waist, beneath his pyjamas. Immediately upon entering the toilet he fastened one end of the bed-sheet rope to the window sill and the other end to his waist. Just as he commenced to let himself down the guard knocked on the door. At the third floor the improvised rope broke and he fell a distance of 30 feet, plunging on to his head and arms. He was severely cut about the face and rendered temporarily unconscious. He recovered consciousness, however, before anyone discovered him and although lame and sore, he attempted to follow the course of escape which he had mapped out in advance. By careful work he managed to evade the two sentries at the mouth of the tunnel, but in making his way along he lost his candle and matches, on which he had depended to guide himself through the thick fog. As he was coming out of the tunnel he was caught between two sentries, who halted him, took charge of him and turned him over to the authorities. For more than a week he was confined to bed, recovering from the injuries he sustained in his fall. Later he was released upon the signing of the Armistice.

Chapter 18

2nd Lieutenant Oscar Mandell, USAS. 148th Pursuit Squadron

Lieutenant Mandell, while serving with the 148th Pursuit Squadron on the British Front, was shot down by ground fire and captured by the Germans. On the morning of 2 September 1918 he started from the aerodrome at Remesnil with four other machines for an offensive patrol over the lines. There was considerable ground haze with clouds at 2,000 feet. After patrolling for half an hour they observed a flight of SE.5 machines ground-strafing further along the lines and nearby a patrol of Fokkers. Meanwhile, the American formation had split up in the fog, but they hung around waiting to jump the Fokkers in case they should attack the Allied planes. Finally they got into a fight. Mandell shot down one plane and was immediately attacked by two others from the clouds. They got above and he could not out-climb them into the clouds. He spent fifteen minutes zigzagging around in a circle until ground fire shot up his machine and stopped his engine. He came down seven kilometres beyond the lines, crashing through some telegraph wires.

Two German infantry officers engaged him in conversation. They finally took him to dinner where they sat him down to good food and a bottle of wine and treated him courteously. He was then taken to the regimental commandant, in whose office he waited three hours until one of the German guards bade him, 'Stand up for an officer!' He looked at him and laughed. He was walked to the rear for six hours, but was stopped for a quiz by intelligence officers at three different places. His fatigue and hunger gave the Huns an advantage over him, which they sought to use as a means of prising from him information about Allied aircraft. They would order a fine meal, place it before him and then try to get him to talk. When he refused to reveal his country's secrets, they would remove the meal.

Altogether, Mandell made five attempts to escape and although none of them was ultimately successful, his persistence and courage constantly kept the Huns on the jump. After two days at Sewarde, where he received good treatment, he was sent to Conde, which was the scene of his first escape. With a British officer by the name of Donaldson (Donaldson was in fact an American officer attached to a British squadron) he climbed through a window and dropped fifteen feet to the ground. They travelled rapidly and soon made their getaway to the lines. En route, about three am one morning, they came across a Hun aerodrome located at La Sentinel, south of Valenciennes. They were suddenly struck with the notion of trying to take out one of the German machines and flying it back to their own territory. They found an Albatros two-seater in a tent hangar and immediately got to work to get it out. They cut the canvas the full length and stripped it from the machine, but they were confronted by the difficulty of releasing it from a series of cables which held it in place. They worked on the job for nearly an hour, tinkering with the machine, loading and testing the guns and preparing the ship for an immediate flight when they were able to release her.

By this time, however, it was four am and a German mechanic came whistling down the field, ready to start his morning task of preparing the machine for the Hun fliers. The bold captives still had one cable to remove from the wheel of the landing gear. Upon seeing the mechanic, Mandell, who spoke good German, remarked in that tongue, 'Ah, here is someone to help us.' The mechanic, however, was not to be disarmed by the remark and immediately became suspicious. The two officers approached him and Donaldson seized him by the arms. The Hun struggled in the grasp of his enemy and pulled a small dagger from its scabbard. Mandell now jumped into the conflict and tripped the Hun, but could not prevent him from jabbing Donaldson in the back with the dagger. The German jumped up with an agile movement and started down the field for help. The officers knew better than to pursue him after the first five steps and mad their getaway.

'It was a damn shame,' said Mandell 'for we had the machine all trimmed up and the gun all set and we were going to run the ship up and down that aerodrome and clean out the whole bunch. As it was, we made a getaway.'

The officers hurried along and got through the German lines to the edge of the water where the Germans had inundated the land in the Douai salient. They were about to swim the overflowing river, after six days in an energetic pursuit of safety, when a German patrol came along. They laid down in the dark and prayed for luck. Luck was in the air, but it went to the Germans, who nearly stumbled over them. They were recaptured, sent back to Fresnes court-martialled and given fourteen days' solitary confinement. They were now attacked by another intelligence officer, who discussed the war in its larger aspects and informed Mandell that Germany was preparing to send a delegation to Japan to procure her assistance in case the United States became troublesome.

On 26 September Mandell escaped again with four others. Three of then started towards the Belgian border, but Mandell, in company with a British corporal made for Holland. They swapped their flying clothes with the French and Belgians, who entertained him royally and secreted them by night. But again luck was on the other side and as they were passing over the Dutch border they were intercepted.

Then Mandell was sent to Aachen, where he spent four days, then to Karlsruhe for three weeks, then to Landshut, where he left on 15 November for the officers' camp at Villengen. After three days there he was released and came back through Switzerland, where the trainload of American prisoners received a wonderful reception.

The three other attempts at escape were very unsuccessful compared to the first two. In the interim he used to keep a little compass in preparation for future attempts and when searched would carry it in his mouth. Regarding treatment, he stated that although he was occasionally subjected to insults, it was on the whole pretty good. Red Cross food and packages of Red Cross gifts were received frequently.

American 2nd Lieutenant J. O. Donaldson, attached to 32 Squadron RAF was taken as prisoner to Douai and kept one night, but due to the heavy shelling by the British he was transferred the next day to a temporary prison at Conde. During the evening another American pilot was brought to the prison camp. This American, Lieutenant Mandell and I escaped that night by jumping out of the second-storey window of the prison and walking through the town. After walking all night and about two hours before daybreak, we came to a new German airdrome. After making sure that there were no guards guarding this airdrome, Lieutenant Mandell and I attempted to steal a machine. After about two hours' work we managed to get a machine almost entirely out of its hangar, but finally had to take the whole hangar down to get the machine clear. Just as we were about to start the machine, a German came out for early-morning flying. We immediately got into a tussle with him and during the tussle he stabbed me in the back and slashed up Lieutenant Mandell's clothing quite a good deal, but did not touch him and we finally hit him on the head with a big electric lamp and ran across the airdrome.

We were not followed and at the first French house we asked them to take us in. They dressed my wounds for me and gave us food for two days. At the end of the second day, German soldiers were to be billeted in this house, so we had to move on and although my wound was quite stiff, after once getting on my feet I could walk all right. After a number of adventures and being halted by sentries about eight or nine times (but due to Mandell being able to speak German, he answered the sentinels as if he were a German officer passing and we passed safely), on 9 September we passed through all the German front-line trenches and stayed in a shell hole in front of their front lines all day. We could see the English guns firing from where we were.

Between us and the English lines there was a small stream dammed up at one end by the Germans. That night, on trying to wade across the stream, we found it too deep and came back and we were taking off our clothes to swim the stream when we were caught by a German wiring party on the front of their front line. They carried us back to Battalion Headquarters. The German NCO who captured us was recommended by the battalion commander for an Iron Cross for catching us. After going through Division Headquarters, Corps Headquarters and Army Headquarters we were finally taken to Valenciennes. We were turned over to our old prison, but the guard refused to take us. Apparently they were afraid we would try and escape again, so they sent us to another prison across the street, where we were placed on bread and water for fourteen days.

On the eleventh day Mandell and I started to think of a means of escape. The only way we could get out of the building below was by passing through the roof. At the end of three days we had a hole sufficiently large for a man to pass through and on the same day two other Americans came into the camp, Lieutenants T. E. Tillingham and R. A. Anderson. That night all four American officers and one British NCO, Corporal George Rodgers, crawled through the hole in the roof, down into the courtyard, over a wall on the other side, swam the canal and set out across country for the Holland border. We travelled for eight days, travelling in the night and sleeping in the daytime, getting food from friendly Belgians.

On the eighth day we struck Brussels and met some rich Belgians who could speak English. Here we were supplied with civilian clothes, maps and other little details that helped us on our journey. After staying two days in Brussels and looking over the airdromes, but finding them too closely guarded to take a machine, we went out across country again to the Holland border. About twenty days from the time we left the prison we struck the Holland border. After reaching the border we were unable to cross for nine days. A friendly Belgian supplied us with insulated wire cutters and also told us the exact location of the electric wire. Two days later we crawled up within 10 yards of the wire, but due to the bright sunlight we had to be very slow. It took us three hours to crawl to the edge of the wire and as soon as the sentinel had come to the edge of his beat and went down the other end, we went up and cut the three lower strands of the electric wire. As soon the sparks had ceased to come out of the wire, we ran across the wire and at the same time the German sentinel yelled and Lieutenant Tillingham claims he fired a shot.

In Holland we proceeded to Rotterdam and from Rotterdam to Le Havre and from Le Havre back to England again. The total time we were in Belgium was about twenty-eight days. Two of the others, Corporal Rodgers and Lieutenant Mandell, departed from us at Brussels so only three of us escaped into Holland. The other two, we believe, are still somewhere in Belgium (dated 11 November 1918).

Chapter 19

2nd Lieutenant Howard C. Knotts, USAS. 17th Aero Squadron

Lieutenant Knotts was a pilot in the 17th Aero Squadron attached to the 15th Wing, Royal Air Force, British Expeditionary Forces and was stationed at the time he was captured near the town of Sombrin, France (Pas de Calais). He was detailed for a ground-strafing expedition and left the airdrome at about one o'clock in the afternoon of 14 October 1918 in a Sopwith Camel Scout. The engine of his machine was damaged by machine-gun fire and he was obliged to descend near Colombes. He purposely descended at the point which he selected for the reason that it was within the zone of concentrated artillery fire, which he knew would soon damage his machine, making it unfit for further use. At that time he had nothing at his disposal to destroy it; therefore, he did not descend into the zone of safety, which he could otherwise have reached with ease. This point was three or four kilometres beyond the enemy lines in their territory. He then planned the best manner in which to reach the British lines and attempted the practically impossible feat of negotiating the Allied shell-fire. He waited for available opportunities between shell bursts and walked and ran from point to point towards the Allied lines, even crossing the enemy lines into no-man's land where he discovered a sunken road, eight or ten feet deep, running first east and west and then turning parallel to the lines north and south. In accomplishing this portion of the flight he was continually sniped at and two bullets penetrated his flying boots, he then carefully reconnoitred and attempted to find a place of safety where he could await nightfall. He discovered a shallow parallel dugout in the side of the sunken road whose partition had partly fallen in, making it possible to creep from one to the other, as will appear.

Knotts entered the first of these parallel dugouts, hoping to hide there until nightfall and then cross over to the British lines. He had, however, been discovered in his flight and noticed soon after he entered the first one a German non-commissioned officer approaching to take him. This German soldier had apparently noticed him enter the first dugout and he looked cautiously into that one, but in the meantime Knotts had succeeded in creeping over into the other one. He immediately jumped upon the

German soldier, who had pulled his pistol and in the succeeding encounter which developed for the possession of the automatic, the German soldier accidentally killed himself with his own pistol. Other Germans, however, had witnessed the struggle and there ensued a pistol duel between Knotts, armed with the dead German's automatic which still held eight or nine bullets and four or five Germans similarly armed.

In this encounter Knotts was overpowered by five Germans dropping down from the elevated side of the sunken road upon him in his awkward position. These soldiers stripped him immediately of his flying boots, flying insignia, watch, Sam Browne belt and ring and a guard of two of them marched him at pistol point to a lieutenant assembling a company in the line. This march was made over shell-shot country strewn with fragments of barbed wire, sharp stones and the usual severe and devastated conditions of a shell-shot country, without shoes, from 3.30 in the afternoon until approximately six in the evening. His feet became torn and swollen on the march so that later he was severely blood-poisoned in one foot and the calf of the leg, the ankle having been slightly wounded by a machine-gun bullet when he was shot down.

He was immediately marched in charge of a guard of soldiers to Divisional Headquarters, seven kilometres away. There were signs and other evidence that indicated that this was possibly the 33rd German Division. Here a German captain, who could not talk English, attempted to interview him, an attempt which failed. Then he was interviewed by a poor interpreter, but Knotts refused to talk. It should be stated here that he had in his possession a flat purse with his identity card and about one hundred and forty francs in notes and a deposit slip from a British bank, which the Germans had overlooked in the examination of his clothes. He carried nothing else. With the money which he retained in his possession he managed to bribe his German guard to purchase a pair of well-worn shoes for him. During this interview he was threatened and browbeaten by his interviewer who insisted that he must have carried secret papers and a British flying map, which they particularly wanted to find.

At approximately 6.30 pm he was marched by one mounted uhlan,[41] sometimes at the point of a revolver and at other times when the guard was changed at the point of a set lance, until approximately three o'clock in the morning without any food from the time of his capture. At this time he reached Maresches, France. His march was accomplished by four reliefs of guard and was made unnecessarily long because of its circuitous-ness. Knotts was particularly familiar with this country and is able to state precisely his eastern route which led to the outskirts of Valenciennes and thence south-east to the town of Maresches, where Corps Headquarters for that Front was located. He is unable to state which corps this was. Here he was taken to the Hotel de Ville and ushered into the presence of a brigadier-general who was in bed. This officer could speak a little English and insisted on Knotts answering certain questions which would identify his unit. He also insisted that he must have secret documents and a map. Knotts replied to this general but gave him no information whatever. This so incensed him that he peremptorily ended the interview and ordered Knotts to be taken to an intelligence officer. This was promptly done. The corps intelligence officer was in the same building. He spoke English fluently. Knotts was here searched again and his pocket book, which was the only thing he carried in his clothing, was discovered. This interview was as futile as the other.

During the interview Knotts had noticed plenty of food and hot tea at hand and although he was asked if he had eaten, he was denied any of it. From here he was taken to the quarters of non-commissioned officers. They were in a state of carousal and desired to prove to him that they had plenty of food, with the result that he had an excellent meal contributed to by many of the soldiers from their own rations. Here he got good treatment for the rest of the night, a comfortable bunk being improvised. Knotts discovered that this guard comprised Prussian Guard troops (this fact might serve to identify the corps). He slept until eight o'clock in the morning.

At that time he was roused and began a march which lasted until three o'clock in the afternoon with an uhlan guard, in a circuitous route which he can identify. He reached St Cast in the vicinity of Bavai at the end of the march. During this march the Germans gave him no food whatever, but a beggar at the roadside gave him a hot baked potato and an apple. At the end of the march he was placed in a typical loft on the second floor of a building filled with German soldier prisoners confined there for mutiny. Knotts was able to state here as a matter of interest that there were approximately one hundred of these soldier prisoners in his building and that practically every available building in the town had large numbers of such mutinous soldiers. It appears that there were so many of these soldiers mutinying daily that it would have been futile to shoot them as fast as they came in.

By this time Knotts' feet were in a frightful condition; moreover, he was hungry. The Germans gave him no rations or medical attention, but one of the prisoners who proved to be sympathetic shared his rations and gave him some salve or grease and bandages which he applied to his feet with considerable benefit. He was imprisoned in that loft for the rest of that day, all that night and the whole of the next day and night. There were no sanitary conveniences. The place appeared to be free from vermin, however. No attention was paid to him during this time.

In the meantime, five former Australian prisoners who had attempted escape were recaptured and brought to this same loft, from which they, in company with Knotts, were escorted by an uhlan guard to the town of Bavai the next day, approximately five kilometres away. That afternoon they entrained aboard flat cars loaded with airplanes. The flat car that Knotts was on was loaded with new Fokker monoplane fuselages. None of the other prisoners was on this car, but there was a German sentry aboard. The wings of these planes were in the car behind with the five Australian prisoners. As the ride lasted until after midnight, it became pitch dark. The guard had been informed of Knotts' condition and paid very little attention to him, permitting him to move freely about the flat car. During his journey he watched for an opportunity and climbed successively into the cockpits of each of the three Fokkers and succeeded in breaking one of the main cross-bracing struts in each of the fuselages, thus completely crippling the three machines under the very nose of the German guard. Food had been given to the six prisoners, consisting of a can of bully beef and a loaf of bread, but Knotts was not permitted to mingle with the other prisoners on the car behind and as they carried the bully beef he was unable to obtain any of it. He ate the loaf of bread, which was all the food he had until the end of his journey.

At Peruwelz, Belgium, they detrained and were marched to a supposed main collecting station (Stallelager), but this camp had been moved further back due to the rapid advance of the British and Knotts and the five other prisoners were taken to the railroad station where they spent the night. They proceeded to Mons, Belgium, the next day. No food was provided for this journey. This portion of the trip was made on regular passenger train. Mons was reached that afternoon. From there the six prisoners were marched into the town to an ancient nunnery which had been converted into a collecting station at which there were approximately 200 British enlisted men, six British officers and one American officer. [42]

Here Knotts was separated in a small room with the other officers, the living conditions being fairly good. No bunks or blankets were provided, but the room was comfortably heated by a coal stove with fuel enough provided for a continuous fire. Here the meals were three in number each day. The morning and night meals comprised plenty of German coffee and black bread and the noon meal was served by Belgian Red Cross workers provided with food by the American Food Commission. This was the fifth day of Knotts' imprisonment and the first day he was permitted to wash. The Belgian Red Cross were permitted to provide the prisoners with a towel, soap, toothbrush and a package of dentifrice. The sanitary conditions were good.

During this four-day stay, Knotts was taken each day to the quarters of a German Air Service officer who was a flight commander. He had breakfast with him each morning. He told him that his name was Schroeder and there were evidences that led Knotts to believe that this was his real name. This man later proved to be extremely familiar with the personnel, operating conditions and losses particularly of two American squadrons on the British Front and of American officers with British squadrons on the Front - hence Knotts' information concerning officers reported missing or dead which might otherwise be impossible to obtain. He describes this man as about 5 feet 7inches in height, weighing about 145lb, with dark brown hair appearing black in the dim light. He was in the habit of wearing his hair as we associate generally with Germans, that is, unparted and close-cropped both sides with the top brushed straight up and the crown graduated to an inch in length, but it is possible that in civilian life or at present he wears his hair differently, as it appeared from a picture he showed to Knotts, taken before the war, which showed his hair long and brushed back from the forehead. It was a side-view portrait and did not show whether the hair was parted.

This man could not have been over thirty years of age. His eyes were dark and flashing. His complexion was sallow. His nose was aquiline. He was always smooth-shaven in the presence of Knotts. His teeth were white and apparently sound. He could speak perfect English. Whether or not he had lived in the United States is not known to Knotts. He habitually wore a German second lieutenant's uniform with the brevet of an observer and eventually a pilot, but, as is customary in the German Air Service, he still wore the observer's brevet. He wore the ribbon of the 2nd Class Iron Cross and the ribbon of either the State of Bavaria or the State of Hanover on the left breast and he wore the 1st Class Iron Cross in the usual position, left-hand side below the belt. The state ribbon was yellow and black mounted with gilded-metal crossed sabres. Knotts believes that he must have been a second lieutenant as he stated and appeared to be, for the reason that in many conversations he exhibited chagrin at never having been promoted, notwithstanding meritorious service, as was evidenced by his decorations and many conclusive remarks.

Lieutenant Schroeder's flight was stationed in the vicinity of Mons at this time. He told Knotts that he had served in the German Air Service in Russia during this war. He also asked Knotts whether he had heard of a German flying officer who had flown over the lines in a French machine, disguised as a Frenchman, landing upon a British airdrome and had taken luncheon with the officers from a British aero squadron. Knotts believed he mentioned the number of the squadron, but inasmuch as he had never heard the story before and considered it fantastic he has forgotten the number, if it was mentioned. This officer also gave Knotts valuable information concerning the graves of two American flying officers, 1st Lieutenant Lloyd Hamilton and Lieutenant Gerald Thomas. Hamilton's grave is north of Lagicourt which is NE of Bapaume in northern France. Thomas fell from a height of 6,000 feet in flames and was completely burned before reaching the ground. Knotts saw this personally on 22 September, so there will be burnt remnants of the machine still there. Knotts was never able to visit these graves, but feels sure that the information given him is correct because it corresponds with known information. It will be found upon visiting these graves that Hamilton's machine was burnt up. Portions of the machine will undoubtedly be found nearby, according to Schroeder. He had complete information concerning all American flying officers with the British who had been taken prisoner and also those who had been killed. This is proven because many facts that were related to him by Schroeder at this time previously unknown to Knotts have been verified by Knotts since his return to the American forces. He had a portfolio with him containing the names and full particulars concerning the status of all American fliers then with the British, or who had been taken prisoner, killed or wounded by the Germans and many others not with the British.

Knotts was not taken to this officer in any sense to be interviewed, but merely through his courtesy. He told Knotts that it was a hobby of his to know everything possible concerning American flying officers and that he was not an intelligence officer; but this assertion would of course be proved untrue if his own statement that he was the German flying officer who had flown in a French officer's uniform to a British airdrome for the sole purpose of obtaining information was correct. Knotts knew nothing else concerning this officer which would be of value to identify him, except that his flight was a two-seater flight comprising various types of machines. He told Knotts that he had one Hannover, two LVGs, two Albatros two-seaters and one Halberstadt. This officer, being a flight commander, was given considerable licence off-duty and lived comfortably in a small, well-furnished house on the edge of the town of Mons, approximately two miles away from the collecting station. Knotts was conducted to this house and returned by a guard for breakfasts during his stay there. He believes that if this officer could be identified and interviewed it would be of the greatest service to complete the investigation of data not now known concerning many of our officers reported missing or killed within the German lines whose graves are known only to him, so far as Knotts knows, unless it be shown that he was really an intelligence officer, in which case it is probable that this data was also forwarded to the German Intelligence Bureau Archives.

At the end of four days' stay here, all the prisoners were moved with the exception of Knotts and the two British boys permanently retained there as cooks since March. Knotts was then transferred to a different room upstairs. Learning from the cook boys that the place was now guarded by a single sentry and as his room was clumsily locked, he watched for a favourable opportunity that evening and escaped. Having become fairly well acquainted with the general directions during his visits to the house of Schroeder and having learned of the advance of the Allied lines to a point he thought he could reach by night marches, he struck out in that direction. He was favoured by rain and fog and walked fully fifteen kilometres before dawn, hiding himself in a clump of bushes. Soon after daylight he shifted his position to a better point of vantage, commanding a view of the main road which he had been following that night and was soon taken prisoner by a German non-commissioned officer into whose arms he almost stepped.

He was promptly returned to the collecting station and interrogated again in the same room from which he had escaped, this time better guarded. He remained here two days longer, during which time several prisoners came in and then was taken to Soignies where he joined the original group of prisoners from the collecting station at Mons, then in a permanent prison camp known as 'English Prison Camp #19' (Englander Geflagen Lager #19). This was a reprisal camp and never a permanent station for very long and was kept just behind the lines at all times, moving back as the lines moved back, locating in factory towns where buildings that were big enough to accommodate 1,500 prisoners could be found. The one selected here was formerly a tannery. Knotts learned that this was a reprisal camp from the many statements of prisoners who were so informed by the German guard. These prisoners were principally Australians and Canadians who were reputed by the Germans to habitually take no prisoners.

There were 1,500 men at this reprisal camp at Soignies, 800 of whom were housed in a building where the officers were also kept. The sanitary conditions were indescribably vile and in fact continued so from that time on. The food conditions were also intolerable. The meagre rations were weakening and there was no medical attendance. There was but one so-called doctor there for these 800 men, who was actually one of the prisoners, a British stretcher-bearer who knew only the rudiments of first aid and nothing about medicine and surgery. Sicknesses of many different kinds developed. The great majority of the prisoners had dysentery. At night the men were obliged to relieve themselves in the yard or court for exercise, an enclosed space approximately ninety feet square. They begged for permission to dig their own latrines, a request which was denied them. The stench was nauseating and permeated through the tannery. Many of the prisoners died. No bunks were provided so prisoners slept on the floor packed in like sardines, bodies touching. All the prisoners had body lice. Knotts killed 167 of them from his own undershirt one morning and about the same number that same afternoon. He states that it was impossible to kill them as fast as they propagated. No means whatsoever for cleaning the clothes were provided.

All this lack of sanitation was unnecessary, for in the town where the camp was progressively located there was always plenty of available German medical skill. At one place the Germans were even preparing to take over the building in which the prisoners were located for a local German military hospital, but no medical assistance was given to the prisoners, even here. At one time Knotts, together with Lieutenant Avery (the other American officer) and the British officers were placed in the meanest, darkest, most unsanitary, damp, cold, unventilated room available in the prison building, for the reason that they refused to sign paroles, the sole advantage of which appeared to have been the promise of a bath. This illustrates well and typically the habitual and inhuman denial of common, civilised, sanitary amenities which were always available to alleviate in some slight manner the miseries of the prisoners.

As a result of this intolerable and weakening treatment which he received in prison from the day of his capture until the early part of November, Knotts' wound became gangrenous and worse until his release on 15 November, at which time he was wholly unable to walk. This state of affairs was preposterous because it could have been avoided from merely elementary assistance and sanitary attention on the part of a doctor whose services could easily have been obtained.

From the time of his incarceration in Soignies until 15 November, Knotts and the other prisoners were frequently marched, as has been stated above, always retreating further and further from the original frontier as it moved back. During these progressive marches the prisoners became weaker and weaker, some of them daily being unable to walk. They had to drag heavy wagons containing the plunder and equipment of a great variety of kinds and one light military wagon containing food. Twenty-five men were detailed to drag one of these wagons. Sometimes some of the prisoners collapsed and were placed aboard the very carts they were assigned to drag. Their fellows gladly undertook the burden of this additional load. At one place the prisoners managed to obtain a carriage in some unknown manner and dragged these prostrate prisoners into it. The guard was often very brutal. The food wagon contained rations sufficient for every one of the prisoners, but the full ration was never issued, as was later proved. An inspection of the large remaining food stock upon the fourth day of the march, for which five days' rations were loaded into the food wagon, showed nearly half of the issued food remaining. This inspection was personally made by Knotts. On 15 November, the day of his release, none of the remaining food was given to the prisoners, their inhuman guards claiming that they needed it for their journey back to Germany.

From 11 November on there were many evidences of laxity in the German guard towards the prisoners and mutiny towards their own officers. As they proceeded along the road the prisoners passed many German troops, abandoned by their higher officers. They encountered no higher-ranking officer than an Oberleutnant. These troops were flying the red flag.

On the last day of imprisonment the group of prisoners with Knotts numbered only 150 to 200. The last day's march was from Maransart, Belgium, to Boucet. The place of their intended release was Holland. They intended to entrain at Liege, five days' march from Maransart. The prisoners were kept off the main roads to avoid encountering the many passing detachments of troops. On the fourth day's march only a half day's rations were issued in the morning, comprising one loaf of bread for seven men - nothing else. At Boucet the prisoners were released without food or guidance. They were in a country plundered, ruined and terrorised, without resources, were too weak to march further and were left in a local hospital. Five are known to have died owing to their frightful condition. This place was 30 kilometres from Liege, 70 kilometres from the nearest town of Holland (Maasterlink). Brussels was 10 kilometres away. The advancing Allied army was 120 kilometres away (8 or 10 days' march). An English captain took back 150 enlisted men and some British officers to the town of Hurmat, 2 kilometres away. Others left for an unknown route.

Knotts and eight British officers, pitifully weak from their inhuman treatment at the hands of their captors, begged to remain in the barn of the chateau. The owner of the chateau was a Belgian, the burgomeister of the town of Boucet and his wife proved to be of the noblest type of womanhood: sympathetic, humane, generous and courteous. It is believed only just that her gracious assistance to an American officer in distress be recognised officially by a letter of appreciation from the military authorities. It is believed by Knotts that a similar appreciation has already been sent by the British military authorities in acknowledgement of her generosity and ministrations to the five British officers housed at her home with him. The name of this woman is Madame Stanislas Seny Oury.

Here Knotts and the five British officers with him were cared for, nursed and fed just as if they were in their own homes. All the available local medical treatment was provided. Madame Seny herself nursed Knotts and it must be understood that for three or four days after these officers were taken into her home the Germans were going by there and some ten German officers and 900 enlisted men were being quartered each night in her chateau and barns, so this care was given to the officers at the expense of having the livestock and the provisions of the farm plundered and stolen by the Germans.

During this time, Knotts and the five British officers had been quartered in the service portion of the barn where heating, bathing and delousing facilities were provided and also a clean change of under and outer clothing. The only reason these officers were not taken into the chateau proper, as was done afterwards, was because each night of the German evacuation so many German officers were quartered in the house that hardly adequate sleeping accommodations were left for the Seny family itself. After the last of the Germans had gone these officers were taken into the house and were treated as esteemed guests.

No Allied troops came through this vicinity except one French division and that offered practically no transportation facilities to the prisoners. It did offer them, however, the advantages of the French military post, which was so slow that it brought no immediate results. After a period of three weeks all the British officers had recovered and started back to their army, which was then only 30 kilometres away, but Knotts was still unable to walk any great distance and was obliged to stay on until word was conveyed by letter carried by the gardener of Madame Seny to the American section of the Permanent Allied Armistice Commission. The commanding officer was Major-General Charles Pdiodes, American Expeditionary Forces. The day after the letter reached Major-General Rhodes, he sent a car with Captain White of the US Medical Services to Boucet so that Knotts was able to report for duty to the American Section of the Armistice Commission on 9 December 1918.

During his sojourn here he was given skilful medical attention. On 14 December Knotts was ordered to report back to the 16th American Aero Squadron through the commanding general of the Third Army Wing Headquarters, which were believed to be then at Coblenz. It was known that Knotts would be obliged to collect his personal belongings left at the squadron and probably be obliged to go immediately after that to a hospital before he was completely restored to health. He proceeded in compliance with his orders to Coblenz, but found that the army commander, Third Army, was at Hayson. Here he received verbal orders which sent him to report to the Army Air Service commander stationed at that time at Treves (Trier), with which order he complied, reaching General Mitchell's office on 15 December 1918. From here he was ordered to proceed to Toul where he reported to his squadron, which moved the next day from Toul to Colombey-les-Belles. Knotts was immediately sent to Camp Hospital #5 at Bariesy-la-Sete. Here he was obliged to remain for six weeks and on 26 January 1919 he left the hospital to receive orders for transportation to the United States, which will be issued as soon as he has completed the special duty for which he was ordered to these headquarters.

Footnotes Chapter 19

41 A member of a body of lancers first employed in the Polish army and later in West European armies. From the Turkish word, ōlan which means 'young man'.

42 This American officer was Lieutenant Walter Avery of the 148th Aero Squadron, attached to the same British wing and operating on the same front as the 17th, Knotts' squadron.

Chapter 20

1st Lieutenant Charles R. Codman, USAS. 96th Aero Squadron

Second Lieutenant Charles R. Codman, a pilot of the 96th Aero Squadron, was taken prisoner while on a daylight bombing expedition over Conflans on 16 September 1918. A flight of seven machines started on this expedition, but all but four fell out of the formation before crossing the lines. The remaining four aircraft bombed Conflans, but on the return trip were met by a flight of twenty-four German pursuit planes. Three of the aircraft were shot down in flames while Codman and his observer, 2nd Lieutenant Stewart McDowell, were brought down out of control with one aileron, the rudder and half of the elevator shot off. Both officers were wounded, McDowell seriously and Codman slightly. Codman stated that he shot down three of the enemy aircraft before his machine was brought down and this awaited confirmation from the statements of three French aviators, also prisoners, who witnessed the fight (the pilots were from the French Squadron C-46).

Codman's aircraft came down in a spiral and crashed in a field near Conflans, in which there were many German soldiers. The aircraft was immediately surrounded. There was no opportunity to set it on fire. The Germans gave first aid to McDowell and he was taken to hospital. Codman was taken to some barracks in a small town near Conflans. From there he was taken by touring car to an intelligence officer in the neighbourhood of Longuyon. There he was questioned for about three hours. Much wine was brought out. No force was used and the intelligence officer was most polite. Next morning he was taken to Mont Medy, a prisoners' camp, where he was placed in solitary confinement for three days and from there he was sent to Rastatt near Karlsruhe and after three weeks at Rastatt was sent to Karlsruhe itself.

In the latter town he spent two nights in the famous 'Dictaphone Hotel' where he was kept with thirty or forty other aviation prisoners, about ten of whom were Americans. Later he was removed to the regular prison camp at Karlsruhe, where he received good treatment and where he stayed about a week. He was then taken to the aviation officers' prison at Landshut, Bavaria. He was allowed to send one postal card on the first and tenth of each month and a letter on the fifteenth and twenty-fifth. In addition he could send all the picture postcards he desired and many photographic cards were given to him and the other prisoners as a sort of advertisement for the camp - largely pictures of prisoners drinking or playing games. At Landshut he was inoculated against cholera, typhus and smallpox. He depended almost entirely on the Red Cross for food and had plenty of that. Newspapers were at hand every day.

On 7 November, a revolution occurred in Bavaria and most of the guards were taken away. The revolution, however, was a quiet affair, consisting largely of a political change while King Ludwig was imprisoned in his castle. Herr Kurt Eisner, a poet and socialist editor in Munich, was made President of the Republic of Bavaria. The revolution lasted only about two hours. Everything had been planned in advance and many of the old regime officials retained their jobs. There was no saluting of officers in the streets.

Relative to other officers in the camp, the Americans were favoured. Lieutenant Codman stated that this was considered by American prisoners as propaganda for American goodwill after the war. Bavarians disliked the Prussians very much. Treatment at the camp was very good and the food was fairly good, the food situation in Bavaria being better than in other parts of Germany. No rubber or leather goods were to be had. Twenty-four American officers (flying) and a few each of the artillery and infantry were housed in Transnitz Castle, where they were well quartered.

The Armistice came as a relief to the German people of the vicinity, but they were bitter regarding the conditions, considering the paragraph regarding railroad carriages especially unjust.

On 16 November, all the prisoners were taken to Villengen except the Red Cross Committee, who stayed to check the Red Cross material. On this committee, in addition to Lieutenant Codman, were Captain James N. Hall, 2nd Lieutenant R. G. Browning and 1st Lieutenant Henry Lewis. The guards disappeared on this date and in the evening these four officers left the camp with a German corporal. They spent the night in a hotel in Munich where no one paid any attention to them and the next day they proceeded by rail with the German corporal to a point on Lake Constance from which they proceeded by boat, landing at Roman's Horn on 17 November. From there they proceeded to Berne, where they spent some days with the American Red Cross, preparing necessary reports on their committee work. Then they proceeded through Geneva to France, arriving in Paris on 21 November.

Chapter 21

1st Lieutenant B. B. Battle, USAS. 91st Observation Squadron

Shortly after noon on 12 June, Lieutenant Battle left his aerodrome in a Salmson to fly as protection for another Salmson which was to take pictures. The photographic mission was accomplished without incident and the two machines were just crossing the lines on the return trip when Battle nosed his machine down and tried out his fixed gun. There was evidently some fault in the synchronisation, for at the first burst the propeller was shattered. Not having sufficient altitude to glide across the lines, he was forced to descend on the German side, landing between the first and second line of trenches. Bearing in mind that the first duty of a captured aviator is to destroy his machine, Battle endeavoured to set fire to his plane, but the men in the trenches opened fire on him and he was forced to desist. He held up his hands as token of surrender, but the fire continued, so he sought shelter in a shell hole. Here he was taken prisoner by an infantry officer of the Bavarian division occupying that sector.

Having landed just in front of the village of Flirey, the nearest German headquarters was at Thiacourt and to this place Battle was marched. During the four days spent at Thiacourt, he was questioned on three different occasions but refused to talk. The intelligence officer finally lost patience and threatened that, unless certain questions were answered, a note would be dropped over the lines stating that 'An American pilot, Lieutenant Battle, has been killed in combat'. He was told to go ahead and drop the note. Shortly afterwards, an armament officer entered and asserted that incendiary bullets had been found in the belt of the Salmson's fixed gun. The intelligence officer then informed Battle that this was against the rules of warfare and that he would be shot unless he gave them all the information requested. This information was again refused.

Shortly afterwards, Lieutenant Battle was placed in a fourth-class coach and taken to Karlsruhe under the guard of an officer and three enlisted men. During the journey he asked to go to the toilet. This was granted, but the guard was watchful and caught him when he attempted to escape through the toilet window. On arrival at Karlsruhe, Battle was sent to the now famous Karlsruhe Hotel, which was fitted out with dictaphones. While here he fell ill but was refused a doctor. The food supplied to sick prisoners was the same as that given to those in good health: thin soup, barley coffee and black bread.

After nine days in this hotel he was sent to the camp for British aviators at Landshut, Bavaria. Here he was locked in a small unventilated room with twenty other officers. A short period of exercise was obtained each day in a small, filthy courtyard about twenty feet square. Food and living conditions were so bad that the officers requested in writing that they be moved to other quarters. After two weeks this request was granted and they were placed in an old castle nearby. The quarters at this place were better and there was slight improvement in the food until ten days before their departure when Red Cross food was received. During his stay here Battle attempted to bribe a German sergeant-major to allow him to escape. This was reported and the American was punished by being placed in solitary confinement for eight days.

Seven weeks after he arrived at the castle, Battle was removed to the prison camp at Villengen.The trip was made by train and took two days. During this time the prisoners were allowed to visit the latrine at eight-hour intervals only. Their shoes were removed to prevent attempts at escape. They received one meal during the trip. The camp at Villengen was reached on 14 September.

On the night of 6 October the prisoners short-circuited the electric light wires of the camp and Battle, in company with four American and one French officer, made his escape by climbing over the fence. He was fired on by the guards but received nothing more serious than a bullet through his haversack. The six officers separated and each took a different route. Lieutenant Battle travelled for five nights through the Black Forest, hiding during the day. He met many people during the evenings, but they apparently supposed him to be some German wayfarer and he was only challenged twice. His food consisted of four pieces of hard tack a day. All went well until he reached the Rhine where he was captured by a police dog. He was taken back to Villengen and put in solitary confinement for eighteen days.

At the end of this time he was told that he had been tried (his presence at the trial was evidently considered unnecessary) and convicted of inciting mutiny. For this offence he was sent to Fort Kurstein, a reprisal camp near Berlin. This place was never reached. At Cassel on 9 November, in the Grand Duchy of Hesse, the train was boarded by revolutionaries, among whom were a number of naval marines and the guards were disarmed and the prisoners freed. Battle struck up an acquaintance with a marine who spoke English and who seemed very friendly. The two of them attempted to make their way to the Dutch border but were stopped by an officer and the socialists who were in charge of the railway station ordered them back to Villengen. Lieutenant Battle talked to many of the revolutionaries and was told by all of them that the war was over and that he would be foolish to try and escape now as all prisoners would be released in a day or two.

Discipline was very lax and he believed that if he had had any money he could have reached Holland with little difficulty.

Boarding a train in company with his acquaintance the marine, Battle went to Frankfurt. Here he met a German officer and got on very good terms with him by giving him some Red Cross food. They went into the station bar together and had some drinks. Everyone was drinking and talking of the revolution, rejoicing that the Armistice was signed or soon would be. A statue of the Kaiser and pictures of Ludendorf and Hindenburg were torn down.

Leaving Frankfurt for Villengen, Battle tried to bribe the guard to take a route which would bring them close to the Swiss border. But the guard still possessed a strong respect for authority and wired ahead asking for reinforcements. When Villengen was reached a strongly armed guard was awaiting him and conducted him to the prison camp. It was necessary to remain in the camp until 25 November when nearly all the American prisoners were released. Lieutenant Battle went to Constance and remained there for three days, receiving excellent food. From there the journey was made across Switzerland and into France

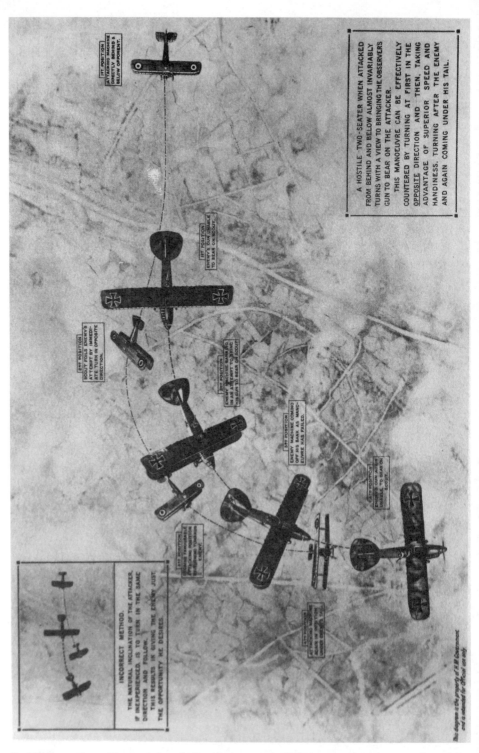

In 1918 a series of instructional diagrams on air fighting tactics was produced for the RAF. This one, entitled 'Outmanoeuvred' advised pilots on the correct and incorrect methods of attacking a German two-seater.

Chapter 22

1st Lieutenant Marian Coldwell Cooper, USAS. 20th Bombardment Squadron

First Lieutenant Marian C. Cooper was assigned to the US Bombardment Squadron at Maulan, France, on 30 August 1918 as a pilot of a DH.4. One month later, on 26 September 1918, with his observer, Lieutenant Edward Leonard, he was part of a seven-plane patrol on a bombing mission of Dun-sur-Meuse and had just completed the mission and was turning for home when the aircraft was attacked by a squadron of Fokker fighters. In less than five minutes five of the bombers had been shot down, including Cooper's. As his aircraft started to burn, Cooper put the aircraft into a dive and then into a slide-slip to prevent the flames roasting him and his observer alive. His observer, Leonard, had been hit in the neck by a bullet and was bleeding profusely and Cooper's hand and face were being burnt by the flames. The aircraft crash-landed and both crew members managed to extricate themselves from the wreckage. One of the Fokker pilots landed alongside the burning machine and accepted their surrender. Troops soon arrived and they were taken to a German field hospital and treated for their wounds. Later they were taken to another German hospital for further treatment and then to a prisoner-of-war camp for the rest of the war. At the signing of the Armistice, they were released and both returned to Paris, France.

Cooper was assigned to duties in Paris with the US Air Service until July 1919 when Ignace Jan Paderewski, the Polish Premier, persuaded President Wilson to allow him to solicit volunteers from the US Air Service to help him form an air force and prevent the Bolshevik Army from invading Poland. Among the thirteen volunteers was Marion C. Cooper, who with the others arrived in Warsaw in September 1919. The volunteers were inducted into the Koscisuzko Squadron, Marian Cooper being given the rank of major. The squadron was a mobile one and consisted of a train of railway coaches, flat cars and box cars for supplies and equipment and as the area of action changed, so did the location of the squadron.

On 10 July 1920 Major Cooper was on patrol over the Bolshevik's front line when he came under heavy ground fire causing his engine to fail and forcing him to land. He was captured by the Bolsheviks and treated quite roughly as they did not take kindly to mercenaries being involved in their struggle. Taken to Moscow, Marian Cooper was put into a prisoner-of-war camp for the second time in his career, this time for nine months. He made his escape at the beginning of April 1921 and after travelling for twenty-six nights he crossed the Latvian border and into safety. Transportation was provided back to Warsaw and at the end of May 1921 he returned to the United States.

His career after that is a matter of record. He became one of Hollywood's outstanding film producers with films such as *King Kong* and *Cinerama*. During the Second World War he joined the USAAC, finishing the war with the rank of brigadier-general.

Chapter 23

Major Frederick Powell

Major Frederick James Powell was born on 13 August 1895 at Patricroft. He was living in Blackpool when he enlisted in the Manchester Regiment. He took his certificate at Farnborough on 2 March 1915 and served on Nos. 5, 40 and 41 Squadrons. He scored two victories on the Vickers FB5 and four on the FE8. Powell served as chief fighting instructor with Northern Groups in 1917. He assumed command of 41 Squadron on 2 August 1917. After shooting down six enemy aircraft, Major Powell was shot down and captured on 2 February 1918 over Auberchicourt by a pilot of Jasta 10. He was repatriated in December 1918. Powell was mentioned in dispatches and received the Military Cross. He flew the Maurice Farman Longhorn, the Shorthorn, Vickers Gunbus, the B.E.2c, the Avro, the single-seater F.E.8, the F.E.2b and the S.E.5a.

I was just nineteen when I joined the RFC. I had been in the Leicestershire Yeomanry, battling with horses. After two months, I joined the Manchester Regiment and whilst I was there, my battalion was asked for volunteers to join the Royal Flying Corps. I transferred and was sent down to Farnborough. I trained there for about three weeks, before doing my first solo on a Maurice Farman biplane. I graduated onto a Maurice Farman Shorthorn and then onto a Vickers Gunbus. This was an armoured fighting biplane. The armour consisted of a little square of armour plating which went under the seat. It was an interesting little aeroplane with a Monosoupape rotary engine. The engine had no throttle on it, so you couldn't go slow or fast; it only had one speed - flat out! I went off those old Vickers fighters and onto the B.E.2c. That was a terrible machine, with a mind of its own! As soon as you put the rudder on it, it banked itself and it slid round on the turns. With the tractors, about three quarters of the visual sight is blanked out by machinery. I always thought pushers were the best fighting machines for the war, though, as the pilot has to be able to see.

My first posting to France was with 5 Squadron, flying the Vickers Gunbus. I had done fourteen hours' solo before I went out to fly, which wasn't too bad for those days; nowadays they do about 500 hours. We used to do two-hour patrols. Our petrol lasted two and a half hours. So we allowed fifteen minutes to get to the lines, did the patrol and then allowed fifteen minutes to get back. The time seemed interminable; it seemed as though you'd been up for three years before the petrol went down and you had to get back.

During my first combat patrols, my laundry bills soared astronomically! After the first few times, though, I felt no more anxiety; it was the most amazing thing. This was made easier by the invention of tracer bullets. There was a little light on the butt end of the bullet and as you fired the machine gun, instead of firing and trying to aim through the sights of the machine gun, you could see this arc of fire going straight off when you fired at the bloke. Once, I was coming down on the back of a Hun in an Aviatik. I fired my gun, I watched these lights and every one was going right into the heart of the pilot. He still went on. It took me a long time to realize that, of course, your eye is wrong! You may be about three or four feet to the right or left before the tracer light goes out. One rumour was doing the rounds at the time, that if you used tracer bullets and were captured, you'd be shot. They regarded them as incendiary bullets, which were against the Geneva Convention and not quite 'cricket'. Occasionally, instead of putting one tracer bullet for every two or three, I used a drum of nothing but tracers so I could really have a shot at it.

We had quite a few entertainments, too. Robert Loraine was a famous West End actor. He was the first man who flew from Liverpool across to the Isle of Man. This was in 1912, when he was producing a play by Bernard Shaw called The Man From the Sea. Loraine's engine failed and he fell down in the sea, which was wonderful publicity. He eventually became a squadron commander, which was a major in those days. I remember we found a Red Cross Army hostel building, with a stage. We saw this from our aeroplane and nobody seemed to be using it and my CO, Loraine, suddenly thought, 'Well, that's a marvellous thing; let's go and take it.' With all our carpenters and mechanics, we took that building, pulled it all down, brought it back to our aerodrome, re-erected it, stage and all. And who should come to visit the squadron but George Bernard Shaw! He came out as a VIP and stayed with us for a week. Loraine produced two unpublished plays of Bernard Shaw's, which were very good. One was called The Inker at Berusalem (sic), which was a skit on the Kaiser. Every Major on the stage always wore an eyeglass. And damn it all, Loraine suddenly appeared in the squadron with an eyeglass! When I was coming back from my first seven days' leave, on the way back, I called in at Harrods and bought a cardboard box full of eyeglasses with broad black ribbons. I issued them to all the officers in the mess and when we sat down to dinner, everybody had an eyeglass. Loraine took it in good spirit.

Another play produced by Loraine was VC, a skit on Michael O'Leary. O'Leary was a piper in a Scottish regiment, who would walk up and down the parapet, playing the bagpipes. This inspired the whole of his regiment; they went over the top and did damned well. I still think the finest VC ever earned was by a man who was a 2nd lieutenant in an infantry regiment. While he'd been out in France, his wife had produced a son and he was due for leave in two days' time. The Boche lobbed a bomb into the trench. He ran for cover, looked round and saw his men, one of whom had fallen over. The men were all piled up and couldn't get out of the way. He came out of his sanctuary and lay down over the bomb. It went off and he was, of course, scattered all over the place, but the lives of his men were saved. By God, nothing's beaten that.

I loved flying. A thrill! Because you'd so few people who did it, you felt rather like a pioneer. It was interesting, particularly if you were at the right age, about nineteen. But I think for an older man it would bore him. After years of instructing, I could see straightaway if a chap would make a good scout pilot. You could tell that boy when you put him in the front seat and you sat behind. You had the controls and you'd say, 'Turn to the left,' and he'd turn, merely doing the correct thing - putting the rudder on and then the bank - but himself keeping straight. I used to say, 'Just like an old GOC bus driver'. He'd never, never be a scout pilot. But when you get the right boy and you say 'turn to the left or the right' and the first thing that moves is his head and he turns round and the machine follows him - there you've got the scout pilot. Quite a different type of mentality - entirely different people.

I knew James McCudden, VC. Quite a different type. He was a little man, who flew Nieuport Scouts with 60 Squadron. He was a brilliant pilot, a young captain and he had the mind of a general. That boy, he used to lead his flight in. They'd do their ordinary work and get into a dogfight with the Boche, McCudden would break away and come back our side and see how his people were doing. If they were not doing so well, McCudden would fight, then break off and come back. But after that, he used to go out by himself. Oh, he was brilliant. Brilliant. He used to get onto the tail of a Boche and the fellow would turn round and they'd go round in circles and as they went round in circles, he'd gradually elongate the circles, 'till he brought the Boche over our lines, then he broke away and shot him down. I think it was December 1916, probably and in that year he shot seventeen Germans down, fifteen on our side of the lines. There's no argument as to whether he shot them down or not. He was the most marvellous pilot of all, you can take Immelmann, Boelcke, Richthofen - in all the fighting air forces, McCudden to my mind was the most wonderful genius of the whole of the air corps.

Albert Ball was a different type entirely. He got the VC, but he was a rotten shot and couldn't hit a haystack at four yards! His idea was to get so close to a Boche before he fired, that it was impossible to miss him. Ball came down many times with German blood on his machine! He was a different type of VC. Mind you, they were all wonderful boys. Comrades' deaths in the squadron were tragic of course. You're sitting rather like in a home and all the brothers are there. And you come in for your meal in the evening and somebody's missing. The Vacant Chair. There would be the vacant chair in the mess. It was the CO's responsibility to keep the cheer up, so there was quite a lot of cheer and quite a lot of booze, too. You had to forget and think, 'Well, probably tomorrow, I'll be the missing chair.' I don't think that really worried us; we were too young and too excited. It was a wonderful thing for boys, a wonderful life. 'Eat, drink and be merry, for tomorrow we die!' There's no finer life than that thought.

I remember the only time I shot a Fokker down. The Fokkers used to fly at about 17,000 feet and our ceiling was about 10,000 feet. One morning I went up in my old pusher, a little F.E.8. I climbed and climbed and I couldn't believe it. I looked at the altimeter and I saw the thing was coming up to 16,500. I'd never been at that height before. And eventually I got damned near to 17,000! I suddenly saw a machine coming straight at me and he was about 100 feet higher. It was a monoplane, so all I could see was the engine above his plane as he came towards me and of course, I couldn't see the markings.

There were two monoplanes, the Fokker and the Morane. So, what was he, Fokker or Frenchman? I had to wait until he fired. Well, he fired and missed, but as I was going to turn into him, I saw his rudder flick and I thought, 'God! He's coming back again!' So instead of turning round to the left and following onto his tail, I turned to the right and pulled up. When he finished his turn and I finished mine, he was about 100 feet below me, so I came down straight on him and fired. And he went down. I remember his face; he was so close I could see the fellow. He looked up and he hesitated, wondering how the hell I'd got up there. He went down in a complete spin, right through the bomber formation he was supposed to be escorting.

I think the Fokker was a very good machine. I never thought well of the Germans in the war, but as engineers they were brilliant. I remember when I was learning to fly at Farnborough, going into the office of the head of the aircraft factory. He was an Irishman named O'Gorman. I looked up and over his desk was a great string coming down from the ceiling and on the end of it was a connecting rod.

I asked him, 'What's that, sir?' and he said,

'Powell, as you know I'm an engineer. That's a connecting rod from a German Mercedes engine. I look at that and it gives me inspiration. One day, we'll make something like that.' And I thought, 'My God. The Germans must be fantastic engineers.'

There was a time when I was sending out more patrols from my squadron and they kept coming back and saying 'No H.A' (hostile aircraft.) I couldn't understand it, because squadrons on my right and left were knocking the Boche out of the sky. I think the SE5a was my favourite; it was a beautiful machine and lovely to fly. It makes me rather sad to think that when I was beaten, I was shot down in the finest machine. Ghastly. That was on 7 February 1918. I organized a patrol of eight machines, myself and three others in diamond formation and another flight of four, 3,000 feet above. I was flying a SE5a. The idea was that WE were the bait and when the Germans came onto us, the chaps above could dive down on them and shoot them up. We went right up to the Front without sight or sound of a Hun. When we got to the very top of the Yser Canal, I turned right, looked up and saw that the whole sky was a mass of black crosses. I came down on the tail of one Hun and had him right in the middle of my Aldis sight. I was about to fire at him, whereupon another Hun was on my tail. 'Pop! Pop! Pop!' He hit everything. He got me through the left arm. My instrument board went up and then there was a cloud of smoke and water. The bullet had gone right through my arm and into the radiator.

We'd no parachutes in those days and I was at 14,000 feet at the time. Miraculously, with three Huns on my tail and no engine, I managed to get down. I landed on a German aerodrome! The chap who'd shot me landed too. I put my cap on and walked over to this German, who was sitting in his plane with the engine still running. He got out of his machine and I walked up to him to shake hands, as one used to in those days. He said, 'Verwundet?' At that moment I looked down and saw blood coming from my sleeve. The force of the shot was so intense, that the bullet had gone clean through my arm; all I felt was just a knock, as if someone had hit me on the arm with the blunt end of an axe. The Germans came running out and carried me to a Casualty Clearing Station, where they dressed my arm. They hadn't got, as we had, real bandages; they used paper bandages. They put my arm in a sling and then took me to see their intelligence officer.

He was a Hauptmann, a captain and wore a delightful sky-blue uniform with a scarlet lining. I gave my name and regiment. Then I was asked my rank. I said, 'Major'. He couldn't believe that a boy of twenty-one was a major, because a German major was usually a fellow with a big, white moustache in those days.

The Hauptmann drove me in a German staff car on the other side of the lines and it was very interesting. As we drove past, there were lots of German troops marching past and as the staff car came they all turned their heads, you know: 'Eyes right!' The Hauptmann said, 'What do you think of that?' I remember saying, 'Well, I think it's marvellous,' remembering that on our side of the lines, as soon as a staff car came past, you saw all the chaps bunch up and go to the side of the road and you knew they were saying, 'Another bloody staff car!' What a difference to go to the other side and see the Germans all click their heads round! We all know the Germans are a military nation, so that's what we'd expect. The Germans never had the spirit that the Englishman has, though. The thing that will beat them, every time, is their lack of a sense of humour.

I was in the PoW camp at Minden until the end of the war. The Camp Commandant there was Hauptmann Niemeyer. He had a great reputation, because some of the boys had gone back to England and the *Daily Mirror* had published his photograph and described him as 'the basest scoundrel in the German army'. Niemeyer had a copy of that and he came in one day and said, 'They know me well in England you know. They have my picture in your papers.' He was very proud of that. I think he didn't understand 'the basest scoundrel in the German army'!

I didn't really miss flying while I was in the camp; in fact, it didn't bother me a bit. What impressed me there was the Germans' lack of humour and the wonderful, intense humour of the British. I was put in a room by myself with the windows whitewashed on the outside. Some wag had been in there before me and done a marvellous sketch of a skull and crossbones, above an inscription: Abandon hope all ye who enter here!

When the war was over, we went back to England in a ship. As we got to the coast, all the little tugboats there hooted like destroyers. We stood on deck, seeing all these people welcoming us back home. I cried. Oh, God, it was marvellous! It was amazing to be back in England again.

My experiences in the RFC and the war changed my life, broadened me enormously and formed my character. I went out to France as a poor little sissy and came back as a man of the world. It was a boys' war, in that to enjoy it, you had to be young. I think if you were an old man, about twenty-four or something, it might have shaken you then. It was a terrific excitement for me, an enormous game. I used to say, 'If I had a squadron of fighters, single-seater fighters, I'd like all of them to be nineteen years old.' You don't want an old man of twenty-four or twenty-five because by that time, he's got intelligence. He's going after a Boche and he's got to be able to go straight to that fellow and shoot him down. But he mustn't have the intelligence to think, 'well if I'm close to him, then he's equally close to me!'

I met so many marvellous fellows in the war. Wonderful men! No, they weren't men; they were boys! It's the comradeship that I miss. That goes for any of the services, Army, Navy or Air Force. It's a wonderful life and what you miss when you come out of the service is the wonderful friendship; you feel lonely to come home as a civilian again. My philosophy is that when there's a war, you have the whole nation, all with one goal and all together. When you get peace, every rotten little man is out for his own. That's the difference between war and peace and I think the only really satisfactory life that humans have is war.' [43]

Footnotes Chapter 23

43 *Voices In Flight: Conversations with Air Veterans of the Great War* by Anna Malinovska & Mauriel P. Joslyn (Pen & Sword 2006). Freddy Powell was interviewed at home at Ivy Cottage, Stalbridge, Dorset on 29 June 1977. He died on 13 March 1987.

Chapter 24

Dice-With-Death Dallas

*June 1st 1918 dawned warm and sunny, with enough low cloud over the Western Front
to tempt daring pilots of Allied planes into one-man sorties over enemy terrain. Near
Lieven three black-crossed Fokker triplanes waited for just such prey. Two of them were
cruising at about 8,000 feet; the third - acting as decoy, was well below. For the flyer in a
British S.E., heading into the sun, this lone enemy appeared a sitting duck. His fingers at
the trips of his forward-firing Vickers, he flung his aircraft downwards towards the Hun.
As he closed, waiting to catch the enemy in his sights, vicious Spandau bullets from the
other two Fokkers raked the S.E.5. Lurching sideways, it spiralled slowly, then, out of
control, plummeted to the shell-pocked earth. Major Roderic Dallas, DSO, DSC and Bar
- leader of the gallant 40th Squadron - had thrown his last dice with death.*

**'Janus' writing in RAF Flying Review, January 1959. Roderic Dallas became
almost a legendary character in the RNAS. He was a pilot of quite
extraordinary skill, a fighting man of astonishing gallantry, a humorist of a
high order and a black-and-white artist of unusual ability. But, above all this,
he was a great leader of men. To be in Dallas' squadron was quite one of the
highest honours open to a young fighting pilot of the RNAS and the high
reputation held by certain of the RNAS squadrons operating with the RFC
was largely due to the training, example and leadership of Roderic Dallas.**

Roderic Stanley 'Stan' Dallas was born on 30 July 1891 at Mount Stanley station
outside Esk, in rural Queensland, to labourer Peter MacArthur Dallas and his wife
Honora. Mount Stanley was an isolated property and journeys to and from Esk
were long and infrequent; Stan was the first Caucasian child born at the station.
His family moved to Tenterfield, New South Wales, soon after the birth of his
younger brother in 1893. They returned to Queensland in 1898, settling in Mount
Morgan, where Peter Dallas became a shift boss at the local mines. Stan attended
Mount Morgan Boy's School from February 1899 and eventually joined its cadet
corps, rising to sergeant. At school he was noted for his intelligence, ability to get
along well with others and quiet sense of humour. He enjoyed the outdoors and
spent many hours in the mountains behind his family's home, observing birds of
prey. In July 1907 Dallas joined the assay office of the Mount Morgan Gold Mining
Company and also enrolled in the local technical college, where he took night
classes in chemistry and technical drawing. He showed an early interest in
aviation, fuelled by the establishment in 1911 of the Mount Morgan chapter of the
Queensland Aero Club. Dallas and his younger brother Norvel built a glider,
which was wrecked by an untimely gust of wind the first time they tried to launch
it. The two brothers continued to build model gliders after this initial disaster,

however and Stan corresponded with pioneer aviators in France, England and the United States. He later transferred to a higher-paying job driving trucks for Iron Island ironstone quarries. Stan and Norvel once again built their own flying machine while Stan was working on Iron Island. They experimented with this seaplane on nearby Marble Island, notorious for its treacherous waters; Stan lost this aeroplane in the sea.

At 6 feet 2 inches tall and weighing 220lb, Dallas would later surprise observers with his ability to fit into the cramped cockpits of fighter planes. Despite his size, he was considered a fine athlete with quick reflexes. Although he could project a loud speaking voice, he was generally soft-spoken and was not known to curse or drink alcohol, nor often to smoke. Dallas stayed fit through regular exercise at the gym and played rugby union football. He had exceptionally keen eyesight, which he had trained by reading small print in newspapers at the six-foot length of his family's table. To balance out athletics, he participated in amateur theatrics, where his strong voice served him well.

Dallas joined the Port Curtis Militia in 1913 and was commissioned as a lieutenant prior to the outbreak of World War I. Believing he had little chance of gaining a place in the newly established Australian Flying Corps, he applied to join the British Royal Flying Corps (RFC), but was rejected. Undaunted, he travelled from Queensland to Melbourne, where he impressed Minister Without Portfolio J. A. Jensen. Jensen gave the young aspirant a letter of introduction to the Australian High Commissioner in London, Sir George Reid. Dallas paid his own passage to England and once there, applied again to the RFC. Rejected again, he turned to the Royal Naval Air Service and was accepted, topping the entrance examination over 83 other students. He was commissioned a flight sub-lieutenant and began training at Hendon in June 1915, gaining Pilot's Licence #1512 on 5 August.

Late 1915 found him wishing himself back with his foot-slogging comrades. His squadron, No.1, was then based at Dover and engaged on routine, wearying patrols over the North Sea, in Short seaplanes. One ambition realised, Dallas had formed another, to come to grips with the enemy, in the air. About this time the RFC were taking a terrible beating from the superior Hun machines and to meet the menace several RNAS squadrons, including No.1, moved to Dunkirk. Dallas arrived in France on 27 November and as a change from the wastes of the North Sea found himself flying with French, Belgian and RFC units, on patrols along the Belgian coast and occasionally over the battlefields of Flanders. There was, at that time, but one available Allied machine capable of meeting German monoplanes on equal terms - the Nieuport 'Bebe' which had an 80hp rotary engine and for armament, a single, wing-mounted Lewis. A few of these French Nieuports were handed over to the Dunkirk-based British units and to his delight Dallas was given one for lone patrols.

On 3 December 1915 Dallas joined No. 1 Naval Wing and began flying combat sorties in single-seat Nieuport 11 fighters and two-seat Caudrons at Dunkirk. Early in his career there, a practical joker imitating his commanding officer telephoned Dallas, who was the duty officer and peremptorily ordered him to take off in a propellerless Breguet. Upon learning that he had been tricked, Dallas joined in the laughter. He not only accepted the resulting nickname of 'Breguet', but also used it as a signature on his letters home later in the war. Having made two unconfirmed claims in February 1916, Dallas scored his first confirmed victory on 23 April. He outmanoeuvred a German Aviatik C and shot it out of control, following his victim down to 2,000 feet, though heavy anti-aircraft fire holed his plane in several places. He went on to score three more confirmed victories with his Nieuport.

On 12 May 1916 he took off in his 'Bebe' and headed for the front line. Fifteen minutes later he came on an enemy Aviatik two-seater and attacked. The moment he caught the Hun in his sights. Dallas pressed his trigger and saw both the pilot and the gunner crumple in their seats. Out of control, the Aviatik hurtled down to smash on the ground far below. Dallas had achieved his second ambition and had emerged victorious from his first aerial fight. Eight days later, near Blankenberghe, he saw five Friedrichshafen two-seaters crossing his front. They were homing after a successful bombing raid over Dover and Dunkirk. Ignoring the heavy odds and though under severe fire from their guns, Dallas flew in and out of the formation and succeeded in breaking it up. This accomplished he pounced on a straggler and sent it earthwards minus a top wing. Before the stricken craft had struck ground another was following it, burning like a torch. The remaining three abandoned the fight and ran for base. Dallas, his ammunition spent and fuel low returned to Dunkirk and to the congratulations of his fellow pilots.

The arduous flights over the North Sea, often in appalling weather, had made him a seasoned and experienced flyer. Now, in combat he was acquiring a technique that was to make him an ace. He was later acknowledged to be, even by the enemy, as one of the bravest aviators ever known. In the early hours of the following morning he shot down an Albatros two-seater which was bombing Dunkirk. And yet again the next day, with another intrepid pilot, R. N. Mulock, he was out again, attacking another formation of Albatros two-seaters. One fell to his guns and Mulock shot up two more, all three spiralling down in flames. The Albatros was no sitting duck, even for the Neiuport 'Bebe'. This particular model, the Albatros C.3 of 1916, was a formidable machine and his speedy accounting for four enemy planes earned Dallas the DSC, which on 9 June he celebrated by a solo stalking of a formation of bombers, protected by Fokker scouts. He had destroyed one of the bombers before the enemy pilots were aware of his nearness. His fire was so accurate that it cleaved the fuselage in two. Far too late, the pilot of an escorting Fokker saw the Nieuport and followed it into the formation. Turning for a second run-in, Dallas caught this pursuer square in his sights. A split-second burst of his deadly accurate fire sent the Fokker groundwards after the shattered bomber - a dead man at its controls.

Two days later the Australian was out with four other pilots of his squadron, engaging a group of Fokkers. In the ensuing dog-fight his plane was literally smashed by bullets. With a sputtering, useless engine, he began to lose altitude, circling slowly as he sought a place to land. Leaving the main fight, two of the Fokkers dived after the stricken Nieuport. Here, the pilots reasoned, was a certain kill, an opinion shared by troops on the ground who had paused to stare up at the twisting, turning planes, like gigantic gnats in the blue summer sky. Had the Nieuport's gun, like those of the Fokkers, been synchronised for forward firing, then Dallas would have been at their mercy. His Lewis being mounted on the wing gave him a chance to fight back. Like giant hawks swooping on their prey, the Fokkers screamed in for the kill. A burst of fire from the leader sent splinters flying from the British plane. Overshooting his target, the Hun pilot turned and in that moment died. Swivelling his Lewis upwards, Dallas had raked the belly of the Fokker as it passed above him. Bursting into flames, it streaked earthwards as Dallas took swift aim and fired a long burst at his second pursuer. Swift his aim might have been, but it was accurate. The monoplane's wing on one side broke away, sawn off by bullets and without further hindrance Dallas followed his unfortunate enemies towards terra firma, to land his wrecked machine behind the Allied lines.

On 23 June Dallas took delivery of the newest RNAS fighter, Sopwith Triplane N500. Armed with a single, fixed, Vickers gun, the new Sopwith was a splendid fighter, fast in the climb and soon won the familiar designation of 'Tripehound.' N500 was the original prototype, having undergone Admiralty trials before being shipped to France. Though still only a test plane, it was flown into combat 15 minutes after its arrival. Dallas named it Brown Bread and it was the first of a series of 'Tripes' that he would fly and fight in over the next year. He achieved his first victory with Brown Bread on 1 July, the same day he was promoted to flight lieutenant. Three days later, he was recommended for further promotion. He scored his last Nieuport-mounted 'kill' on 9 July, earning the Croix de Guerre and a mention in despatches for coming to the aid of a French Maurice Farman biplane. On 7 September Dallas was awarded the Distinguished Service Cross, 'for the specially gallant manner in which he has carried out his duties' since first seeing action in December 1915. By the end of 1916 he was among the earliest RNAS aces, with eight confirmed and four unconfirmed victories and had been raised to the rank of flight commander.

Dallas became one of the best-known pilots of Sopwith Triplanes in the RNAS. He opened 1917 by setting an altitude record of 26,000 feet in the Triplane while testing a prototype oxygen set; he endured frostbite and oxygen intoxication in the process. By now No. 1 Wing's fighter squadron under Squadron Commander F. K. Haskins had been renumbered as No.1 Squadron RNAS and had totally re-equipped with production Triplanes. It also moved airfields from Veurne in Belgium to Chapilly in France, leaving behind RNAS control by transferring to No.14 Army (Air) Wing, 4th Brigade of the RFC. Formation flying became the order of the day, as the practice of fighter pilots soloing into combat dwindled. The last three weeks of March were also filled with Dallas's responsibilities for flight and gunnery testing. April 1917 found Dallas, flying a Tripehound in the thick of the grim aerial fighting in which Manfred von Richthofen earned immortal fame by alone destroying over twenty Allied machines. As British losses in the air began to mount during Bloody April, Dallas and his squadron moved airfields once again, to La Bellevue. They were thus positioned to take a prominent part in the subsequent Battle of Arras, where the intense aerial fighting saw Dallas add to his burgeoning score.

With another 'Tripehound' pilot, Lieutenant Thomas Culling, Dallas was out over St. Elio on 21 April. By then the name stood for nothing more than a heap of shell-torn rubble. Spotting a formation of Albatros two-seaters under the protection of D.3 fighters, they decided to attack. The D.3 pilots saw the two Allied triplanes heading for the Albatros observation machines and dived to intercept them. For fifty minutes Culling and Dallas were engaged in an all-out aerial battle with the pick of German men and machines Careering through the formation Dallas saw his tracers whip into one scout, which hung dead for a second, then burst into flames. As it began to spin down he banked and was in time to see Culling literally shoot the wings from other. Abandoning the scouts they then turned on the D.3s. Dallas sent one hurtling down in flames and Culling, equally inspired in his shooting, raked two more. One was seen to crash and the other, out of control, faded from the fight. They had engaged heavy odds and by now the triplanes were flying wrecks. Dallas and Culling made a run for base where Culling, in landing his machine, knocked out two teeth on his dashboard. Both machines were write-offs, but otherwise the men who had flown them had escaped injury. For his part in this fight Dallas was again mentioned in dispatches and by the French, awarded the coveted Croix de Guerre.

The combat of 23 April became known as one of the classic air battles of the war. Dallas and his wingman Thomas Culling took on a squadron-sized formation of 14 German aircraft, having gained an altitude edge over their foes. The naval aces exploited this edge by making quick diving attacks from opposite sides, culminating in short bursts of machine-gun fire. Using the Triplane's superior climbing ability, they would then bob back up to position themselves for the next assault. In contrast to the usual hit-and-run tactics of most dogfights, the RNAS duo launched at least 20 gunnery runs over 45 minutes. The Germans were forced progressively lower, into disarray and then chased back over their own lines. While they shot down three of the Germans, Dallas and Culling also achieved a more important outcome by blocking and then breaking up a determined enemy effort against the British ground offensive. The action led to the award of a Bar to the Distinguished Service Cross for Dallas and a Distinguished Service Cross for Culling, which were gazetted on 29 June.

By May 1917 the initiative had again, passed to the Allies. On 16 June Dallas added to his score by shooting down an Aviatik he found reconnoitring behind the British lines. On the 22nd he was awarded a Bar to his DSC when he destroyed an A.E.G. two-seater under the protection of six or more scouts near Chapilly. That engagement had been before lunch. After lunch he came upon another A.E.G. with the crew busy taking photographs. This, too, he sent crashing down in names. Dallas was experienced enough to anticipate that this aircraft was under escort but to what extent he did not know. Bullets zipping close above his head told him that the enemy were on his tail. Unknown to him there were five, all Halberstadts. The leader flew diagonally across and slightly above Dallas to draw his attention away from two more, coming up beneath him. Catching the decoy in his sights Dallas gave it a ten-round burst through the cockpit. With the pilot slumped over its stick the machine flew wild, before plunging down and baulking the attack from those below. In the general confusion Dallas slipped away behind low cloud and made his way home.

By June 1917 Dallas had achieved over 20 victories in aerial combat. This experience and his leadership ability, led to his appointment as commanding officer of 1 Naval Squadron on 23 June. The unit had been forced to cut back its operational strength from 18 aircraft to 15 due to lack of pilot replacements and a shortage of spare parts for the aging Triplanes. It had also moved airfields, to an unprepared site at Bailleul and was attached to the 3rd Army. As a leader, Dallas made a point of shepherding new pilots through their first flights and even setting them up with their first victories by manoeuvering enemy aircraft into a good position for the rookie to take a shot. On the ground, he proved to be an efficient organiser, designing and directing construction of the new air base. It was also during this time that he wrote a treatise on air combat tactics, extracts of which have survived. Both the air base layout and the treatise displayed his talent as a sketch artist. At Bailleul 1 Squadron came up against a redoubtable enemy formation, the first of the famous Jagdgeschwader operational groups of four staffels, under von Richthofen. Large scale aerial battles now became daily occurrences and under Dallas, 1 Squadron continued to give a good account of itself. He proved an exceedingly popular CO and won the respect and loyalty of all who served under him. The increased responsibilities of being a CO did not give Dallas the individual scope he had hitherto enjoyed. Nevertheless, during the autumn and winter, his score rose to 26 enemy aircraft destroyed.

On 2 November 1 Squadron moved airfields once more, to Middle Aerodrome, which put it back under overall RNAS control. The unit received its first eight new Bentley Sopwith Camels on 9 November as replacements for the Triplanes. On 11 November Dallas was again mentioned in despatches, this time by Field Marshal Haig. After gaining its full complement of Camels, 1 Squadron was transferred to England and took up home defence duties at Dover.

On 16 February 1918 Dallas led his squadron back to France, where it was based at Téteghem supporting units on operations along the Belgian coast. He commanded it for another six weeks, until 31 March. As part of the amalgamation of the RFC and RNAS to form the Royal Air Force on 1 April 1918 Dallas was promoted to major and given command of 40 Squadron RAF, flying S.E.5s. This famous squadron boasted a number of aces in its ranks and had a splendid record as a fighting group. It had arrived in France during August 1916 flying the F.E.8 'Pusher' scout, replaced in March 1917 by the Nieuport. The roll of 40 included many famous names, those of men like Mannock VC and McElroy. If McElroy did not serve in the squadron at the same time as Dallas, they were well known to each other and McElroy, who rejoined in June 1918 flew one of Dallas's old machines. Dallas replaced a gallant officer, Major Tilney, shot down on 6 March 1918 by the ace von Tutschek. The former RFC members were suspicious of Dallas's naval background. However, he was able to overcome their misgivings and established himself as the new CO with his personal demeanour and courage; the nickname of 'Admiral' that they bestowed upon him was an affectionate one. Ten days after taking over, Dallas had adapted well enough to his new mount with its inline engine to score his first victory with his new unit. His men also saw that he would not only look out for his rookie pilots, but would not shirk the dangers of ground attack sorties. The arrival of Dallas as CO of 40 Squadron coincided with a decisive moment of the war. The Germans had launched their last supreme bid for victory - the great spring offensive - against the British 3rd and 4th Armies and every flyable aircraft was in constant demand. The S.E.5A he now flew had a double armament, both a Vickers and a Lewis. In one of these, a few days after arrival, Dallas destroyed a Rumpler two-seater.

His studious bent continued to serve him; he kept notes on his methods of attacking enemy aircraft, which often exploited their structural weaknesses and used them to tutor pilots under his command. Ground fire was as great a hazard when flying over enemy territory as anything to be encountered from opposing aircraft. His offhand attitude toward wounds to his thigh and heel he received during a strafing attack on 14 April, after which he made 'a perfect landing' especially impressed his subordinates, as did his appreciation of all ranks for their hard work. Dallas was briefly hospitalised but he sneaked out four days later to rejoin his squadron. His departure may have been spurred by news of the capture of his friend Richard Minifie.

By 26 April Dallas had increased his official score to 37 and been awarded the Distinguished Service Order for operations at Dunkirk. He had also several times been recommended for the Victoria Cross but it was never approved. His casual attitude towards claiming victories was noted by a member of 40 Squadron, Cecil Usher, who related that Dallas once remarked of an opponent, '...he went down belching a lot of black smoke and after he had gone down someways one of his planes came off, but I didn't see him crash so I shan't claim him.' On 2 May, during a lull in the fighting at Flanders, Dallas took off in his favourite S.E.5, D3511, to taunt his foes. The fighter was distinctive with the new camouflage, instead of the olive green body and wings and cream undersurface that had hitherto been normal. This soon won it recognition in both camps. He strafed the German base at La Brayelle to 'attract attention' before dropping a package on the aerodrome with a note reading, 'If you won't come up here and fight, herewith a pair of boots for work on the ground, pilots for the use of'. He then circled in mist until troops came to examine the bundle, whereupon he dropped two bombs and again shot up the base, causing 'general panic'. News of this singular exploit reportedly provoked laughter from Field Marshal Haig and RAF founder General Sir Hugh Trenchard, two men not known for their sense of humour.

On 8 May, with another pilot, Dallas engaged a large formation of Pfalz and Fokker scouts near Bailleul. He had shot the wings off a Pfalz before the enemy knew he was being attacked. Before they could recover from the surprise, Dallas was gone again. Three days later he shot down another Pfalz and on May 23 a Fokker and a Rumpler. By the 28th his personal score stood at 39. While adding to his score and leading his squadron into combat, Dallas had begun thinking beyond the war. He was pleading with his father to quit the dangerous job of mining, with hints that he would support his parents by pioneering aviation in Australia. He also harboured a long-standing ambition of flying from England back to Australia, which would be a record-setting journey.

Dallas was promoted to lieutenant colonel and appointed to the command of a wing, but he would never see the message from headquarters that arrived on 1 June 1918 advising him of the promotion and ordering him to cease flying. For the Commanding Officer of 40th Squadron there was nothing to distinguish 1 June from any other day. It was a warm and sunny morning with inviting low cloud for cover and walking towards his waiting S.E.5, displaying the streamers of a leader, he probably thought conditions ideal for a seasoned man like himself to seek out and destroy reconnoitring enemy scouts, collecting information that could spell death for thousands of hapless men in the trenches. Acknowledging his wave as he took off in a cloud of dust his mechanics might have wondered what the day held for him. Would he return with his score at 40, or - the alternative was practically unthinkable. No matter what odds he encountered, Dallas always returned. No trick, no subterfuge, that enemy pilots might employ, could be new to Dallas and we must believe, knowing what we know of the man, that Dallas realised the lone Fokker triplane was a decoy. That somewhere, hidden by low cloud or against the sun, waited others. He had encountered this deceit before and won through by his daring and his amazingly accurate fire. When he turned down the nose of his S.E.5a to attack, it must have been with awareness of the dangers. But this time the hoary old Reaper was not to be cheated. As Dallas's fingers moved towards his gun-trips the enemy bullets riddled his body. It was a man already dead that plummeted earthwards in the shattered S.E. Dallas's score was to remain at 39. [44]

It was later learned that he had been killed over Lievin during combat with three Fokker Triplanes from Jagdstaffel 14, probably by its commander, Leutnant Johannes Werner. There are various theories as to how he died. The common elements are that he was on patrol near the front line when he pounced on a German fighter flying at a lower level, that there might have been another unknown British pilot in trouble and that the Germans who shot Dallas down had dived from a still higher altitude. Medics near his crash site at Absalom Trench ventured into no man's land and retrieved his body, while a patrol of eight volunteers salvaged his personal effects from the fallen aircraft. He was buried at the Pernes British Cemetery, France. News of Dallas's death was greeted with shock and disbelief by his squadron, one pilot recording: The world is upside down ... Dallas has been killed ... Too good for this world I suppose.'

For his record in aerial combat and his leadership skills, Dallas has been compared to the 'Red Baron', Manfred von Richthofen. The former flew combat for 29 months and the latter for 31 months, if his three months in hospital are deducted. Dallas successfully led two different squadrons during his career and was killed just before assuming command of a wing. Richthofen led first a squadron and then a wing during his twelve months in command, again excluding hospital time; he achieved more victories, but had the tactical advantage of fighting over his own lines with the wind in his favour. Dallas flew a score of different types of Allied aircraft as well as captured German planes; he was also instrumental in developing the Sopwith Triplane. Richthofen flew the Fokker Dr.1 and helped develop the Fokker D.VII, but did not live to fly it into battle.

Footnotes Chapter 24

44   His score of aerial victories is generally regarded as the second-highest by an Australian, after Robert Little; however there is considerable dispute over Dallas's exact total. While his official score is commonly given as 39, claim-by-claim analyses list as few as 32 and other research credits him with over 50, compared to Little's official tally of 47.

Chapter 25

A VC's Story

Air Commodore Ferdinand Maurice Felix 'Freddy' West VC CBE MC, was born in London on 19 January 1896, the son of an army officer killed in 1902 during the Second Boer War. Growing up in Italy, he attended the University of Genoa in 1913 and during the 1914 vacation he acquired a post in banking. When war broke out he joined the British Army, initially in the Royal Army Medical Corps in 1914 as a private, before being commissioned in May 1915 and joining the Royal Munster Fusiliers. He arrived in France in November 1915. After a flight in early 1917, West decided to transfer to the RFC, training as an observer at Brooklands and sent back in France in April 1917 to 3 Squadron, becoming a fully qualified observer in July 1917, having accumulated over 100 flying hours. After six months and 225 flying hours he was posted back to Britain to undergo pilot training at Grantham. He was then posted to No 8 Squadron in January 1918, flying Army co-operation duties with the infantry and tanks. Crewing up with Lieutenant John Haslam in March, West flew a series of hazardous sorties over the front, culminating with both men being awarded the Military Cross on 1 May 1918. On 18 June 1918 West's aircraft was attacked by four Pfalz D III scouts. West personally claimed one shot down and skillfully evaded the rest to return to base. The next day West was bounced by a group of Fokker DVII scouts and he dropped to 200 feet altitude and flew through a network of kite balloons to escape.

'In 1914 I was 18 years old, a law student but secretly hoping for adventure and excitement. War broke out between Britain and Germany and I immediately volunteered for service in the Army. In November 1915, I arrived in France as a second-lieutenant in the Royal Munster Fusiliers. After a few days in the trenches my disillusion about warfare was complete - it wasn't the mud or the rats that upset me but the tedious routine duties which consisted in keeping a continuous watch on the few hundred yards which separated us from the German lines. All I could see was masses of barbed wire, shell holes and several corpses in various stages of decay - I was bored. But I was thrilled whenever I saw aircraft manoeuvring in the vastness of the sky and fascinated watching air combats. I felt that airmen went to war like gladiators - I wanted to be one of them - but how to achieve this?

Towards the end of 1916 the Royal Flying Corps, in France, suffered heavy casualties and the Army called for officers with war experience to volunteer to transfer to the Royal Flying Corps for duties as observers. This was my great chance and I immediately volunteered. After training in England I was posted on 22 April 1917 to No 3 Squadron in France, which co-operated with Army units of the 4th Army.

The Squadron was equipped with two-seater Morane Parasols. On my first flight in France my pilot, Lieutenant Edgar Golding, taxied rather fast over a patch of rough ground, the aircraft turned over on its nose and I was catapulted to the ground. Lieutenant Golding scrambled out of the cockpit and having ascertained that I was not hurt told me 'Sorry about this, West. The Moranes are delicate on the ground but most manoeuvrable in the air. Have you heard that Lieutenant Warneford destroyed a German airship with a Morane Parasol and got the VC for it?' Golding tried again, this time successfully. My impression in the Morane Parasol was that I was sitting on the back of a bird and that any hit would cause the aircraft to go down with us in it - parachutes were known but not yet used in aircraft.

Golding gave me about four hours' flying experience over our own lines, during which he made me fire my Lewis gun several times; satisfied with my progress he flew me over the German lines. The Squadron duties consisted of artillery spotting, general photographic reconnaissance, bombing specific targets and firing in to enemy trenches.

I gained my baptism of enemy fire in the air a week later. Whilst Edgar Golding was trying unsuccessfully to destroy a German observation kite-balloon, I suddenly spotted two German aircraft flying above us - I distinctly recollect seeing the 'iron crosses' and yellow and green stripes on the fuselage. They split, one banking to the right and the other to the left of our aircraft. I estimated that they were almost 300 yards behind and about 100 feet above us; Golding shouted to me 'I shall keep a steady straight course and you open fire before they do'. I did exactly what I was told to do as the German fighters dived singly on our tail I opened fire before they did and both German pilots broke combat. This incident made a deep impression on me; I felt that observers should only observe for enemy fighters and at no time concentrate on observing activities on the ground. I must say, however, that there was no general agreement on this in our Squadron.

During the following weeks Golding attacked enemy troops and transport from low heights - our aircraft was often hit by rifle or machine gun fire but luckily not in vital spots. The Squadron suffered a considerable number of casualties and replacement pilots and observers arrived from England. The Commanding Officer split the experienced crews, placing experienced pilots and observers with new pilots and observers. As a result of this action, Golding and I were separated. A week later Golding was fatally wounded and crashed in enemy lines - we had become close friends and his death hit me hard. Fortunately, within a few days I was notified of my selection for training as a pilot in England.

I wanted to be a fighter pilot, but I was told that on the basis of my experience as a soldier in the trenches and as an air observer in the air, I would be more useful in an Army Co-op Squadron. My flying training commenced at Grantham on 1 October 1917 in No. 15 Training Squadron commanded by Major Leigh-Mallory. [45]

My first aircraft was a two-seater de Havilland 6 Trainer better known to pilots as the 'Sky Hook' or the 'Clutching Hand'. I received my wings two months later and found myself with an additional uniform, that of the Royal Flying Corps. It consisted of a double-breasted khaki tunic buttoned up to the throat - familiarly known as the 'Maternity Tunic' - and we wore a Sam Browne belt and khaki forage cap. Dressed in this uniform I was sent for by Leigh-Mallory who told me that he had just been posted to command No 8 Squadron in France and that he had arranged for my posting to this Squadron. I told him how grateful I was for this posting - I liked Leigh-Mallory very much and this was the beginning of a long friendship.

I arrived in France shortly after Christmas - No 8 Squadron was situated in the Amiens area which I knew so well as a soldier in the trenches and as an air observer; I felt quite at home! No 8 Squadron was equipped with Armstrong-Whitworth FK8 aircraft powered by a very reliable 160hp Beardmore engine. The aircraft was known colloquially as the 'Big Ack'. It was a general purpose two-seater with a maximum operational speed of about 95mph. The armament comprised a fixed Vickers machine gun for the pilot, while in the rear cockpit the observer had one or occasionally two Lewis machine guns mounted on a movable Scarff Ring. Leigh-Mallory told me that he would place me in C Flight - my observers would be Wilkinson, an Australian and Beaton, a South African. 'These chaps are very tough and independent,' he added, 'but probably very good in a scrap. Remember, West, that you are the pilot and in command of your aircraft - not them.'

For two days my flying was restricted to an area near the aerodrome - this to enable me to get accustomed to my new type of aircraft, especially its manoeuvrability. I did not have an observer with me but just a few sandbags securely strapped into the rear cockpit and as I taxied out ready to take off, I noticed the Australian and the South African observer sitting on the grass watching me. When I completed my test flying no comments were passed - I was told later by other pilots that this was a very good omen.

The routine of our Squadron was two sorties daily - one in the morning and one in the afternoon. We were detailed for any of the following duties: photographic reconnaissance, spotting for artillery batteries, bombing and machine-gunning enemy troops and transport. Of these various duties photographic reconnaissance was most unpopular; flying at about 6,000 feet on a steady course we were an ideal target for anti-aircraft gun fire - hardly a photographic sortie was accomplished without damage to our planes. The most popular job was the machine-gunning of enemy troops from a low height. Throughout the month of March No 8 Squadron had been very active. The information brought back by all the pilots was of increasing enemy activity. Photographs taken by us clearly showed many more batteries in the Amiens-Bapaume battle zone - we were junior officers, our knowledge and experience was confined to our particular front area, but all of us were convinced that the Germans were 'up to something', probably an early offensive. We repeatedly told this to Leigh-Mallory who agreed and kept 4th Army HQ informed of our reports. On 21 March 1918 the German offensive in the Amiens area was set in motion with considerable initial success. Several other squadrons were then moved into our area - the Germans also brought in air units, amongst them the well-advertised 'Richthofen Circus'. We were told that the circus consisted of their most experienced pilots. Leigh-Mallory concentrated his Squadron effort in ground stafing from low heights. During the period of the relatively short German offensive, the weather was foggy and misty and this in one way protected us from the German fighters. Ground fire, however, was intense and practically every aircraft of our Squadron was hit by either rifle or machine-gun fire. The German offensive was halted by our Army - activity on our front greatly diminished and the Squadron returned to normal sorties.

On 21 April, whilst flying behind our lines in the Amiens sector, I saw a considerable number of flashes from our batteries indicating that German fighters were in our area. I then saw, a few miles east of Amiens, three red Fokkers diving through the smoke of shells bursting around them. I saw one of them diving on what I thought was one of our machines and then to my astonishment the German continued to dive, crashing into the ground near Corby village. There was a rather large field in that locality and after reconnoitring from about 50 feet I landed on it. It took Lieutenant Grice, who was with me on this occasion and myself almost an hour to reach the spot of the crash. We were greeted by a large number of cheerful, enthusiastic Australian artillery officers and men who told us that they had shot down the famous Baron Richthofen. Before leaving I was given by the Australians, as a souvenir, a small piece of Richthofen's cowling roughly cut in the shape of Australia. [46] Leigh-Mallory told me a few days later that there was much controversy about who shot down Richthofen. His death in any case was a psychological blow to German pride and morale. Later a staff officer at Corps HQ told Leigh-Mallory that a Canadian pilot shot down Richthofen. Although this was not what I had seen, I was not surprised with the news as situations in the air arise and often end in a matter of seconds and of course I was a few miles away, concentrating on my work and flying at heights of not much more than 3,000 feet. [47]

The Germans and the French gave much publicity in their radio and press to the exploits and victories of their fighter aces - we in No 8 Squadron were told the names of Richthofen, Goring (German), Guynemer and Fonck (French) but we were not told the names of our own aces. I do not know if this was a deliberate policy or, as I suspect, just bad staff work. It is only after the war that I have read with pride the feats and air victories of McCudden, Bishop, Barker, Proctor and Mannock.

In April 1918 the Royal Flying Corps was renamed Royal Air Force, having amalgamated with the Royal Naval Air Service. The reaction in our Squadron was wonderful - it was a joy and an inspiration to us to belong to a new arm of the Forces. It was up to us flying crews to win spurs and build up the reputation of the new Force. Leigh-Mallory, about this time, informed me that I was to take over command of B Flight and that my promotion to captain would be published in due course in the London Gazette [on 8 November 1918]. As I was leaving his office he asked me to get hold of J. A. G. 'Alec' Haslam MC, an outstanding and brilliant artillery officer who was my observer in the majority of my sorties during the month of April. When I returned to the office with Haslam, Leigh-Mallory said 'It is with great pleasure that I inform you that you have both been awarded the Military Cross - well done - thank you'. It is difficult to explain my feelings that day; to be in a new Force, in the rank of Captain with an MC! I felt I could walk on clouds until I came across the Australian boys who greeted me with 'Feel important?' That brought me down to earth. On 2 June Leigh-Mallory informed me that No 8 Squadron had been attached to the Tank Corps for specific cooperation duties and that my flight would undertake this task. He added that Captain Inglis and Captain Tappet of the Tank Corps would join me the following day. These two officers explained to us that visibility in tanks was rather restricted and they thought that we could be their eyes. We carried out many experiments but were soon confronted with many snags. The main difficulty was how to establish a means of communication between aircraft and moving tanks. The tank crews tried to use various coloured flags, but these often were covered with grease and dirt and could not be easily identified from the air. We thought /T would probably be the answer but if the rumours of a summer offensive were true we would not have the time to try this out. Then the best temporary solution was for pilots to fire Very lights above or near enemy gun emplacements. The tank officers agreed with our suggestions and we trained on these lines.

On 9 July our Squadron was at Auxi-le-Chateau; at about 6pm on that day one of our fighter aircraft landed, probably for refuelling. After about ten minutes the pilot took off again - when he climbed to about 100 feet he turned steeply to the left and in so doing, stalled and crashed. The pilot was killed. Our medical officer told us that the dead pilot was wearing the purple ribbon of the Victoria Cross. The following day we were told that he was Major McCudden - he was buried with full military honours in the small British cemetery at Wavans a couple of miles north of Auxi-le-Chateau.

On 7 August General Sir John Salmond, the head of the Air Force in France, visited our Squadron, now situated at Vignacourt in the Amiens area. We were not told beforehand of his visit. I was so busy detailing crews for various duties and showing on a board the latest air photographs, pinpointing location of enemy batteries, that I did not notice the various visitors in our marquee. Apparently Major General Sir John Salmond, two Army Staff Officers and Leigh-Mallory had been listening in the background for several minutes - Leigh-Mallory then called us to attention and Sir John came forward, saying 'I have some important news for you - tomorrow the Army are launching the biggest and probably the last offensive of the war. They expect the Germans to throw in their considerable reserves. The Army C-in-C needs the earliest possible information of where these reserves are massing or moving to - I ask every one of you to do all you can to get this information - Good Luck'. The morale of the Squadron was marvellous. On the following day, my observer Lieutenant J. Haslam and I took off at dawn. There was a thick mist on the ground but at about 1,000 feet the sky was blue and cloudless. Hundreds and hundreds of gun flashes and hundreds of lights of various colours were piercing the mist and creating a kind of red glow. It was a beautiful sight - the whole front, on the ground and in the air, was alive but unfortunately the movement of German troops and transport was taking place under a blanket of mist. On 8 and 9 August we had narrow escapes both from the ground and from enemy fighters. On the 10th however, weather conditions changed and whilst flying [Armstrong-Whitworth FK 8 C8602] low at about 1,500 feet we saw a large concentration of German troops around vehicles and lorries.[48] This I knew was what the Army needed to know so I decided to return immediately to our aerodrome to pass on this information.

The sky was full of enemy fighters and on that day the RAF suffered heavy casualties, Haslam and I amongst them. A German fighter of the Richthofen Squadron shot us down. On the same day I suffered the amputation of my left leg, well above the knee, in a disused monastery situated a few miles behind our lines and which had been converted into a casualty field post [No 2 Red Cross Hospital] and Haslam, who was wounded in the legs and wrists, was sent to a hospital further down the lines. [49]

On 14 August West wrote a brief letter to a friend on No 8 Squadron:

Dear Keslerton

Now that the doctor has finished with bandaging me up I take the opportunity to write a few lines.

Do you know about these fairy tales you read in magazines, where pilots open fire at 30 yards where you can easily describe the face of your opponent etc - well I never believed it myself and always made a joke of it, unfortunately I did experience it.

After a very exciting morning flying near Roye I came across 7 Huns - I was flying then at 1000', about the height of the clouds -I knew at once that my only-chance was to wander from cloud to cloud making for the lines. Unfortunately I found myself, a few minutes later, in a small gap, one hun, who was 500 feet higher than I, must have followed me out of the cloud then dived and fired 80 yds to 25 yds from my machine - his first burst got me - about 5 explosive bullets went through my left leg and above my knee. I saw his machine, his face - his face -I heard Haslam's guns working, saw his tracers going well through the fellow's machine - Haslam's guns jammed and the hun was still at it -I switched off, peeled off etc - and doing lots of flat turns -I then noticed that my left leg was lying almost across the joy stick - I know I was fainting and saw the ground getting nearer made an effort, pushed my left leg away from the stick - the great pain caused brought me back to reality and landed the machine. It was a bum landing -I fainted immediately - Canadian infantry men who watched the whole show came up to us at once thus saving my life, as the bleeding was enormous owing to the arteries being cut - Old Haslam was great - though wounded in the ankle and foot refused to be attended to until I was fixed up - Haslam always was a great fellow and proved himself great - the journey to the CCS was awful but the worst was the journey down to Rouen - they kept us lying in the open, no shelter – Now we are in a fine hospital, the nurses are charming, the food is adequate -unfortunately we got bombed during the last two nights. If you knew how uncomfortable it is to lie in bed, not being able to move when bombs are coming down.

When the sun rises again, everything is nice - I feel happy once more. I lost my leg but I am through with the actual fighting and after all I feel I have done something for my country - well old bean hope you will do me a favour and gather all my kit in both places (quesues le Coute) put the best half in the suit case, don't forget if you can, to put the watch, the black book, pass-book, best tunic - send this suit case here address all the rest to Messrs Holt & Co. The address here is: N2 Red Cross Hospital, AP02,

W1, France.

Let me know how you are getting on old bean, drop me a line every now and then
- you know how much we do appreciate to receive news from the lines - I understand
that Boomer is taking over the flight - is that correct? Whoever the flight commander
is I wish him the best of luck and hope he will realize how good a flight he is taking
over –

I will be kept here 3 or 4 weeks before going to Blighty. If you or Sinclair are on
leave when I am in London, please call on your old flight commander.

Give my love to Spence, Davies, Reffers - I am writing an update line to Reffers.
Good bye old boy, I wish you the very best of luck.
(I may have one leg but I shall always be cheerful)
F WEST

Alec Haslam also wrote a letter to 8 Squadron.
On the 'Essequibo' or some such 14. viii. 18
Dear Swales

I hope this will find you back again to pleasanter parts and with no other gaps in
the Flight.

In case this is the first intimation you've had of what happened to us, I will presume
sufficient curiosity in you to warrant my setting forth the story.

We had been watching and watched by 7 Fokker Bips from the time we arrived on
the line; however 6 Bristols and some others were close at hand and though we couldn't
persuade them to attack the Huns, even by flying practically into the Hun formation
ourselves, they certainly gave us great security.

We then changed our patrol and had a look at the large junction of E. of it and
found it well worth a visit; time being short we turned for home and were at about
1000' and over our lines when a Fokker Bip appeared in the clouds about 1000' above
us. We continued towards home and he flew after us. I don't know whether he'd seen
us before but anyhow he came along faster, still keeping well above us. So West flat
turned and made him look a bit silly. He was straight above us and stalling to pull up.
So I thought a few rounds wouldn't be wasted, especially as I didn't think he would
attack, we being very low and right over our lines. However, he came round on our
tail and started in. We were getting along splendidly at about 150 yards range when
he decided to close in and at the same time an empty click came from my guns. Of
course he was encouraged and came in and did the dirty on us just in the time I was
changing drums. By the time I had another drum on he had buzzed off and West was
just about landing:- he made an excellent forced landing and I then remembered having
felt my leg hit in the scrap and realised that it was and found that old West had been
hit a nasty one in the left knee - right early on he said - but had crossed his right leg
over and so brought us down; which was a pretty stout effort as, in addition to getting
it right in the bone etc of the knee, he had lost a lot of blood before he landed.

Well, all's well that ends well. We'd landed nearly on top of 2 motor ambulances,
so we buzzed right off. And before we moved off I heard that the Hun had been fetched
down tout de suite - God, I hope I helped!

'All's well that ends well' - I hope West is OK. He was taken before me at the FA
and I've not seen him since. But the doctor there at the CCS later told me that it would
not leave him any the worse. I hope it's true.

I collected a beauty through the left calf - clean through and no bone injury. Rather a large and lurid exit otherwise the perfect Blighty.

The Hun was using explosives - I saw one burst on the empennage and another apparently on my gun, but that must have come through somewhere else as I feel certain my gun wasn't hit. By the way if you want your observer to have a good pair of guns I recommend my old ones -22... 6 and 22395 - the latter is the 'elder and better' - if there is anything in it; they work at 11½ lbs tension not less.

If and when you get back to the old place you will find -I think in the lockers under the window on my side - a large F'cap size A B bound in blue paper board - like the Mess ale book. Kinnear, whose place you took, apparently left some letters in and written in this book and has written to me asking to destroy them. So will you do it for me!

And Mess ale reminds me that I gave Kay a cheque from West on the EFC for 100 frs and 100 frs in cash for the Mess and regret to say I did not intend it as the means to a Mess gramophone.

Kay himself financed the Mess for the last shopping before I came away - I don't know to what extent. Pour la reste, Shirlaw owed 100 frs and Davies 30 frs and everyone else square up to the 9th - except the Bolitho (a friend of Shirlaw!) owes 50 frs which will taken out of him in a dinner to the Flight, I hope.

By the way, 'dabou, donation dedication' - and please notice the epistolary Imperfect - all furniture I possess in France with the exception of my own bed and the bed I lent to Peppers, to you; to Peppers the said bed - which isn't mine really, but belongs to one Haddemore (?) -I don't know how to spell his name.   There is, I think, some money in the RA jacket which I had at V......... If the cost isn't already packed will you please give Ball 50 frs of it and my best thanks for looking after me so well.

Let me have news of you and the flight - and of West as soon as you hear of or from him more than I've told you in this.

I should think you'll be wondering whether I wasn't hit in the head too after reading this.

Well, the very best of luck to you and all the Flight.

        HASLAM

P. S. Met Young at CCS and again at No 3 Gen Hospitel Le Treport. I think he's probably there still as I haven't seen him here. He seemed pretty fair - hit in the arm and thigh I think. Give A Flight the address of the hospital.

For his part in this gallant action Alec Haslam was awarded the Distinguished Flying Cross.

Towards the end of September Freddie West's name was removed from the 'Dangerous List'.

'I was then transported to the London Hospital in Whitechapel; whilst in that hospital, awaiting to be invalided out of the RAF, I resigned myself to resuming my law studies. My hopes and dreams of a flying career had suddenly vanished. Life, however, is to a certain extent like a roulette game - you never know in which slot the ball of destiny will fall. Shortly after Armistice Day I met a Mr Desoutter, a Swiss Engineer, maker of precision instruments. He told me that he had lost a leg in a car accident, after which he designed for himself an aluminium leg which enabled him to climb mountains and fly an aircraft. He then told me that he had recently fitted an English actor, Herbert Marshall, with one of his aluminium legs. This actor was very happy with it and had resumed his acting on the stage. If you can spare about £80, he added, I will fit you with one. Fortunately I accepted the offer. General Sir John Salmond and Sir Hugh Trenchard, I don't know how, heard that I could walk reasonably well with my new artificial limb. Sir Hugh Trenchard sent for me at the Air Ministry and in his very deep voice straight to the point told me 'Do you think that you could fly with that tin leg of yours?' I replied 'Certainly, Sir'. He then said 'Good'. 'Sir John Salmond,' he added, 'told me about your work in France. I want you in my new Force - I shall have problems with the medics but I will see that you will get a permanent commission in the RAF.' My name was in the first list issued to the London Gazette in 1920 and to my delight also Leigh-Mallory and Haslam's names were also on the list. [50]

I began flying again at Northolt. I didn't visualise it then, but in September 1939, as a group captain, I would fly to France in command of No 50 Wing, consisting of Nos 4-13 and 5 Squadrons, flying a Blenheim, in the very same area which I had seen war service both on the ground and in the air. [51]

Footnotes Chapter 25

45   Trafford Leigh-Mallory was born in Mobberley, Cheshire, the son of Herbert Leigh Mallory, (1856–1943), Rector of Mobberly, who legally changed his surname to Leigh-Mallory in 1914. He was the younger brother of George Mallory, the noted mountaineer, who died on Mount Everest in 1924. He was educated at Haileybury and at Magdalene College, Cambridge where he was a member of a literary club and where he made the acquaintance of Arthur Tedder, the future Marshal of the Royal Air Force. He passed his Bachelor of Law degree and had applied to the Inner Temple in London to become a barrister when, in 1914, war broke out. Trafford married Doris Sawyer in 1915; the couple had two children. Leigh-Mallory immediately volunteered to join a Territorial Force battalion of the King's (Liverpool Regiment) as a private. He was soon commissioned and transferred to the Lancashire Fusiliers though officer training kept him in England when his battalion embarked. In the spring of 1915 he went to the front with the South Lancashire Regiment and was wounded during an attack at the Second Battle of Ypres. After recovering from his wounds, Leigh-Mallory joined the RFC in January 1916 and was accepted for pilot training. In July 1916, he was posted to 7 Squadron, where he flew on bombing, reconnaissance and photographic operations during the Battle of the Somme. He was then transferred to 5 Squadron before returning to England for promotion to Major and assignment as a squadron commander. Leigh-Mallory's first combat command was 8 Squadron in November 1917. In the period after the Battle of Cambrai, 8 Squadron was involved in Army cooperation, directing tanks and artillery. At the Armistice, Leigh-Mallory was mentioned in dispatches and awarded the Distinguished Service Order.

46   This was displayed for many yerars in the Torbay Aircraft Museum.

47   60 years later a very large painting of Manfred Freiherr Von Richthofen and a small one of me, painted by the same artist, Mr Henry Campbell, were unveiled in the RAF Museum in London. The same day Kommodore E. Willing, Commanding Jagdgeschwader 71 'Richthofen', telephoned me at Sunningdale inviting me to attend the 60th Richthofen anniversary dinner at their Station in Wittmund, Germany. My friend, the later Air Marshal Sir John Stacey at the Allied Forces Central Europe, also telephoned me to say that the Germans were most anxious to have as their guest a British RAF Officer who was actually flying in the Amiens area when Richthofen was shot down and who saw his body and apparently I was the only ex-RAF officer available to attend the dinner.)

48   They were to co-operate with British tanks advancing towards Roye. Flying through mist in the

Han-Bombleux area West and Haslam found a large concentration of German troops and they flew low to assess the strength. Unsatisfied that he that they had pinpointed them accurately, West dived through the mist , only to be attacked by several German scouts; one of which put a burst into the FK 8, wounding West in the right foot. In spite of this he relocated the enemy troop concentration and turned for home with this important information. However, the FK 8 was then set upon by more German scouts. Haslam kept up a brisk fire from the rear cockpit in spite of being wounded, but in the front cockpit West was struck in the left leg by five explosive bullets which almost severed the limb. In spite of intense pain and severe blood loss, West managed to bring his aircraft back to a crash landing in British lines where he insisted on making his report before receiving medical treatment.

49   It was for this action that Captain West was awarded the Victoria Cross. The most effective way to perform the essential task of locating major enemy formations proved to be to fly low and attract their fire. This Captain West and his observer did for three consecutive days. On the third day he came under sudden and heavy fire from a wood, clearly indicating the unsuspected presence of a large concealed enemy force. Having flown over his target three times to confirm this fact, he set course for base to bring back this vital information. But enemy fighters were also well aware of its importance and he came under heavy and continuous attack from them, during which he was shot through the right foot and his left leg was almost completely severed by explosive bullets. He suffered enormous loss of blood but managed to improvise a tourniquet with his underwear and eventually contrived to make a safe landing behind our lines, where his machine continued to be strafed by enemy fighters in an unsuccessful attempt to silence him. After being rescued by Canadian troops, he insisted on transmitting an accurate and detailed account of his reconnaissance before allowing himself to be taken to hospital for treatment. Sir John Salmond, then Major-General Commanding the RAF in France, later Marshal of the Royal Air Force, has justifiably described his conduct as 'of superb gallantry'.

50   In WWII he was Air Officer Commanding (AOC) No. 12 (Fighter) Group and shortly after the end of the Battle of Britain, took over command of No. 11 (Fighter) Group, defending the approach to London. In 1942 he became the Commander-in-Chief (C-in-C) of Fighter Command before being selected in 1943 as C-in-C Allied Expeditionary Force under General Eisenhower for the D-Day operation on 6 June 1944. In November 1944, en route to Ceylon to take up the post of Air C-in-C South East Asia Command, Air Chief Marshal, Sir Trafford L. Leigh-Mallory's aircraft crashed in the French Alps and he and his wife and eight others were killed.

51   West was awarded a permanent commission in the RAF during 1919. Posted to RAF Uxbridge, he gradually returned to flying duties. He commanded 4 Squadron in 1936 and during World War II he commanded No. 50 Wing in France during 1939. From June 1940 he was the Air Attaché at the British Embassy in Rome and thereafter was part of the British Legation in Berne, where he assisted Allied airmen who had escaped into Switzerland. At one stage the Gestapo put a price on his head because of his underground activities. At the end of the War he was awarded a Commander of the Order of the British Empire for his work. West later achieved the rank of Air Commodore. He finally retired in March 1946 and joined J. Arthur Rank Overseas Film Distributors in January 1946. He became Managing Director in 1947 until 1958 when he retired as Chairman. The last surviving British holder of a VC from WW1, he died on 8 July 1988 aged 92.

Alec Haslam retired as a Flight Lieutenant in June 1927, later taking Holy Orders and becoming a don at Cambridge. He was recalled to the Service during WW2 and retired again in 1945 as a Group Captain. Haslam died in December 1990. See *A VC's Story* by Andrew Thomas, writing in *Intercom* Winter 1992/93

Chapter 26

Balloon Buster

One wheel nearly touched the sandbag of the gun emplacement as the American pilot flew in and flipped the last grenade over the side of the cockpit. He was heading back for another strafing run when it finally happened. He kicked left rudder and stood the Spad on its wing. There was a rip in the fabric by the cockpit and the force of hot metal tearing through his shoulder twisted him around in his seat. The airplane fell off and headed for the ground. But now the immediate shock of the wound was over and the pilot eased back on the stick, sweeping over the still-blazing enemy gun emplacements. His own machine guns chattered in return as waves of nausea began to well up in his stomach. He emptied his guns in this last diving pass and pulled up just high enough to spot the closest clearing. An open field lay dead ahead. The high whistle of the wind abruptly replaced the engine's roar as he cut the throttle and side-slipped down, fighting off the throbbing dizziness. The little plane bounced off the uneven surface of the field, then settled back and rolled to a shaky stop. It was late in the afternoon of 29 September 1918, near the village of Murvaux, France. The American pilot was a twenty-one-year-old second lieutenant from Phoenix, Arizona, whom Eddie Rickenbacker called 'the most intrepid air fighter who ever sat in an airplane.' His name was Frank Luke and he had just made aerial history.

James C. Law, writing in *Air Force*, journal of the US Air Force Association, July 1956. In seventeen days between 12 September and 29 September, in just nine days of combat flying, ten missions and only thirty hours of flight time, Luke was credited with shooting down 14 German balloons and four aircraft (seven aircraft according to some sources). This feat was unsurpassed by any pilot in World War I.

One of nine children of German immigrants, Frank Luke, Jr. was born on 19 May 1897 in Phoenix after his family emigrated from Germany to America in 1873 and settled in Arizona. Frank was his family's fifth child and he grew up excelling in sports, working in copper mines and participating in bare-knuckle boxing matches. As a boy he was an excellent athlete and he is reputed to have been a considerable shot with both rifle and pistol. He was a lively, inquisitive youngster, collecting tarantulas with his sister Tilla and birds' eggs with his pal, Albert 'Pidge' Pinney. He grew up to be strong and good-looking, the natural leader of a trio - himself, Pidge and Bill Elder. The three boys went hunting in the hills, or, on occasion, liberated melons, chickens and other commodities from local farmers. Guns were a way of life and Frank was a crack shot, at birds, small game and (on one memorable occasion) the senior class pennant flying atop the high school flagpole. He played rough-and-tumble football against the Indians at St. John's Mission. During high school summer vacations, he worked the Cornelia copper mine in Ajo. It was hard work, with hard men. When the miners heard that the blonde teenager actually gave dancing lessons, only Frank's pugilistic victories over characters like the Irishman Breen and 'Battler' Haney from San Francisco saved his reputation as a tough guy.

Following America's entry into World War I on 6 April 1917, Luke enlisted in the Aviation Section, US Signal Corps on 25 September and he received pilot training in Texas and California. At Austin, Texas, School of Aeronautics he finished the regular nine weeks' course in seven weeks. At North Island, San Diego, he was first in his class to solo. After being commissioned a Second Lieutenant on 23 January 1918, in March he deployed to France where he finished final flight training at Issoudun at the head of his class in flying and number-two man in gunnery. His first duty was ferrying aircraft at Orly; a task which improved his flying skill but frustrated his aggressive spirit. On 25 July he obtained a posting to the 27th Aero Squadron operating at Saints near Chateau-Thierry along with eight other replacement pilots, among them Joseph Frank Wehner, a flier from Everett, Massachusetts. Joe had been suspected of being a spy because of his German background. During the first week Luke flew only routine patrols, for new pilots were ushered away from areas where there was likely to be trouble. On 30 July Luke witnessed his first aerial combat casualty. On 1 August eighteen planes went up that morning, to protect two reconnaissance Salmsons. Fokkers jumped them and cut them to ribbons. Six pilots of the 27th were lost that morning. Frank Luke learned early that to fight the way he wanted to fight he would have to go it alone and he decided that at the first opportunity, he would head straight for the enemy lines.

On 16 August he broke formation against orders and did just that. He had not even seen an enemy plane, so his idea was to head for the one spot where they were sure to be found. He pushed the little biplane to its ceiling and headed for the nearest German airfield. He throttled back while crossing over the front to avoid detection, but once he was deep into enemy territory, he eased the Spad down, scanning the earth. Finally he saw a cluster of hangars and the dirt runway of the field near the horizon. And ahead of him, at a lower altitude, were six enemy Albatrosses. They were flying in formation, heading toward the field from the same direction as Luke. He pushed the stick forward and dived down to their altitude. Then he opened the throttle and began to close the gap. The German fighters continued serenely on, confident of their safety this far behind their own lines. Finally Luke was within twenty yards of the closest German ship. He was actually part of their formation and they still had not noticed him! He unloaded a long burst of incendiaries into a startled German's fuel tank and then stood the Spad on its nose.

He had drawn his first blood and yet, because he was so far behind the lines that no other Allied planes or observers could confirm the action, he could not officially claim the kill. This was to be the first of many brushes with authority; Luke was impatient of discipline and was constantly in trouble with his superiors. He was not a good mixer and his tough self-confidence did not endear him to his fellow pilots, who considered him a conceited braggart. He was, however, a born combat pilot, whose marksmanship and flying skill were equalled by his aggressive spirit. He became an embittered 'loner' and formed a close friendship with only one other pilot, Lieutenant Joe Wehner.

There were later occasions, when he fought deep in enemy territory, where there could be no official confirmation of his victories. This was only part of the price he paid for his brand of fighting. But that is the unofficial record. The official record began on 12 September 1918 and it became a fighting record that has never been equalled. From his first official victory on this date to his last day in action, ending in the field near Murvaux, just seventeen days passed. And yet in this short time, Frank Luke became the leading American ace in the war. In this seventeen day period he had eighteen official victories! Rickenbacker flew at the front for more than eight months and was the leading American ace with twenty-seven victories at the end of the war, yet even then, Frank Luke's record in only seventeen days of fighting placed him second.

September the 12th marked the opening day of the St. Mihiel offensive and Luke's squadron was busy patrolling its prescribed sector of the front. The ground troops had begun their advance at dawn, but were immediately slowed by accurate German artillery fire. Frank Luke spotted the observation balloon that was directing the deadly fire. It was strung up about two miles behind the front at the right of the American lines, just outside of his patrol sector. He returned to the airfield to report his find. Here he was told that the balloon had already been seen by the squadron in whose patrol sector it was located. It had, in fact, been under constant attack for most of the day, but without success. Luke asked permission to enter the neighbouring patrol sector and attack the important balloon. A good friend of his, a Lieutenant Wehner had just landed to refuel. When he heard about Luke's request, he asked to go along to fly cover for the attack. Balloon attacks were rarely made on a volunteer basis, simply because there were rarely any volunteers. The observation balloon was the most dangerous target in the air. It measured about fifty by two hundred feet, a huge, sausage-shaped bag filled with highly inflammable hydrogen. The observer hung below in a wicker basket. With powerful binoculars and radio communication to the ground, he was an effective observer, usually operating at about 2,000 feet. A lorry on the ground, with a winch on its flatbed, would reel out the balloon at dawn, tow it to wherever it was needed and pull it back in at sunset.

It was a big, stationary target, to be sure. But few who attacked it survived and of those who did, few repeated the attempt. For on the ground, around the balloon in a huge ring, were batteries of anti-aircraft and machine guns. Knowing the exact height of the balloon, they set their shells to explode accordingly. So an attacker had to fly through a wall of exploding shells and machine-gun bullets, pour a long burst of incendiaries into the balloon, since a short burst would seldom ignite the gas, then fly through the fiery wall again on the way out. In addition enemy fighters were usually hiding in the sun somewhere above and in any encounter they would have the advantage of altitude on the balloon attacker.

The requests of Luke and Wehner were granted immediately. When they reached the balloon, Luke peeled off and Wehrner began to circle above to cover him from fighter attack. Luke pulled out of his screaming dive beside the balloon and opened fire, but a machine gun had jammed. He pulled up over the balloon and found himself in the midst of a ring of fire. His plane was jarred by explosions on every side but he whipped around and came back at the balloon, his remaining machine gun chattering. The balloon burst into flames and Frank Luke headed out through the ground fire while his first official victory dropped to earth in flames. Luke landed his SPAD so badly damaged that it was written off - the first of five aircraft which he 'used up' in his meteoric career.

His first success at fighting the drachen was a solid confirmation of his fighting skill. When he volunteered two days later for another balloon attack, he was given a flight of planes to fly cover for him. But his job wasn't easier. For there was not a balloon, but a cluster of three! They were strung up near Boinville and were important to the Germans. They were hung at an exceptionally low altitude to discourage attack. In fact, they were low that the observers in the balloon could not use their parachutes, only recently developed at this time, to save themselves. Because the balloons were so valuable to the Germans it was almost certain that fighters were on guard. As Luke and his escort approached the target, Luke rocked his wings at the flight leader, pulled away from the formation and nosed his Spad down. He had just begun his dive when a pack of Fokkers dropped through the broken clouds, jumping Luke's squadron mates with blazing guns, trying to break through to stop his one-man attack. While they fought off the protective patrol of Fokkers Luke made his run, pouring tracers into the grey bag, but the balloon did ignite. He came back for a second, a third pass and the sky was filled with the smoke of shell bursts. With each dive the ground fire came closer, but he ignored repeated hits and bored through the withering curtain of steel. This was the killing assault and the balloon collapsed into a mass of flaming canvas. Now he turned on his attackers. He defiantly hurled his Spad back into the deadly perimeter and proceeded to strafe the gun position with his remaining ammunition. Finally he headed for home, struggling to keep his battered Spad airborne. When he landed, the ground crew shook their heads in amazement. The plane was completely riddled, no longer fit for flying. One slug was found buried in his headrest, not six inches from Luke's head.

A new plane was made ready and the covering flight returned and was reformed. By late afternoon they were heading back for the two remaining balloons. On this attack, because the first balloon had proved so stubborn, Wehrner was to follow Luke down. The quicker you could get in and out of the zone of fire, the better your chances to live and tell about it. And this way, the chances of any dangerous return passes would be lessened.

Again enemy Fokkers engaged their protecting group and again Luke continued toward one of the balloons, this time closely followed by Wehner. As they drew near the balloons they spied still another enemy formation. The

Germans had figured they would break away from the covering planes for the balloon attack. Eight Fokkers were bearing down on them. Luke and Wehner pushed their throttles wide open and dived, racing the Germans to the balloon. Even before they got within range the balloon's observer jumped, pulling his ripcord in spite of the hopelessly low altitude. They were beating the Fokkers to the balloon but there was time for only one pass. The ground fire was blistering on all sides of the balloon, but they were diving from almost directly above. Luke had time for only a short burst before he had to pull out, but with the first bullet the great gas bag exploded. They passed through the billowing, expanding smoke, levelled off on the deck and flew for home, leaving the burning balloon and their eight pursuers somewhere behind.

At dawn the next day Luke was in the air again, scouting the Boinville area and planning his attack on the third balloon. While doing so, he spotted a new balloon that the Germans had hurriedly sent up at Bois d'Hingry.

He reported back at the field, told what he had seen and a new attack was quickly planned. Three five-plane patrols were to rendezvous near the target as he began his first dive. Then, within sixty seconds of his attack, they were to dive after him. So that any victories resulting could be confirmed, our own observation balloons in the area were alerted to watch for the attack. The time was set for 5.05 that afternoon. As the time drew near, observers began their watch of the lone remaining Boinville balloon. Suddenly the German anti-aircraft gunners jumped into action. Out of the clouds above them came Frank Luke, five Fokkers on his tail. On time to the second, he dived straight at the balloon. According to plan, the three flights of Luke's escorts appeared, diving after him. This placed them on the tails of the German planes, just as they had anticipated. Meanwhile, Luke had once again successfully penetrated the deadly ground fire and observers saw the sausage-shaped outline of the Boinville balloon disappear in a ball of fire. But then they saw his plane still heading toward the ground. It vanished below the horizon. It seemed impossible that he had not crashed. Actually he had pulled out of his dive only a few feet from the ground. Rather than climb up into the still-blazing anti-aircraft fire, he immediately landed on the uneven battle field. His wheels had hardly stopped rolling when he spied the Bois d'Hingry balloon faintly visible in the distance. He jammed the throttle forward and dodged shell craters and ditches to take off. He held his Spad a few feet off the ground, flying between splintered trees and over barbed-wire entanglements until he reached the balloon post. He flashed over the muzzles of the surrounding guns and took them completely by surprise. He pulled back on the stick and climbed upwards toward the balloon, firing as he went. The second balloon to appear in his sights that day, not twenty minutes after the first, fell in flames.

He landed to find that this plane also had been practically shot out from under him. But a patrol had just returned with news of a new balloon, north of Verdun. There was a little daylight left so Luke headed for Verdun in a new plane. He arrived over the balloon at dusk and for the second lime that day surprised the Germans. They were hauling the balloon down for the night when Luke's tracers ripped into it.

There was no flying the next day. The whole front was closed in by bad flying weather, but the day following, 18 September, the weather began to break. Luke and Wehner took off together and began scouting the front. They spotted a group of three balloons just going up near Labeuville. It was unusual for the balloons to be launched this late in the morning. They were normally sent up in the last minutes of protecting darkness before dawn. But there was good reason for the change in procedure. The Germans knew that the balloon killer, who appeared suddenly and was dropping their valuable balloons like over-ripe plums, would not pass such a tempting target. Luke took the bait and Wehrner headed for his covering position above the first balloon. Luke's Spad got one balloon and headed immediately for the second. Meanwhile Wehner was in a scrambling, falling dogfight. When Luke began his first dive, six Fokkers dropped from their hiding place beneath the clouds and headed after him. Wehner charged in and broke up their dive. Now, as Luke exploded his second balloon, Wehrner was slowly losing the one-sided fight he had entered. As Luke hurried to reach him, Wehrner's Spad burst into flames and spun into the ground. Wehner was dead and Luke continued his climb towards the other four Germans now diving to meet him. His engine sputtered. His main fuel tank was empty. He switched to his reserve tank - ten minutes of fuel, which had to be hand-pumped to the engine.

Luke held his climb towards the diving Germans. They were all firing at him now. In another second, they would meet head on. Luke didn't budge from his course. The Germans had to break formation and roared on past. Luke half-rolled his Spad. Pulling the stick back, he split-S'ed after them. As the Fokkers pulled out of their dive, Luke caught the lead ship with a long deflection shot and the pilot slumped forward. Luke's dive had carried him through their formation. Pulling the nose up, Luke tried to line up the second ship in his sights. The Fokker went into a tight turn to the right and Luke turned inside of him, sending a shower of bullets through the Fokker's top wing and into the engine. The plane fell off sluggishly on one wing and then started to spin to the ground. But the two remaining Fokkers were closing in on Luke. He quickly cut his engine, pulled up sharply and the Germans flashed past and headed for home. Almost as suddenly as it had begun, the battle was over.

On his way back to the field Luke spotted a white cluster of exploding antiaircraft shells. Allied gunners were firing at a German LVG, a two-seat reconnaissance plane. Luke headed for the enemy plane, though he expected to run out of petrol at any moment. The German rear gunner opened up but Luke dived below the tail of the LVG and out of the line of fire. He then pulled up and raked the bottom of the ship from nose to tail killing the German pilot. The two balloons and three planes brought his total to eleven positive victories. Six days had passed since his first confirmed kill. He had passed Rickenbacker. His buddies began to call him 'indestructible' and the way he fought, it seemed as though they were right.

As the leading American air ace, Luke had earned a seven-day leave to Paris but he soon returned to combat. Frank Luke remained an outcast and a loner, practicing his marksmanship, riding a motorcycle around the airfield, tuning up his Spad and typing up blank confirmation statements for his future kills. In the first week of September, the 27th Aero Squadron moved from its comfortable quarters at Saints to a closer, but less luxurious, airdrome at Rembercourt, near the Marne, 18 kilometres north of Bar-le-Duc. On 26 September when the Meuse-Argonne offensive opened he added another plane to his score but again lost his wingman, Lieutenant Roberts. Deeply depressed, Luke went AWOL for a day. He destroyed another balloon and shot down a two-seat Hanover on an unauthorised flight. On 28 September, after achieving his 14th and 15th victories, he landed his SPAD XIII at the French aerodrome at Cicognes where he spent the night, claiming engine trouble. The French treated 'the indestructible' royally that night. Next morning he walked out into the cold dawn and climbed into his ship. The 220hp Hispano-Suiza engine was already warmed up and idling. The French mechanics had refuelled the plane and armed the twin Vickers machine guns. They had even left a bag of hand grenades on the floor of the cockpit for him. When he returned to the 1st Pursuit Group's base at Rembercourt he was confronted by Captain Alfred 'Ack' Grant, his squadron's commanding officer; a disciplinarian, who ordered the squadron to fall out in formation at reveille. Luke's persistent flouting of orders had become a disgrace and a grounding and arrest order was issued; but it was destined never to be served. Despite being under threat of arrest by Grant for being AWOL, Luke took off without authorization and flew to a forward airbase at Verdun, where his sympathetic Group commander, Major Harold Hartney, a Canadian who instinctively understood the undisciplined ways of fliers, cancelled the arrest order and gave Luke tacit approval to continue his balloon hunting. That evening just before sunset, Luke flew to the front to attack three balloons in the vicinity of Dun-sur-Meuse six miles behind the German lines. He first dropped a message to the American balloon headquarters in Souilly and dropped a note reading, 'Watch three Hun balloons on the Meuse, Luke.' The balloons were floating a few miles back of the front, near Murvaux.

The observation post watched him nose over for his attack. Suddenly the air was full of Fokkers. There were ten of them. They had been patrolling in relays 12,000 feet, waiting all day for him. First one, then another of the Fokkers dropping out of the fight in flames. Luke was kicking the little Spad in and out of the swarming Germans like a wild man. For a full five minutes he fought them off. Then his Spad appeared to go out control and tumble toward the ground. His plane was falling directly over the three balloons at Murvaux, but Frank Luke wasn't dead. The German gun crews stopped their cheering and watched in stunned silence as he levelled out and opened fire. The first balloon had already burst into flames at Dun-sur-Meuse before the gun crews recovered. The air around him began to explode as they angrily opened up. Luke hit second balloon at Briere Farm and he flew on to Milly and shot the third down in flames. Three thick columns of smoke were observed beginning to rise but Luke was severely wounded by a single machinegun bullet fired from a hilltop above him, a mile east of the last balloon site he had attacked.

He dived to strafe German troops in the streets of Murvaux but ack-ack caught him and he eventually crash-landed on the outskirts of the small village. As he waited for the German troops in the little field outside of

Murvaux Luke knew that his war was over. He had emptied his machine guns and the hand grenades were gone. The pain in his shoulder had eased a bit, but he couldn't fire up the engine himself. He could only wait. As German troops spilled into the field near the Ruisseau de Bradon, by a stream leading to the River Meuse Frank Luke pulled himself out of the cockpit. He stood by his Spad waiting for them. They surrounded the ship and the German officer called out to him to surrender. Frank Luke drew his Colt Model 1911 pistol and emptied the .45 at the enemy. That was his answer and a signal Germans to cut him down with arms fire and he died instantly. He had fought with all he had and he was not quite indestructible but Frank Luke came as close to it as anyone can get.

On 30 September the Germans buried Luke in the Murvaux cemetery. For three months, nothing was known of Luke, except that he had disappeared. Not until 3 January 1919 did the American military authorities have definite word of his death. His grave was located and the story of his last fight pieced together from eyewitness accounts. After the US Army obtained sworn testimony from French and American sources, Luke was awarded a posthumous Congressional Medal of Honor. The presentation was made to Frank Luke, Sr., in Phoenix in May 1919. His son's habit of making unauthorised sorties has led to some confusion over his actual score, recorded accounts varying between 17 and 21. [52]

Eddie Rickenbacker said of Luke, who was second only to Rickenbacker among pilots serving only with the AEF: 'He was the most daring aviator and greatest fighter pilot of the entire war. His life is one of the brightest glories of our Air Service. He went on a rampage and shot down fourteen enemy aircraft, including ten balloons, in eight days. No other ace, even the dreaded Richthofen, had ever come close to that.'

Footnotes Chapter 26

52   17 of Luke's 18 victories were officially recorded as destroyed, versus only 11 of Rickenbacker's 26. Americans flying with the Royal Flying Corps/Royal Air Force from April 1918 who exceeded Luke's score were Frederick W. Gillet (20 claims, all destroyed); Lieutenant Harold A. Kullberg DFC, 1 Squadron RFC (19 confirmed) and Wilfred Beaver (19 claims, 12 destroyed). Tied with Luke at 18 was William C. Lambert (18 claims).

Chapter 27

August To November 1918

H. F. Taylor[53]

Harold F. Taylor was commissioned in the RFC in January 1918 at the age of eighteen and after the usual training was sent in July 1918 to 205 Squadron, operating on the Somme. He flew the D.H.4 and the D.H.9, carrying out reconnaissance, photography and bombing, sometimes flying two and three raids a day and visiting St. Quentin, Busigny, Namur and Dinanl among other towns. Richthofen's famous 'Circus' was still lively. Though three observers were wounded when flying with him, Lieutenant Taylor emerged unscratched to the end of the War. Moving up after the Armistice, his squadron was engaged on the earliest air mail, carrying mails from Cologne to the French coast. He was demobilized in April 1919.

August 8th, 1918. Who of those who were on the Somme will forget that day when we started to push the enemy back along the long, straight road which leads from Amiens to Peronne? I had just joined my squadron as spare pilot. It happened that an observer had been wounded the previous day and my flight commander asked if I would act as an observer for a time. Of course I said 'Yes.' What else could I say? Thus it was that on August 8th I had my first experience of a bombing expedition over the lines. The objective was an ammunition dump somewhere along that same long, straight road. Fourteen machines flew in V-shaped formation, so close that an observer on one side could make faces at his friend flying on the other.

For an hour we circled on our own side of the lines, gaining height. Referring to my map, I found I could look down on the Forest of Crécy, where centuries ago another army of ours had fought, but with what different weapons! Now we were heading east, sweeping along at ninety miles an hour, three miles up. At such an altitude, details below cannot easily be picked out and because of my lack of experience we were over the target and dropping bombs before I realized we had crossed the lines. At a signal from my pilot, I pulled the two wires and released the bombs from their rack below the fuselage. Then I leaned over the side to watch them fall.

Have you ever looked down from a high building and felt as though you must throw yourself down? As I watched those two bombs falling, second after second, getting smaller and smaller until they became invisible, I felt an almost irresistible impulse to slip over the low wall of three-ply wood that was the side of the cockpit and follow them. I had to turn away.

So far, we had had the sky to ourselves, but as we turned for home I became aware of a number of black specks on our left, rapidly growing into a flight of enemy scouts. They did not dive on us, but hung behind, peppering away at the end machines of the V formation. Every one of us opened up with his two Lewis guns and I had my first sight of a machine sent down in flames. Who hit him it was impossible to say, since he was the foremost in the attack and the target of at least six guns. He suddenly dived. Petrol vapour streamed out like smoke behind him, then burst into flames. I watched as he rushed downwards, to fall to pieces 1,000 feet below. His companions disappeared and we were left to go home in peace. In the distance I noticed a number of machines carrying out most wonderful evolutions. There must have been twenty, twisting and turning like worms writhing in a fisherman's bait tin.

At the lines we dived and broke formation. My pilot flew low, perhaps 100 feet up and we looked on the ground that had been fought over that morning. The earth was torn up. Here a tree stump, there a heap of ruins, a wrecked gun, a dead horse and a deserted tank half buried in the mud. It is impossible to describe how desolate the scene appeared. Soon we were back at the aerodrome, taking off our flying suits.

'Poor old Baker's done,' said my pilot. 'Didn't you' see him go down?' I had not noticed any of our men drop out, but it was true. Only thirteen buses landed. I was no longer a spare pilot.

'Those fellows were having a good time stunting, just before we got to the line, weren't they?' I asked.

'Stunting?' said Johnson grimly. 'That was a dog fight. Our bombers and Jerry's scouts. That's what would happen to us if we didn't keep formation.'

'Why didn't we go and give them a hand?'

'Nothing to do with us. Our business is to drop bombs and get home as quickly as possible.'

One soon gets to know people in an Air Force squadron. There was Mills, who always stayed in bed until the last possible moment and at the cry 'Raid on!' would hastily don his flying kit over his pyjamas and climb into the machine. There was Macdonald, who, unknown to the CO, was so short-sighted as to be unable to judge his height and had to give the controls to his observer when about to land. Biddard, who rouged his cheeks and reddened his lips; and Machin, whose father was a boot manufacturer and kept his son supplied with an extraordinary collection of footwear.

I was soon to see changes. One by one as the days went by, familiar faces disappeared and new ones came. Mills went off one day alone, on a photographic expedition, returned with a dud engine and was well cursed by the CO for not getting the job done. He went off again and never came back. Whether he was killed or spent the rest of the war roaming a prison camp in pyjamas, I never knew. It was not the CO's fault. He was being hurried by the wing commander, who in turn, no doubt, was responsible for the photos to someone higher up. One machine and its occupant was a small price to pay for them.

Macdonald was lucky. He went home after six months' flying with 'nerves.' Biddard came down one day in a raid on Namur and was taken prisoner, unhurt, but no doubt sadly missing his rouge and lipstick, which he had left behind. That evening in the mess, raid orders were posted up just like the football teams we used to put up at school only a few months before. Machines, with pilot and observer, were set out each in its position in the formation. Being a new pilot, I was given a comparatively safe position near the front.

At dawn next morning we were awakened by the cry 'Raid on!' and hurried out for a quick breakfast of boiled eggs. The engines were being run up by mechanics and we were soon in. A heavy mist hung over the ground. One by one the engines were opened out, the machine moved forward, gained speed and at last rose up. Soon we were in formation, circling to gain height. Below us stretched a sea of cotton wool, the earth being obscured by ground fog. Ahead, we steered into the rising sun, straight for the lines. I had no difficulty in keeping in formation; we had practised that when in the training squadron. Nothing happened as we crossed the lines and neared our objective. Then suddenly, a dirty yellow cloud unrolled itself about 20 yards on my right and a hoarse 'Woof followed. It was 'Archie,' an anti-aircraft battery.

Another and another followed and we were soon flying through slowly dispersing clouds of smoke. It seemed impossible to avoid being hit and before I realized it, I had soared 200 feet above the rest. I was no better off. As I turned to avoid one burst, I would see another appear in front of me. The range had been changed and while the formation sailed peacefully below I was catching the lot. However, we left it behind and I resumed my place. On several subsequent occasions, I have seen young pilots do the same thing, to fall easy prey to Fokkers lurking above waiting for 'Archie' to disrupt the formation.

Over the target we dropped our cargo and then as we turned, we met the enemy scouts as before. Why they did not dive on us from the front and split us up I do not know, but their policy was always to hang on behind. Our observers opened fire. Streams of tracer bullets shot out from each gun and our machines began to sway from side to side and up and down, yet still keeping in the V shape, which it would have been fatal to lose. For fifteen minutes it went on. Above the roar of the engine could be heard the sharp rattle of machine guns. Little rags of fabric would spring up in the wings as bullets tore them and all the time the pilot must keep his hand on the throttle and his eyes on the machine ahead, swinging and dipping until collision, seemed imminent, yet always keeping a little above and to one side, so that the guns in front might protect his blind spot under the tail.

We reached the lines and our attackers vanished. We could fly steadily now and I had time to look behind. My observer was leaning on the side, white-faced and gazing longingly at the ground below. I realized he had been wounded and the awful thought flashed through my head that he might fall across the controls, setting the machine into a dive from which I might be unable to pull out. Hastily I motioned to him to sit down and dived steeply for home. Every minute I expected to feel his weight on the elevator wires and I was never more thankful than when my wheels touched the aerodrome. My engine stopped as I landed and I stood up and waved. The ambulance, always ready, dashed across and my observer was carefully lifted out. I never saw him again: wounded men were always hurried away, lest the sight of them should affect the nerves of the rest. I looked at my bus. The planes were torn and the ailerons sagged loosely. It was half an hour before the next man came in, then one by one the stragglers arrived. Three messages came later, reporting forced landings up and down the country, but four of our machines were never heard of again. That was my first air raid as a pilot.

Of course it wasn't always like that. We made two and sometimes three raids a day. Sometimes we had trouble with aircraft or 'Archie' or both; often we had none. Twice we took over new aerodromes, following our slowly advancing infantry. New faces appeared and old friends dropped out and in three months I found myself senior pilot of my flight.

It was late in the afternoon of a day in October. We had done our two raids and imagined our work was over for the day, when a message came from the wing commander, asking for volunteers to bomb Peronne, the possession of which our troops were stoutly contesting. Everybody volunteered; we couldn't refuse. We were assured that it was an easy job, that there would be no 'Archie' left in the town and that we should be back before dark. There was no time to gain height and we must do our job at 2,000 feet, a most unusual thing for us, with our engines specially designed for use at high altitudes. We approached the lines as dusk was falling. All around us guns flashed incessantly. It seemed that the air must be full of projectiles. I have no idea how high a shell travels, but I went in fear of being knocked to pieces any minute. Then 'Archie' started. At such a range he could be very effective and we had experienced nothing like it before. Still we kept steadily on, to meet a new horror as we approached the town. Long strings of balls of fire began to float up. Sometimes slowly, then accelerating, one could not judge their speed. Sooner or later one must become entangled and fall to a hideous death.

Now we were over the town. I signalled to my partner to drop his bombs. As he did so, the engine began to splutter and the nose dropped. I looked at the revolution indicator: the engine had fallen off to half its speed. Hastily I swung round, so hastily, indeed, that for some seconds my compass card continued to swing and I could not be sure in which direction we were flying. Our only hope now was to clear the lines. We could no longer fly horizontally; the only thing was to glide at as small an angle as possible and trust to luck.

Now we were alone 'Archie' recommenced and so near were his shots that in the disturbed air we were tossed like a leaf in the wind. Tracer bullets pelted from below as we crossed the lines only a few hundred feet up. We kept up as long as possible, but a very convenient field not badly scarred by shell holes enabled us to make a safe landing. Even then we were not really sure we were among friends until a khaki uniform appeared. My observer was so overjoyed that he wrung the hand of this bewildered artilleryman and then complained of a wound in the head. Gingerly we untied his helmet. Not a scratch! It was a case of shell shock. 'Archie' had been a bit too close.' I spent the night with a battery of howitzers nearby and after phoning up my squadron got my engine repaired, it was a minor mishap and I flew back next day.

As I say, these particular flights were exceptional. The one I remember best was the last one I ever did. It was uneventful, but I was panic-stricken the whole time. I was to go on leave next day and I could not drive away the fear of catching a stray bullet on this raid, after having done over 100 without a scratch. However, I did come back safely and next morning, as I waited for the car to take me on leave the CO popped his head out of his hut and said:

'The war's over!' It was November 11th.

Chapter 28

Epilogue

Oh it's Tommy this, an' Tommy that, an' Tommy go away';
But it's 'Thank you, Mister Atkins', when the band begins to play,-
The band begins to play, my boys, the band begins to play.
Oh it's Thank you Mister Atkins', when the band begins to play.
Rudyard Kipling

Toward the latter half of June 1940 appeared the following announcement:
'Awarded a Bar to the Distinguished Flying Cross. Pilot Officer Louis Arbon
Strange DSO MC DFC.' The decorations after the name of a Pilot Officer were
unusual. They connoted brilliant ability and outstanding courage, yet the rank
was the lowest commissioned rank in the Royal Air Force. Thoroughly
intrigued, I pursued the matter and learned of the experiences of an
Englishman who was so anxious to help his country in the war that although
he had played his part in creating the Royal Air Force and had retired with the
rank of Lieutenant Colonel and Wing Commander he was happy to rejoin as
a Pilot Officer. At the age of forty-nine he was as keen to strike a blow for
England as he had been at the age of twenty-three. Moreover he has proved
himself capable of striking as strong a blow in these latter days as in the earlier
days, as the award of that Bar to his Distinguished Flying Cross, which was
won in 1918, serves to show.

He was once asked what his real rank was. 'What does it matter?' he
replied, a gleam of amusement in his blue eyes. He is tall and slender with
greying hair and thoughtful lines on his lean brown face and his words recall
the words of Burns - 'The rank is but the guinea stamp, a man's a man for all
that.'

Here is an Englishman who loves his country and is doing his best for her;
one who loves the soil which his forefathers have cultivated for generations;
one who has seen the whole panorama of aviation unfold and has helped to
unfold it; one who at the age of fifty loves flying as much to-day as he did
when he took his Royal Aero Club certificate No. 575 on 5 August 1913 and
applied for a commission in the Royal Flying Corps. In those days he was
farming 600 acres, but flying won him over to join the Royal Flying Corps and
it was arranged that his brother should look after his farm.

'When farming pays, I fly for a hobby,' he said. 'When farming doesn't pay,
I fly for a living and make farming my hobby.'

His friends were amused one day to find him referred to in the same official publication as Lieutenant Colonel L. A. Strange DSO MC DFC and as Pilot Officer L. A. Strange DSO MC DFC, so someone was apparently rather bewildered. As he has since attained the rank of Squadron Leader this puzzle may be solved by referring to him as Colonel Strange.

Born at Blandford in Dorsetshire in 1891, he was educated at St. Edward's School, Oxford, where Wing Commander Douglas R. S. Bader was educated in later years and in May 1914 - nine months after taking his pilot's certificate - he donned the uniform of the Royal Flying Corps. Three months later, on 16 August 1914, he flew over to France in a Henri Farman biplane which was fitted with a Lewis gun on a mounting of his own design, the first aircraft to be fitted with the gun which afterwards became the main fighting weapon of the air.

Unable at his first attempt to climb within 1,500 feet of the enemy, he was ordered to take out his Lewis gun and use a rifle for fighting in the future. To use a rifle the observer was compelled to stand up in the cockpit and it was difficult to aim straight owing to the movements of the aircraft, so the inventive mind of Colonel Strange overcame this drawback by fitting a safety strap to the leading edge of the top plane. With Lieutenant E. Rabagliati as his gunner, he went up on 2 October to try out his idea, the success of which led to its adoption in other aircraft.

Within twelve days of landing in France he experimented with the forerunners of fire bombs in the shape of petrol bombs which set fire to two German lorries; on 6 October he dived down on German troops to attack them with a machine-gun in what was probably the first ground strafe; towards the end of November he originated leaflet raids by dropping. French news bulletins, printed by a French priest, over occupied parts of France; he designed the standard mounting for the Lewis gun used on the army biplane known as B.E.2C; and being one of the earliest advocates of arming aircraft who preached the importance of the gun and the gunner, he may truly be regarded as a pioneer of air warfare.

The army of those days had little faith in aeroplanes and the men who flew them. On 4 September when Colonel Strange and other pilots in his squadron saw Von Kluck swerving away from Paris, the Higher Command could not credit it, with the result that the 'Old Contemptibles' were compelled to continue their desperate retreat from Mons for a day longer than they need have done. It was all so plain to the pilot in the air, but it took twenty-four hours to convince the Higher Command on the ground.

Colonel Strange happened to be the first to observe the initial German gas attack at Ypres on 22 April 1915. He was flying in the evening when he saw what appeared to be streams of yellowish-green smoke rolling from the German front trenches toward the British lines. A German soldier captured ten days earlier had mentioned a forthcoming gas attack, but as no signs of preparation could be detected from the air the information was discredited. Looking down, Colonel Strange was puzzled by the phenomenon; then he remembered what the German had said and flew full speed back to his base, whence he was rushed straight into the presence of General Plumer to report.

Of his adventures in peace and war there is no end. Once during his training days at the Central Flying School, Upavon, a petrol tap in his Bleriot snapped at 5,000 feet and the fumes rendered him unconscious. The Bleriot started to side-slip out of control, but in side-slipping the spray of petrol was blown away from him and the fresh air brought him round. Seeing the way to salvation, he continued to side-slip down to the aerodrome - an unforgivable crime in the eyes of the commanding officer who, thinking he had been deliberately stunting in defiance of orders, gave forth a flow of admonition which shocked the semi-conscious pilot back to his senses. The pilot, who was expecting praise for saving his life and the aircraft, was surprised to get a wigging. Not until his commandant had exhausted his vocabulary was he able to explain what had happened and prove it by his petrol-soaked clothing.

It recalls an amusing incident in which Colonel Strange administered the reproofs when he was in charge of the Central Flying School at Upavon three years later. One day he saw a pupil turn upside down at 2,500 feet and glide in this position with propeller stopped down to the golf course, whereupon the tail swung over and the Sopwith Pup turned right way up again. The pupil simply got out of the cockpit, swung the propeller and took off again as though landing upside down were quite the normal thing. Colonel Strange gasped. Climbing into the nearest aircraft, he sped after the pupil and waved him down.

'What on earth do you mean by flying the aircraft straight off again after landing upside down?' he queried.

The pupil looked at his commanding officer in amazement. 'The last thing I remember was starting to try a roll,' he said. 'Then I woke up to find myself sitting on the golf course and as it is forbidden to land there, I started up and took off again.'

Even more amusing was the meeting of Colonel Strange with a brigadier who was posted to a camp on Salisbury Plain and told to take charge of 8,000 men in four days. The camp proved to be one bell tent, one sergeant and three men. Rushing to London, the brigadier bullied the right clerks into signing orders for equipment and when he found the stores were sold out, he calmly rubbed out the names of the firms who had no supplies and wrote in the names of firms who had the goods. Ordering his sergeant and three men to guard the equipment and rations until they reached Salisbury - he was afraid someone else might scrounge them - he had his camp ready in four days. When the men turned up he found all their names began with A and B and there were so many Adams and Browns that he ordered every man to be given a nickname, so the men were given nicknames which stuck to them for the rest of their service. That brigadier was a genius in the gentle art of improvisation.

Colonel Strange himself proved no mean exponent of the gentle art, for he was once given a sergeant and three men, an Avro, a Bleriot and the remains of two Henri Farmans and told to form a squadron. He did it, too, by making the brilliant pupils teach the slow coaches; but his great accomplishment was obtaining from headquarters orders for three new training Avros. Knowing that someone else would take them from under his nose, orders or no orders, he sent three pilots down to the works to remain there until the aircraft were through their tests and then to fly them straight away. He was taking no chances. His chagrin can be imagined when the day before he was due to take his new Squadron No. 23 to France; he had to be rushed to hospital for an immediate operation for appendicitis. To make matters worse, a swab was left inside him after the operation and kept him fourteen weeks in hospital and below par for months after.

That led to some of his finest constructive work for the Royal Flying Corps, for he was given charge of the Machine-Gun School at Hythe which later became No. I School of Aerial Gunnery. When he took command the school turned out five pupils a week and on leaving it was turning out five a day. Directly bad weather prevented his pupils from living under canvas, he requisitioned the Imperial Hotel. He knew what he wanted and took it. Removing the aerodrome to Lympe compelled the pupils to go three miles for target practice and they could not waste time walking six miles.

Transport was essential and it was not to be had. Selecting pupils who could drive, Colonel Strange went down, to the bus depot of Messrs. Tilling and Stevens and as each bus came in it was requisitioned and driven off. The company claimed £150,000. But the country got its air gunners who shot the Germans out of the skies.

'Every man who goes into the air on a fighting machine is a gun-layer first and last and so his success and the success of his squadron and the whole RFC depended on his gun-laying ability,' he wrote in his book 'Recollections of an Airman.' 'Without the supreme efficiency of the man behind the gun, all other work done by the RFC and other arms of the service, seemed bound to be nullified, because photography, wireless, bomb dropping, etc, could not be carried out without the protection of fighting machines manned by efficient gunners. I therefore threw myself whole-heartedly into the development of the gunnery schools that were to teach and improve shooting from the air and assure the RFC the supremacy over our opponents.'

A new generation fighting the same old enemy has learned that the man behind the gun in the aircraft is still the deciding factor, as Colonel Strange preached and practised in the last war. The far-sighted Englishman who joined up as a Pilot Officer in this war laid down the foundations of gunnery for the Royal Air Force.

His escapes in the air have been legion, but the most hair-raising of all took place on 10 May 1915 when he was fighting a German at 8,500 feet over Menin. An empty ammunition drum jammed in his Lewis gun, so he controlled his aircraft, by holding the stick between his knees while he started to tug at the drum with both hands. At that instant the stick slipped and the Martynside stalled and flicked over into a spin. He was still gripping the jammed drum with both hands when he was flung clean out of the aircraft and he hung there with only that jammed drum between him and instant death.

'I knew it might come off at any moment, however and as its edge was cutting my fingers badly, I had to get a firmer hold of something more reliable. The first thing I thought of was the top of the centre section strut which at that time was behind and below the Lewis gun, but as the machine was now flying upside down, I had sufficient wits left to realize that it was behind and above me, though where it was exactly I could not tell,' he wrote in his book.

'Dare I let go the drum with one hand and make a grab for it? Well, there was nothing else for it but to take the risk; I let go and found the strut all right and then I released my other hand and gripped the strut on the other side. I was then in a more comfortable position and at least I felt rather more part of my machine than I had done in my original attitude.

'My chin was rammed against the top plane behind the gun, while my legs were waving about in empty air. The Martynside was upside down in a flat spin and from my precarious position the only thing I could see was the propeller (which seemed unpleasantly close to my face), the town of Menin and the adjacent countryside. Menin and its environs were revolving at an impossible angle - apparently above me - and getting larger with every turn.' I began to wonder what sort of a spot I was going to crash on.

'Then I got angry and cursed myself for a fool for wasting time on such idle speculations, while at the same time it dawned on me that my only chance of righting the machine lay in getting my feet into the cockpit. If I could manage it, I knew that I was bound to fall automatically into the cockpit when the machine came over. I kept on kicking upwards behind me until at last I got first one foot and then the other hooked inside the cockpit. Somehow I got the stick between my legs again and jammed on full aileron and elevator; I do not know exactly what happened then, but somehow the trick was done. The machine came over the right way up and I fell off the fop plane into my seat with a bump.'

Even then he was in dire danger, for he crashed right through the seat and jammed all the controls. It became a desperate fight to pull out the bits of seat from the controls before the aircraft crashed. He had, of course, kicked all his instruments to bits in trying to get his feet back into the cockpit. He just escaped death by a few seconds. 'I rose and cleared the trees on the Menin road with very little to spare,' he added, to round off a double escape as dramatic as any in the history of aviation.

In 1918 Charles Findlay DFC AFC a Bristol Fighter pilot on 88 Squadron, a newly formed unit, served under Wing Commander, Lieutenant Colonel Louis Strange. He described him as 'a grand senior officer.' 'The fact that the average life of a pilot on active service had been estimated at three weeks failed to damp our enthusiasm, because we had confidence in the new Bristol machine which was powered by a Rolls-Royce engine, the Falcon. In August when the Allied armies had begun a victorious advance our Wing co-operated with the Fifth Army on the Lille front. To reduce hostile interference, sweeps were organised. Two or three squadrons would rendezvous over a well defined landmark, each at a different height and the formation would then penetrate enemy territory and search the sky. Hostile aircraft were forced to land at their aerodromes, where they were attacked by machine-gun fire. Though successful, the effect of the operation was temporary. Our Lieutenant Colonel Strange produced a new idea. His suggestion that our wing should attack thoroughly one aerodrome at a time was approved. Several days' observation confirmed that the majority of enemy machines were grounded every day at lunch lime. Haubourdin near Lille was selected as the first target. Four squadrons took part, comprising in all sixty-five machines. Bristol Fighters, Camels and S.E.5s; the formation was led by the Wing Commander. All machines were loaded with explosive and incendiary bombs and as much machine-gun ammunition as they could carry.

'The impressive air fleet met over Reclingham aerodrome at 12.30 pm, each squadron at its allotted height and crossed the lines at La Bassee. On arrival at Haubourdin, after making wide sweeping arcs to deceive the enemy, the Camels attacked first, the other squadrons circling overhead to give air protection while waiting their turn. A solitary enemy machine was engaged in circuits when we arrived; the pilot panicked when he saw the silently gliding armada approaching and promptly crashed into a tree on the edge of the aerodrome. The leader of the Camels, flying past the entrance of each hangar, his wheels nearly touching the ground, discovered that three of the hangars were packed with machines. Zooming up to about 200 feet he dropped a bomb on each as a signal. Then the fun started. When the Camels had unloaded, the SE5s descended and joined the party and the hangars were soon ablaze. We, the Bristols, continued to circle above at a few thousand feet, having a grandstand view of the proceedings. When our turn came we attacked with 25lb bombs any target that seemed to have escaped attention. A building that appeared to be the Officers' Mess was left in flames.

On the ground utter confusion reigned; personnel streamed across the landing ground in a struggle to reach a building marked with a Red Cross. They came in for attention en route. Troops in the adjacent railway station were attacked with machine-gun fire, many casualties resulting. Two Staff cars tried to escape but were shot-up, one of them running into a ditch and climbing a bank. A train was shot at and stopped. Haubourdin aerodrome received a mighty pounding and the operation destroyed a considerable number of hostile aircraft and personnel. All our machines returned intact.

The following day a similar raid was made on Lomme aerodrome with equally successful results. The element of surprise was confirmed on arrival when we saw two pilots, panic stricken, crash their machines on the landing ground before a shot had been fired or a bomb dropped.

By October I had learned many lessons in the art of air combat. I had been in France without any leave, except for a few days in Normandy. After every flight my machine was wheeled to the butts and I personally re-aligned the Aldis sight with the machine-gun, a matter of supreme importance to obtain accurate shooting. I had found that the vibration of flying and landing often threw the sight out of alignment. Gun and sight were synchronised to be accurate at a distance of fifty yards, as I knew that it was a waste of ammunition to fire at a hostile machine much beyond that distance. Practice taught me to fire consistently short bursts each of ten rounds and never to trust the visible trajectory of tracer bullets; the burning phosphorous regularly flew off at an angle after travelling a short distance.

My observer and I had recorded some successes (nine to the front gun and five to the rear one) and our Bristol had never been hit by a hostile bullet. A success was never claimed if the enemy was only out of control, because it was known that the simulation was often used as a stunt to escape.

In August my Flight was given a roving commission to operate on the Amiens front during the battle. The famous German 'Circus,' commanded by Lowenhardt, who had succeeded Richthofen, was working there and our task was to search for the multi-coloured formation. The leader always flew in a red machine. On two successive days we fought them and several were shot down without loss to ourselves. On the second day I found myself in deadly combat with the leader when my ammunition was nearly spent. Suddenly the enemy presented a perfect target for my observer, Lieutenant Digby-Worsley, who poured a short stream of bullets into the cockpit with his Lewis gun. The red machine side-slipped and turned over and over as it fell to the ground. The following day a German news bulletin announced that Lowenhardt had been killed the previous day on the Western front.

The day of days for the number of enemy aircraft shot down was October 30th, less than a fortnight before the Armistice. The RAF Communiqué placed the total at 68 aeroplanes and one balloon, a record for the war. It was now rare to encounter hostile aircraft flying in small numbers. Our young pilots felt on top of the world, burning with exultation and eagerness to meet the opposition. Constant improvement in the power and performance of our machines had nourished keenness and boosted morale.

On the morning of the 30th - weather fine - I led an offensive patrol at 15,000 feet over Tournai, Leuze and Ath, an area rich in military targets which were being pounded by our D.H.9A bombers. Our formation consisted of fifteen Bristols, arranged in flights of five machines each. We flight commanders took it in turn to lead squadron patrols.

'Wind in aerials; close in,' I called over the wireless telephone.

I had spotted a large number - about fifty - hostile fighters cruising towards us. Our attack was made in succession of flights, machines in line ahead for protection of each other. This orderly procession, however, lasted only a short time and the inevitable dog-fights developed. Several machines fell out of the sky at the first contact, some in flames and others out of control.

One vivid picture remains etched in my memory. For a split second I glimpsed through whirring blades, the goggled eyes of a Fokker pilot glued to the sight of twin-Spandau guns which were spurting streams of bullets. They missed. In a flash, zooming up in a climbing turn, I was on the Fokker's tail for a few precious seconds and my front gun riddled the cockpit. The enemy plunged to the earth in flames. But there was no time to exult; I was just in time to take violent evasive action during an attack by another hostile machine. As the Fokker speeded past in pulling out of the dive, my observer raked the gaily-painted fuselage from nose to tail with a burst from his Lewis gun. It reared up, sideslipped and dropped below, burning like a torch.

The enemy leader now endeavoured to bring cohesion to his battered formation and fearing that the Bristols might be running out of ammunition, I did the same. Gradually our machines responded to my signal to resume formation and the enemy sheered off. We returned to the aerodrome and found that one machine was missing and that several had been damaged. Later in the day we learned that the missing Bristol had been chased down by six hostile fighters and compelled to land just our side of the lines. Pilot and observer were wounded but recovered in due course. A total of sixteen enemy machines had been destroyed in the encounter; confirmation came from our own troops who had witnessed the engagement from the front lines.

In the afternoon we rode aloft to resume the battle but searched the sky in vain. Reluctant to return without inflicting some damage on the nearly broken enemy, we descended to ground level and peppered with machine-gun fire the important railway yard at Ath, in Belgium. All our machines returned intact.

When the Armistice was signed, many of us felt that we were just getting into our stride in the challenge for the sky over the Western Front.'

Retiring from the service in 1921, Louis Arbon Strange devoted his energies and remarkable organizing ability and knowledge of flying to the development of civil aviation, in conjunction with Whitney Willard Straight, the wealthy young American - a Grand Prix motor racing driver, aviator, businessman, and a member of the prominent Whitney family of the United States. In a few years they developed a fine business - the Straight Corporation Limited, which operated airfields throughout Britain and ran flying clubs as well as new types of aircraft that included the Miles Whitney Straight. At the outbreak of war Whitney Straight was at once called up for service in the Royal Air Force - his experiences in Norway are worth a chapter to themselves - and official instructions were issued that all the resources and ground organization of the firm were to be devoted to 'work of national importance.' That work consisted mainly of teaching young men to fly for the Royal Air Force.

Colonel Strange, who was the managing director, buckled to the task. His only remaining director was a retired officer of the Royal Air Force who was eventually recalled for duty, leaving Colonel Strange to shoulder the burden alone. No one will ever know what he endured. The firm, which he had worked so hard to build, was not taken over by the Government, but its commercial activities were entirely suspended with the consequent closing down of its usual source of revenue. A large staff had to be paid every week, but to get money out of the Treasury was extremely difficult.

'I must have next week's wages. I must pay the staff their wages,' he insisted to the Treasury officials responsible for dealing with the matter. 'If you don't give me a cheque for the wages I'll ground the aircraft!' he threatened more than once. Then a cheque for the week's wages would be forthcoming and Colonel Strange would be able to devote a little time to working for the country before wasting more in wrestling with the Treasury officials for the next wages.

After struggling along in these conditions for six months, the notice arrived that the Government was requisitioning the entire organisation. 'This means that the firm has ceased to exist,' said Colonel Strange when the order came through. 'The interests of the trustees must be protected. We've got no aircraft now, so we've got no business left. We must close down. We shall have to write 600 letters giving everyone a week's notice.'

This was done. He actually sat down and wrote a letter to himself giving himself a week's notice to terminate his employment as managing director of the business which he had nurtured. It was the legal thing to do and he did it.

That was worthy of W. S. Gilbert at his best.

'Now,' he thought to himself, 'I shall be able to fly for the country.'

So, having put in his application to rejoin the Royal Air Force which he had served so nobly in the past, he called one day upon the selection board for an interview just like thousands of other unknown men who were burning to serve their country. The officer, to whom the name of Louis Arbon Strange meant less than the name of Adam, glanced at the tall bronzed figure and wasted no time. He was very busy.

'How old are you?' said the officer.

'Forty-nine,' was the reply.

'You can't fly at that age!' said the officer bluntly.

'But I do,' insisted Colonel Strange.

'You can't do it,' repeated the officer.

'But I do,' insisted Colonel Strange.

'We can't take a pilot over thirty. You'll have to do administrative duties,' was the rejoinder.

'No, I want flying duties,' protested Colonel Strange, who was adamant.

'All right' came the reply at last. 'Give him a test on a Tiger Moth.'

In the most serious way Colonel Strange was made to pass tests on all types of training aircraft, even the types which his own organization had developed and launched in the air. That is the simple truth. So the man who had been in charge of the Central Flying School and who had helped to create the modern gunnery schools of the Royal Air Force and had been the Wing Commander of the 23rd Wing went to have his test on a Tiger Moth. The youthful pilot who was ordered to test him grinned when he saw him.

'What are you smiling at?' asked Colonel Strange.

'Well, sir,' was the reply, 'I've got in my pocket my father's pilot's certificate and it is signed by you. It's rather funny!'

Which goes to show that the youngsters in the Royal Air Force have a sense of humour.

234

Index

236

Voss, Werner   140-142

Wallsend   16
Warneford, Flight Sub-Lieutenant Reginald
    Alexander John   16-17
Wavell, General   135
Wehner, Lieutenant Joe   215-218
Werner, Leutnant Johannes   202
West, Air Commodore Ferdinand Maurice
    Felix 'Freddy; VC CBE MC   203-212
Whitlock, Brand   53
Wilson, Corporal Ralph   11-13
Wingfield, Lawrence A. 'Lawrie' MC DFC
    105-114
Wintgens, Leutnant Kurt   20
Zeebrugge   128
Zeppelin raids   16-20, 26-27, 115-118, 120,
    123